HERE COMES EVERYBODY

HERE COMES EVERYBODY

THE STORY OF
THE POGUES

JAMES FEARNLEY

CHICAGO
REVIEW
PRESS

An A Cappella Book

Chicago Review Press, Incorporated

814 North Franklin Street

Chicago, Illinois 60610

ISBN 978-1-55652-950-4

Library of Congress Cataloging-in-Publication Data

Fearnley, James, 1954-, author.

Here comes everybody : the story of the Pogues / James Fearnley.

   pages cm

"First published in Great Britain in 2012 by Faber and Faber."

Includes index.

ISBN 978-1-55652-950-4 (trade paper)

1. Pogues (Musical group) 2. Rock musicians—Ireland—Biography.

I. Title.

ML421.P645F43 2014

782.42166092'2—dc23

 [B]

                          2013047366

Cover design: Jonathan Hahn

Cover photo: Andrew Catlin

Printed in the United States of America

5 4 3 2 1

In memoriam Philip Chevron

Illustrations

One

30th August 1991

Shane had gone to his room, stuck phosphorescent planets on the walls and drawn the curtains. Since checking into the Pan Pacific Hotel, on the seafront at Yokohama where we had come to perform at the WOMAD festival taking place in the Seaside Park nearby, none of us had seen hide nor hair of him.

We had arrived in Yokohama from Tokyo the day before, after a brief stopover in London, on our way from a festival in Belgium, the last of a series of European music festivals. Increasingly, our performances had become a matter of determinedly turning a blind eye to Shane's fitful, fickle behaviour on stage. To keep time, we had resorted to foot-stamping. To find out where we were in a song, we had been forced to commit to prolonged, wretched and discomfiting eye contact.

I was adrift with jet lag. Incapable of staying awake any longer, I'd been waking up just an hour or two after nodding off, to turn the television on and watch CNN, the only channel in English. In the last few days a hundred thousand people had rallied outside the Soviet Union's parliament building, protesting against the coup that had deposed President Mikhail Gorbachev. The Supreme Soviet had suspended all the activities of the Soviet Communist Party. That the Eastern Bloc was disintegrating seemed apposite to the situation in which we found ourselves.

Yokohama was blazing with sunshine. Against the blue of the

1

sky, the exterior of the hotel was white as sailcloth. It had been a glorious day. I had spent it plying between the hotel and the rumpus of the festival, the hubbub of musicians, techs, drivers, roadies, in the souk of the backstage area, among the caravans and canvas. I adored, in the afternoon sunlight, Suzanne Vega, her hair magenta, accent Californian, pallor Manhattan. I tucked into the crowd with Jem to watch the Rinken Band, a headbanded, muscular bunch from Okinawa. We laughed out loud at their choreography of flexed biceps. They played, to our delight, instruments called shamisens. The thwacks of the plectrum were like firecrackers. It was a joy to spend the day at such a festival, relishing the summer sunlight and the warmth of the evening. I ended the day in jet-lagged, sake-infused awe of Youssou N'Dour, having forgotten for the time being about Shane. Now, as the afternoon turned to evening, I was waiting in my room for the phone call to summon me to a meeting in Jem's room, to talk about what to do. Though there had been no single catalytic event to join our minds and harden our will regarding Shane – it was just time.

I pictured Shane up in his darkened room somewhere in the hotel as a freakish combination of Mrs Rochester and Miss Havisham, with *The Picture of Dorian Gray* thrown in. Whenever I thought of him alone in his room, a feeling of impending catastrophe sank my otherwise buoyant spirits. His solitude had started to symbolise the human condition of disassociation, irreducible loneliness, the separation of person from person. What I imagined him doing up in his room, condemned to wakefulness and watchfulness and a horror of sleep – the wall-scrawling, the painting of his face silver, the incessant video-watching – made me fear for us all, for humanity somehow, that all we were heir to was eternally unfulfillable desires and the inevitability of death. I was jet-lagged, was my excuse. Jet lag, along with hangovers, beset me with anxieties that loomed larger than maybe they should. I was filled with worry too at the improbability of putting on a reasonable show tonight, let alone the gigs we had coming up in Osaka and Nagoya before going home.

I had had no desire to go up and see him, no compulsion to drop by. I used to before the Pogues started. His flat was situated at a sort of nexus of my itineraries to and from guitar auditions. I had been drawn to the unmistakable, mardy power he had. Once the Pogues started, I entered into near-constant orbit round him, a decade in which the exigencies of life on the road, the cramped minibuses, the confined dressing rooms, studios, rehearsal rooms, enforced our physical proximity.

Over the past couple of years I had found I didn't want to be near him. Mostly I didn't have to be. The Pogues' continuing success had done away with the tiny vans in which we used to ply the motorways and autobahns and autoroutes at the beginning of our career. By this stage in our lives together, our success had furnished us with relatively commodious tour buses, with a kitchen, bunks, a lounge in the rear. We occupied single rooms in more or less luxury hotels. We played venues, more often than not with ample facilities backstage, with sufficient space for Shane to find a room for himself. By now, I found myself not so aware of Shane's gravitational pull. I had come to consider myself free of an incumbent responsibility for him, only to be beset by the opposite: a revulsion, a self-protective termination of whatever duty I thought I should have felt towards him, particularly on stage, when the evidence of the torture of his worsening condition over recent years, as he seemed to hurtle to his own self-destruction, had become manifest. I had ended up hating him.

The phone rang. We were to meet in Jem's room in half an hour. The occasion for a meeting had become rare enough to be a novelty. It had been several years since we had abandoned our skills at decision-making, suffering as they had from a modicum of success: the hiring of a manager, the signing of a record contract, the engagement of lawyers, an accountant, an agent, the venue for meetings having become the polished desks in lawyers' premises or the corporate sterility of record company offices or a melamine table with a tray of water, still and sparkling, in one of the conference rooms of the hotel we were staying in. The cumulative effects of our success seemed to have detached us from the ability to husband our creative source.

I was tempted to get excited about the prospect of doing business, taking our careers in hand and sorting things out. Reminded of the circumstances that had prompted the meeting though, I chastised myself. Summoned to the meeting this afternoon in Jem's room, at a time of day when, given the line-up at the festival, and given the almost pristine beauty of the weather, I would probably have been out at the festival site, whatever excitement I might otherwise have enjoyed sitting around in Jem's room with my compadres, my brothers-in-arms, my adoptive family, was eclipsed by a feeling of sickness and doom.

They were my compadres. They were my brothers-in-arms. They were my family. Since the chaotic first show at the Pindar of Wakefield in King's Cross in 1982, we had been together for nine years. It seemed longer than that. We'd gone through a gamut of human experience. We had survived impecuniousness, evictions, sickness and destitution. We had fused our fortunes together in a series of confined spaces: passenger buses, ferryboats, bars, dressing rooms, cabins, restaurants, pubs, hotel rooms. I had lived with these people longer than I had with my own parents, Jem pointed out to me once. I closed the door to my hotel room behind me and climbed the echoing stairwell up to Jem's floor.

He opened the door. Light from the net curtain at the window lit the corridor. I couldn't help but try to detect a certain hesitancy or a hint of pessimism in the smile which puckered the corners of Jem's eyes and revealed the minute serration of his front teeth. In the ten years I had known him, the genuineness of his smile had always been reliable. He stood against the wall to let me in. Even under circumstances such as these, there was a formality about Jem, an understated attention to the matter of putting one at ease. It gave me the feeling that things were going to have a good outcome. I took a seat at the foot of the bed. We awaited the rest of the band. There was a smell of toothpaste in the room.

Whenever there was a knock on the door, Jem got up to greet whoever it was, in the same way he had greeted me. Terry came into the room, carrying, as he did, a pair of glasses in a sturdy case and the book he was reading. He wore jeans and a dramatic black and red short-sleeved shirt, tucked out to hide his stomach. Though he wasn't a tall man, Terry exuded eminence. He was older than us by a few years. He had curls which were once boyish - a 'burst mattress', I used to tease him - but were now greying. He sat on one of the two chairs in the room, his hands folded over his book on his lap, his lips pursed, the expression on his face one of sad seniority, full of the expectation that his years in the music business would be put to use.

Darryl came in and sat in the other chair across from the table, tapping his thighs. His cheeks were laced with capillaries. His bay hair, which he had now begun to dye, fell in brittle unruliness over his forehead. Fatigue had gouged a brown half-moon in the corner of each eye.

Andrew lumbered in. He had grown his hair long. It was beginning to show filaments of grey. He sat heavily on the bed next to me and stared at the carpet. He began to turn his wrist in a hand ivied with veins. His mouth was a lipless line.

Philip came in and wiggled his hand to have space made for

him. He perched awkwardly on the corner of the desk-cum-dressing table with his legs crossed, a shoe tucked behind his calf, his frail arms similarly twisted. His hands trembled as he shook a cigarette out of a packet. His mouth was thin, recessive, dwarfed by his fleshy, slightly curving nose. His face was suffused with pink from tiredness.

Spider was the last to knock on the door, apologising for being late. His lips were dry and, with his dark tousled hair, he looked as though he'd just got up. He had a boyish face, even more so this afternoon as he paced back and forth, a hand on his hip, his arm bent awkwardly behind him, the skin on the underside of his forearm wan and subtly grained with the blue of his veins. He clapped his long-fingered hand to the back of his neck, looked down at his shoes and paced between the bed and the wall.

There wasn't a lot of room. We sat shoulder to shoulder on the ends of the beds or on the dressing table. Terry had the chair and Darryl the armchair by the curtains. By the time we were all gathered the atmosphere was almost funereal.

We talked about our circumstances, what had led us to this meeting, the state of Shane.

In the course of the past two years, our gigs had been decimated by his fits of screaming, his seemingly wilful abandonment of his recollection of the lyrics, his haggard, terror-stricken appeals which we had mistaken for panicked requests for a cue, his maddening and petulant refusals to come out on stage with us.

Jem lamented the fact that Shane no longer accompanied us anywhere, preferring to shut himself in his room, appearing only at show time, more often than not with seconds to spare and hardly in a condition to do much. He lamented the fact that, at one time, Shane would have loved to come to such a festival, the hotel so close, the people interesting, the organisers ready to bend over backwards to help.

6

'I miss him!' Spider complained. 'I do!' He laughed at the thought and ruffled his hair with his hand. 'I miss the cunt!'

'I'm simply not enjoying myself,' Andrew announced. We all turned towards him. We knew Andrew well enough. The silence that followed was a precursor to something else. He lifted his eyebrows in weary anticipation of what he knew he was going to say next, resolved to the implications it would carry.

'He's spoiling everything.' He drew in a long breath and cleared his throat. 'I have a family,' he continued, 'what's left of it.' Four months before, days after giving birth to their son, Andrew's wife Deborah had died from an aortic aneurysm.

Terry nodded, and mouthed 'Andrew' in sympathy.

'We all have families,' Andrew said. 'Well, most of us.'

He propped himself up, hands on his knees. We waited.

'I have childcare to pay,' he went on. 'I have a mortgage. I earn my living playing music. I can't do it any more with – him.' He nodded at the door of Jem's room to signify Shane, somewhere in the hotel, in his darkened room. Andrew fell silent long enough for us to know he had finished.

'What do we want to do?' Jem said then.

'Let him go,' Andrew said with a brutality that shocked me.

'Let him go,' Spider said.

We went round the room. Philip, Darryl, Terry and Jem were all of the same mind. I didn't want to let him go. It frightened me to lose what I had become used to, to relinquish pretty much everything I'd wanted since first setting a guitar on my knee and painfully framing chords on it when I was thirteen. I also wanted to punish him. I wanted to drag him round the world with us some more. I wanted to rub his face in his own shit to teach him a lesson.

'James?'

'Okay,' I said.

7

I hadn't expected our meeting to arrive so swiftly at such a conclusion, or at any conclusion.

'Who'll tell him?' Jem said. Jem was the perfect candidate. Jem had been the one whose opinion Shane had once sought, and with a meekness which bordered on the reverential. Jem was the one who had badgered him to write, who had set everything up, organised everything. Jem had been the one on whose resolve we had all depended.

In the end though, the task of letting Shane go fell to Darryl. It felt like an act of cowardice, to give the most recent member of the band the job of releasing our singer. But, overriding that, Darryl had the least history with Shane, had less of an axe to grind, was the least judgemental. Of all of us, Darryl was the nicest.

When the time came, I was shocked that Shane should arrive at the door with such alacrity. Jem got up to let him in. Shane nodded at us all and stood dithering in the short vestibule between the toilet door and the wall.

'Awright?' he said. It was a greeting that was as familiar as it was ridiculous in such a context.

There was an endearing vulnerability to him as he turned this way and that, sniffing, taking us all in but unable to meet eyes with any of us with the exception of Jem. Shane followed Jem with a devoted gaze, as he returned to his seat on the end of the bed.

Shane's hair was filthy. His beard was blasted. His face was the colour of grout. A bib of necklaces, beads and talismans hung from his neck. He was wearing the black short-sleeved shirt which had not been off his back for the past couple of weeks. It was dank with the wearing and had calcimine stains down the front.

'Can a lady have a seat?' he said. He dropped into the chair

8

that was found for him and rested a palsied, trembling hand in his lap.

'Shane,' Darryl started in. 'Well, we've been having a talk.'

At the end of Darryl's speech, Shane clopped his tongue to the roof of his mouth and nodded and sat up in the chair and looked at no one.

'You've all been very patient with me,' he said. He wheezed his laugh of letting air escape where teeth used to be. 'What took you so long?'

Two

30th June 1980

The studio at Halligan's rehearsal rooms was narrow. The brown carpeting was sulphurous under the track spotlights in the ceiling and wormed with cigarette burns. A bottle-green set of drums crowded the way in. A guy called Terry sat behind it. He stood up to shake my hand. Beyond, on the brown-carpeted dais at the far end of the room, another guy squatted against the knotted pine dado wiping his nose with the back of his hand. Across from him, a girl leant back against the weight of her white Thunderbird bass. As I worked my way down the room with my guitar, past the edges of the cymbals, the girl appraised me unashamedly – and my new black strides. It seemed she knew how recently I had thrown my flares in the bin. The guy sitting on his heels, in T-shirt, jeans and sandals, forearms on his knees, looked as though he'd had a long afternoon. He pulled on a cigarette and wiped his face. He had watery blue eyes and looked as though he had come off the worse in a fight or two. I could see where cartilage twisted under the skin of his nose and where a kink of scar traipsed from an upturned lip into a nostril. He breathed through his mouth.

'Hullo,' I said.

'Nng,' he said and nodded.

I laid my case on the floor and took out my guitar. Terry pointed me to the amp I was to use.

'What's the name of your band?' I asked.

'It didn't say in the *Melody Maker*?' Terry answered.

'It just said "name band", ' I said.

'The Nips,' the singer said lazily.

'The Nipple Erectors,' Terry said.

'The Nips,' the singer repeated.

As soon as he stood up I realised who the singer was. There couldn't have been many people who hadn't seen the photograph on the front of the *NME* of a guy called Shane O'Hooligan having his earlobe bitten off by one of the Mo-dettes at a Clash gig at the ICA in 1976.

We went around our names. The girl bass player I was told was called Shanne. I wondered if the similarity of her name and O'Hooligan's was by design rather than chance.

I took my guitar out and slung the strap over my shoulder.

'Telecaster,' O'Hooligan said. I couldn't tell if the guitar was a disappointment to him.

I was proud of my Telecaster. It was the blonde pre-CBS Telecaster with a rosewood fingerboard and a £220 price tag which I'd pulled again and again out of the rack at Barratts on Oxford Road, Manchester, to put back again and again, paralysed by the thought of forking out that kind of money for a guitar, or for anything for that matter. I had saved the money working for three months on one of Fearnley & Sons Ltd's building sites. Being the boss's son, it wasn't particularly hard-earned, but it was a lot of money nonetheless. Part of me wanted to find fault with the guitar, an excuse to put it back and walk out, not so much on account of the expense, but to spare myself the presumption of thinking that buying such a thing was ever likely to change my life. At the same time, I dreaded walking out and away from a vocation I had always had.

I left Barratts, walked through the pelting rain and phoned my brother.

'Get it,' he had said. 'It's your ticket out.'

I plugged into the amp Terry had pointed out.

'Telecasters are good,' Terry said. 'We haven't seen one of those all afternoon.'

'Yeah,' O'Hooligan said. 'Telecasters are all right.'

They had me play a song that was all downstrokes: A to D to E. It was easy enough. The chorus consisted of slashing out A and D chords. Now and again I looked across at Shanne the bass player's hands in an attempt to predict when a chorus was likely to come up. Her face was inscrutable. O'Hooligan was in a world of his own, singing to the wall, tall, cocking his head from time to time. I had to rely on Terry, his mouth in an O, to nod me into changes in the songs, not that there were all that many of them.

O'Hooligan sang with his eyes half-closed. His nostrils flared as he lifted his head up to the microphone, positioned higher than his gaping mouth, which was full of crowns white as mortar with blackened joins where they met the gums. Where one of his crowns was missing stood a tiny brown prong.

He sang with abandon. He would clutch the microphone with both hands and then buckle away from it at the end of a verse, as if it repulsed him. His voice was guttural and artless and he sang in a London accent.

When the song came to an end, O'Hooligan stepped clear of the microphone, sniffed, wiped his nose on his wrist, cleared his throat with a cough, looked over at Shanne, remembered a packet of cigarettes on the ledge, shook one out, patted his pockets elaborately for a lighter, wheeled around to see if there was one nearby. At the end of the sequence, he caught my eye and nodded and quickly looked away. He lit the cigarette and looked round for guidance from Shanne as to what to do next. I took something in their exchange of looks to be an indication that the audition was going well.

We finished a couple of other songs which were indistinguish-

able from one another. Puffing on a cigarette, O'Hooligan stepped down from the dais. He came to stand close to me. He was tall and his proximity was threatening.

'Can you do disconnected shards of industrial noise?' he asked me, in such a way as to imply that he doubted I could. I relit my roll-up.

Once I had bought my guitar, I had gone back down to London. The 'guitarist wanted' ads in the *Melody Maker* sent me all over the city. In Harrow I had played soul music – in Carshalton, rhythm and blues – in Covent Garden, metal – in Teddington, new wave. I thrashed punk in Camberwell. In Islington, I chugged blues. I crossed and re-crossed Central London.

I had shown up at my appointed times – at a classroom, a Sunday school, the back room of a pub, the offices of a record company for an interview for Billy Idol's newly renamed Gen X, where I was only asked if I would be prepared to wear leathers, to which I said, 'Yeah, why not?' and then was sent away. I'd spent an evening cross-legged on a beaten leatherette sofa opposite an owlish Glaswegian, meshing guitar riffs until the last train while he recorded on an old TEAC. I had gone to Wood Green and handed my guitar down through a hole in the floor of a dilapidated front room, shimmied down a pole into a tenebrous basement to find myself standing among mute creatures wearing black jeans and sagging cardigans, with shocks of black hair hanging over their faces.

I had been waiting my turn at an audition in Covent Garden when I had heard the thud of a jack going into an amp, followed by a cascade of harmonic distortion interspersed with wails and shrieks. The noise ended just as abruptly as it had begun.

I didn't play that stuff. I stuck to percussive, metronomic rhythm-playing, the plectrum close to the bridge, going against the grain every now and again in a way I hoped sounded like Steve Cropper, Mick Green or Wilko Johnson. Chords I knew. I had done my time sending burning spasms into my extensor muscles over Mickey Baker's *Complete Course in Jazz Guitar*. My fingers bore dark, ingrained calluses because of it.

But if O'Hooligan wanted something that called for the stretching of my fingers into jagged and discordant chord shapes and torrents of splintered notes, I could do that.

'Can I do disconnected shards of industrial noise?' I answered O'Hooligan. 'I can do disconnected shards of industrial noise. Where do you want them?'

The song went from A to D to A to D for the most part. It was moronically simple. I whacked the chords out, watching Shanne's fingers on the bass, alert to when the solo was going to come, but not wanting to appear too eager to launch into it, in case it might be mistaken for showing off. O'Hooligan suddenly pointed to the ground.

I thrashed into the solo, chafing the strings with my guitar pick, dragging it back up towards the bridge where the sound was harsher, bundling and splaying my fingers in discordant configurations on the fret board, spidering up the frets, clustering in one place or another, my head down. I had no idea what I was doing. Remembering O'Hooligan's comment about my guitar, it occurred to me that perhaps a Telecaster mightn't be the best guitar for this kind of thing.

Then O'Hooligan hurled himself into the chorus, about how he didn't care, how he was getting nowhere and how, when everything was going wrong, he'd sing a happy song.

At the end, he nodded.

'Awright,' he said and rubbed the side of his nose with an onion-coloured finger.

A small, balding guy came in, churning his eyes I guessed on account of his contact lenses and the smoke in the room. He was introduced to me as one of the Nips' duo of managers and was called Howard. The other manager I'd met on my way into the audition that afternoon was a guy called John Hasler, a tall hollow-cheeked man with blond hair and a comic-book countenance about him. Howard needed to bring the audition to a close. There was another guitarist waiting.

I packed up my guitar in the bare-boarded lobby with the strip lighting and the lock-up cages and was about to leave to go back to Kingston-upon-Thames where I'd been living for the past ten months, working at a bakery, the band I'd been in having gone to shit, to wait for a phone call – or not – when Howard came out of the rehearsal studio.

'They want you to hang about.'

In a pub down Holloway Road, Howard asked me where I was from, what bands I'd been in, what bands I liked. He didn't really listen. He folded an arm across his chest, propping up the other, his fingers either prodding his eyes or squeezing his earlobe. He had a round, fleshy face, which he kept at a continually oblique angle to me, and wet lips.

'You all right here for a bit?' he said.

I was excited by what looked like the prospect of being in another band – a band back in the city, in North London too. After an hour, the door to the pub opened. I looked up to see Howard leaning in.

'You're still here,' he said. 'Good. They let the last guy go,' he added. 'They want to play some more with you.'

On the way back to the rehearsal room, Howard asked: 'How old are you?'

'Twenty-two,' I lied.

'We won't hold that against you,' he said.

Back in the rehearsal room, Terry the drummer's geniality, in the interim, had changed into unalloyed effervescence. O'Hooligan and Shanne on the other hand were reluctant to give so much away. They seemed sheepish about having brought me back to the rehearsal room: Shanne's face, despite its lack of expression, now allowed the briefest eye contact; O'Hooligan was gawkily executive and impatient to play. I plugged back in.

We went through a couple more songs. They were called 'King of the Bop' and 'Hot Dogs with Everything.' They were fast but easy to learn.

At the end of the afternoon, with nothing left but the prospect of packing up and seeing what was supposed to happen next, I started chiming an A chord on the guitar. The rhythm I struck out had little context or purpose other than the fact that I liked the sound of it. Immediately, O'Hooligan stepped back over to the microphone and started to sing, flipping the rhythm unexpectedly into a backbeat I hadn't been thinking of.

Sun arise she come every mornin'

It was just him and me for the first verse. Shanne joined in. I opened the song up into a three-time rhythm. Terry took up with two on his bass drum and a backbeat. Halfway through, we broke it down to the A-chord figure that started the song and then built it up again. I had loved Rolf Harris's 'Sun Arise' since I was a child. Though it should have been laughably out of context in the circumstances, we played the song with an ingenuousness that seemed to go hand in hand with the lyrics.

'Fuckin' hell!' O'Hooligan said, when we'd finished.

Howard sent me to wait in the pub again. When he pushed open the door, O'Hooligan was with him. We sat at one of the tables in the corner.

'You want to be in the band?' Howard said to me.

'I have a condition,' I added.

'What kind of condition? A medical one?'

'I'll join the band if they give me somewhere to live,' I said.

The band I'd been in, in Teddington, had been gravely new wave and fronted by a singer called Geoff, small in stature, intense, quick and as insecure as a rodent. *A Clockwork Orange* had provided the band's name – The Mixers – and had vaguely inspired Geoff's dress sense, at least when it came to the few gigs we did. His wife, Jan, was his polar opposite – compliant, long-suffering, but with a mettle that wasn't all that far beneath the surface.

One night at Geoff and Jan's flat, Geoff trudged upstairs to bed, tired and drunk. While Jan and I were clearing up, we fell on one another with an abandon that shocked us both. The affair advanced from glances and brief touches of the hands behind her husband's back, to meticulously scheduled phone calls in a phone box at the end of my street, to meeting in a park on her lunch hour, to borrowing the key to the house of one of her co-workers. My affair with Jan was months old when the band broke up. The wave of destruction which had been bearing down on their marriage crested. I arrived at their flat one afternoon. Geoff turned me round at the top of the stairs and ushered me back down to the street.

'Are you having an affair with my wife?' he demanded.

By the end of a month, Geoff had gone to live in Thames Ditton. Jan kept the flat above the car repair shop. One night when she and I were in the Royal Oak opposite the flat, a mate of Geoff's followed me into the toilets. He stood waiting until I'd finished, and then said that if he'd come across me in the pub on my own he'd have given me a kicking. He told me not to bother ever coming back to Teddington.

I viewed my ten months in suburban London as an aberration. I burned with regret at having wasted so much time. I didn't want to go back to Teddington.

'You want somewhere to live. Shouldn't be a problem,' Howard said. 'He wants somewhere to live.'

'Shouldn't be a problem,' O'Hooligan said.

·✠·

O'Hooligan took me out drinking. After a pint or two on Holloway Road he took me down to a couple of pubs near where he lived in King's Cross. We had hardly settled in the Skinners Arms on Judd Street, before we had to go to the Norfolk Arms on Leigh Street. In the Norfolk Arms our pints were half-empty before we were up again. As we went from local to local, I thought his restlessness was a sign of boredom with me. To compensate, when we had pints in front of us, I found myself talking. I was inflated by my success at the audition and the more pubs we

18

went to the drunker I got. I ran at the mouth. I painted for him a life of privilege: my middle-class parents, my private schooling, my father's chairmanship of the family building company, the shares I owned in it.

The evening went on and we downed more pints. By the time we got to the Harrison on Harrison Street, despite my initial ambivalence about O'Hooligan, I wanted to impress him, at least with self-revelation, and found myself divulging secrets, among them details of my affair with Jan, which had resulted in my turning up for the Nips' audition that afternoon, together with the rumour that my grandfather had flushed a baby down the toilet in the Sixties. He cackled with delight.

He rose to the exchange. The next thing I knew, I was struggling not just against the amount I had drunk, but to pick my way through a tangle of allusions to his childhood. He'd been born in England where his parents lived, but appeared to have been brought up by family in Tipperary. From the little I could comprehend, his first six years in Ireland had not always been happy. He laughed. It was a strange sound: a protracted Donald Duck quack.

When the pub closed, I staggered down the road after him with my guitar. He weaved a little across the pavement, his hands dug in his pockets. We turned into a dead-end street, cobbled and lined with iron railings. With the exception of No. 32, where there were a couple of lighted windows on the upper floors, the street was dimly lit, the houses dark and clad in scaffolding. Shane let us in. He showed me a room with a mattress in it and left.

I wondered if I would have cause to reprimand myself for having talked too much about myself. So ironic had been his laughter about his own disclosures that I told myself I had no worry on that account.

Three

'Well, you were told wrong!' a girl's voice bellowed down the stairway. 'There's no room here! Go round to Burton Street, that's where Shane lives!'

I stopped on the landing, halfway up the narrow stairs, leaning on my speaker cabinet, panting. Through Howard Cohen, Shane had let me know that there was a room above a bookshop on Marchmont Street in Bloomsbury. A friend had driven me and my belongings – my Telecaster, my acoustic, my amp and speaker cabinet, record player, typewriter, a suitcase full of clothes – up from the bedsit I had been living in in Kingston-upon-Thames that morning in a Transit van. I lugged the speaker cabinet back down the stairs, to the street and back into the van. I didn't want to go back to the suburbs. I was finished there.

Burton Street was a dead-end Victorian terrace. Just two houses were occupied: No. 32 and the one facing it, which had a BMW parked outside. No. 32 was administered by a local housing association. The guy living in the house opposite had made the mistake of buying his. The remainder of the street was a building site, the darkened brick façades hidden by scaffolding and dust sheeting. It was a Saturday and the street was quiet and, with the exception of the BMW and a couple of skips full of splintered wood and dust, empty. It was a grim sort of place, a backwater of Woburn Place and Euston Road.

My arrival at No. 32 Burton Street threw the girls on the top floor – Jackie and Cath Cinnamon – into consternation. Of course, Shane wasn't in and I obviously hadn't been expected, but seeing as I'd turned up with a Transit van full of my belongings they couldn't really send me away, though I suspected they wanted to. They laughed when I said I had an agreement with Shane.

Jackie and Cath took pity on me. They showed me a room usually occupied by a guy called Jem who happened to be on a camping holiday in France. They were sure something could be figured out when he returned. I hauled my amp and speakers up the narrow stairs and leant my guitars against the wall. The room overlooked the street. It was scant of furniture. There was a mattress on the floor and a wardrobe. The Transit van pulled away from the kerb and drove off.

The kitchen was a tip. The window-frame had been jimmied out and thrown onto the roof of the bus depot behind the house. A half-burnt chair lay at an angle in the hearth. Filthy mugs, milk cartons, plates, spoons crowded the table. The cooker was black with grease. I was standing in the room, taking in the squalor, when a girl called Jasmine came in.

'Hello,' she said. She was wearing an eggshell-blue dress and white ankle socks. Her dark hair glistened with washing. I was amazed that anyone could be so clean, living in a place like this.

I was relieved to be back in London, amid the clamour of King's Cross. To the north was the racket of Euston Road and the railway stations, Euston, St Pancras, King's Cross. To the south, beyond Bloomsbury and the British Museum, it was a twenty-minute walk to Covent Garden and the West End. The entire area reeked of literature. Charles Dickens had lived nearby on Doughty Street. The Woolfs had lived on Gordon Square, E. M. Forster on Tavistock Square and W. B. Yeats on Woburn Walk, at the top of Burton Street.

In a couple of days the guy came back from France. Jem had wiry hair and prominent brows. There was an urbanity and an apparent suspension of judgement about him that was appealing. I liked his air of quiet capability. He didn't seem to mind all that much that I had been using his room and actually sympathised with my turning up on the doorstep at Shane's invitation.

I moved into a room off the top landing that Jackie and Cath had cleared out. It was nothing more than a cubicle with a mattress in it, a window at one end and what remained of a door at the other. I dragged my gear up the stairs and parked it in the corner of the room. I stationed my typewriter and my radio on the windowsill. I set my suitcase of clothes against the wall and draped a woollen blanket over the door for privacy.

No. 32 Burton Street was a noisy place. On weekday mornings, labourers' vehicles came to park up and down the street and in minutes the houses on both sides were ringing with hammering, shuddering with impact drills and braying with Capital Radio.

Nearly every night, in his room on the floor below mine, next to Jem's room, rant music from Shane's record player – relentless intoning against a thumping reggae beat – pounded the walls and timbers throughout the house. I tried to keep it out of my ears by pulling the bedding over my head. I went downstairs to implore him to turn the music down.

'Sure,' he said. He lifted a finger in a gesture of docility. I got back into bed, relieved that it had been that easy to get what I wanted from him. I lay in my bed, naïvely imagining that the delay in getting up to go to the volume knob of his record player might be due to the rolling of a joint, the putting out of a cigarette or something. The ululation went on unabated, pounding through the floor in my ear.

It wasn't just Shane's record player that kept me up. There

were arguments, door-slamming, the sound of breaking glass and occasional shrieking as someone or other fell foul of the bicycles which were stacked in the front hall outside the room occupied by people called the 'Beards'. One night, a beam-shuddering crash started me awake, followed by shouting, the precipitation of footsteps down the staircase and the slam of the front door. Soon, I became aware of the clatter and tinkling of objects striking the corrugated roof of the bus repair depot behind the house. I crept downstairs to see Cath Cinnamon sitting on the overturned kitchen table, throwing items of cutlery, one after the other, through the window.

⚜

I got a sweeping-up job at a repair shop in Soho where they became used to my taking time off. In the afternoons, for a few days a week the Nips rehearsed at Halligan's on Holloway Road. We spent a lot of time waiting for Shane to turn up. When he did, he was drunk – a couple of times so drunk that he had fallen asleep on the tube, overridden his stop and ended up at Wood Green or Cockfosters. It was funny to begin with. After a while it began to annoy me that he should turn up so late and incapable of doing much. I brought it up with him.

'You don't understand!' he said, clawing at his face in disbelief. Shane worked as a barman at the staff bar of the National Hospital for Nervous Diseases. He implied that his lateness and drunkenness were collateral damage that came with the job. He trumped my complaints with the fact that his inebriation happened, actually, to be in the service of nurses and doctors, for whom, if they wanted a drink after hours on a weekday afternoon, he was there to oblige. When Shanne beseeched him to try to turn up to rehearsal on time, and sober, there was a surprising kindliness in the way she dealt with him. I gave up. I was a new boy. I yielded, and spent the afternoons at Halligan's going over what I and Terry the drummer and Shanne were capable of doing by ourselves, waiting for Shane to make an appearance.

As rehearsals went on, it became clear that Shane was in love with Shanne. In the course of going through the songs, he sought her approval on everything. Shane and Shanne were so obviously the core of the Nips, their union exemplified by their near-as-damn-it homonymy, that after a couple of weeks I was shocked to understand that Shanne and John Hasler – one of the duo of managers – had married the previous May and that Shane had been debarred from the wedding. By September, Shanne Hasler was four months pregnant.

When I also learnt that Terry Smith was the tenth drummer the Nips had had, and that I was the fifth guitarist, I wondered how long this group was going to last.

The first gig I did with the Nips was at the Rock Garden in Covent Garden. I didn't know what to expect. I kept my head down. My experience of gigs, so far, had been ordeals of un-requitedness, a series of sporadic confrontations with an audience's neutrality. Playing to one which actually knew better than I did what was supposed to happen was shocking. When I stepped up to the microphone to sing backing vocals – on 'Hot Dogs with Everything' – I was taken aback by the fact that the crowd had already begun shouting out:

'Lah, la-la-la-la-la lah la-lah, lah la-lah, la-la-la-lah!'

We did a gig somewhere in South London, the floor incompliantly empty throughout our set, the audience having retreated to the walls, behind iron pillars. Halfway through, Shane, wearing a plum-coloured, quilted smoking jacket, hurled himself from the stage to writhe on the flagged floor, his legs working his body

round, singing the whole time. To watch him as if at the nether end of an exorcism, surrounded by what there was of an audience, some of them giggling nervously, scared me.

The gigs in what seemed to be the Nips' stamping ground of North London were raucous, teeming, claustrophobic events. I recognised faces I'd seen around the neighbourhood. Jem Finer was a familiar presence at Nips gigs – at the Hope and Anchor, Dingwalls – and held Shane in some esteem.

When we weren't playing our own, there were gigs to go to – at the Greyhound, the Lyceum, the Moonlight, the Marquee, Camden Palace, the Rainbow, the George Robey. There were clubs like Billy's, the Wag, Beatroute and Blitz. I went out a lot with Shane, Howard Cohen and a girl called Mandy who worked for an agent and had the words 'super ligger' embroidered on her zip-up jacket. Often enough, though, Shane and I ended up going out by ourselves.

I had to exert myself to follow him through the cold London streets, in the yellow fog. He was always ten or fifteen feet ahead of me. I had never known anyone to walk so fast. It was as if the matter of getting from pub to pub, from double port and lemon to double port and lemon, snakebite to snakebite, was a bothersome chasm in the evening that needed bridging as swiftly as possible. His long legs strode down the street. He pushed his hands in his pockets against the cold. He was oblivious to the fact that I continually lagged behind. I had to skip to catch up, my hands in my pockets like him, hoping he wouldn't see me cheat, hoping he would think I could walk as fast as he could.

If we had to take the tube anywhere, we sat opposite one another in the brash light of the train. We were careful not to meet each other's eyes. If we did, he'd let out a cackle the significance of which I didn't understand, but I would reciprocate, as if I did. He'd wipe his nose against the back of his hand and abruptly stare down the carriage, a meekness in his eyes, embarrassed at what he thought was an exchange of intimacy between us.

One night he took me up to Dingwalls at Camden Market. I felt privileged to go with him. Neither of us was on any guest list but we got in anyway without paying. The kid behind the glass at the box office summoned an older guy, who waved away the kid's reluctance when he saw who it was. He nodded Shane and me in.

The band Shane had brought me to see was already playing down the far end. The bar was fairly empty. There were a few people sitting on stools along the walls or leaning on the shelves round the pillars. I was too proud to be in Shane's company to pay much attention to the band. Shane didn't seem to show much interest either. I followed him across to the bar. The lack of words between us I hoped passed for an understanding it looked like we had.

'What you having?' I said.

'A Black Zombie,' he replied, but over my head, directly to the barman, a large man with a pink implacable face. I wondered if I detected a weary familiarity in him with Shane.

'You?' the barman said to me.

'He wants one too,' Shane said on my behalf. The barman raised his eyebrows and went about putting the drink together. He crooked his finger under each of the optic dispensers to release, one after the other, a double measure of each of the white spirits – gin, vodka, tequila, Bacardi – together with a double shot of pastis into the plastic pint glass. Finally and unceremoniously, he upended a bottle of Coke into it. He pushed the drinks across the bar. I paid.

I held the Black Zombie up to the light. The plastic glass was scuffed to the point of opacity. The drink was black right enough, but with a noxious-looking, muddy iridescence in it. It looked evil. Shane drew the Zombie to his mouth and, in a succession of elaborate gulps, swallowed all of it. I wished I could do the same, but my adenoids recoiled from the first vaporous mouthful. I set the drink on a ledge for the time being.

I looked at him, standing in the half-empty bar, dark against the lighting behind the bar, his hair dark, his donkey jacket black, black jeans, the black drink gone. The clop of the empty plastic glass on the counter signalled the end of my naïve and besotted expectation of any real brotherhood with Shane.

'I'm getting another one,' he said. 'You?'

⁕

I knew how to get home. It was a question of putting one foot in front of the other, difficult as that might be. It was a question of taking your time, standing for a moment considering your options, a question of rummaging in your pockets for the packet of fags and getting one out without spilling them all over the pavement, finding the lighter, holding the flame steady at the tip of the cigarette. It was a question of quickly rectifying the sudden and unpredictable shifts in your centre of gravity, while taking in a drag of smoke, taking in the night, the sky the colour of Bakelite, the darkened windows of the houses, the yellow light of the streetlamps – and then of setting a flopping foot forward in the direction of home. If my equilibrium was ever abruptly and unceremoniously swiped away and I was flung leg over leg to crash into something – a tree, a parked car, a garden wall – I would sit for a minute, put a finger to the broken skin or the frayed hole in my trousers, and then get up and carry on.

I was good with drunks. I looked forward to delivering Shane successfully to his room and to his bed. I had an instinct for the dividing line between what was expeditious and what was just fun at someone else's expense. I knew to wait a few paces ahead, alert to danger, scanning the high street for traffic in case he lurched out into the roadway, to steer him away from a breadcrate in one of the doorways, to stand at a kerb ready for the unexpectedness of the step down to cross a street, to brace myself for his inability to predict a sudden gradient. I wasn't successful. Shane's legs were gone. He staggered down Camden High Street, sidestepping, lurching, coming to an abrupt but teetering standstill before precipitating forward, the soles of his shoes slapping on the pavement.

He kept working his hands into his pockets and working them out, letting out great sighs of frustration at his progress down the street, stopping now and again to hawk phlegm from his throat, but doubling over, gagging with the effort, sucking saliva back into his mouth and wiping his face with his hands. He stopped to light a cigarette, teetering in the middle of the pavement, thumbing the lighter over and over and, once he'd managed to get it to light, circling the flame round and round the end of the cigarette. He took a drag and set off again, but the smoke must have gone to his head because he lost his balance and sidestepped against a shop window. I cowered against what I expected to be the crash of him going through it with his shoulder. The impact though, forceful as it was, only threw him to his knees and set the window quivering for seconds after.

'Ow!' he wailed. 'Ow! Ow!' I stepped forward to help him up.

'Fuck off!' he screamed. 'Just fuck off! I don't need any fucking help! Cunt!'

I stood back to let him struggle up from his hands and knees, but with my arms at the ready in case he met with failure. When he set off again he hurled himself against the side of one of the cars parked up and down the street, pushed himself upright and launched into a stagger onward down the road. I walked a few paces ahead, to give him some distance, but not so much that I wouldn't be able to rush back to assist him if he got into more difficulty.

'Cunt!' he shouted at me, but then laughed.

We successfully made our way down most of Eversholt Street. When Euston Station came into sight and the spire of St Pancras Church, beyond which was our turnoff into Woburn Walk, I must have allowed myself to relax. I heard a crash somewhere behind me, but a crash which seemed to come from one of the buildings set away from the street. I looked back to see the pavement empty of Shane. I ran back to where I'd missed the open gates of a forecourt on the corner of Wellesley Place, where the concrete sloped down to a loading bay and some bins. He was clutching the railings halfway down the incline, swaying from side to side, voiding his stomach onto the concrete. I went down the ramp and, thinking it to be a universally accepted gesture of support and brotherhood, put my hand on his back. He swiped me away.

'Fuck off and leave me alone!' he cried out. 'Why can't you leave me the fuck alone? Fuck off! You sanctimonious cunt! Cunt! Fuck off! Fuck off! FUCK OFF!'

I wove across Euston Road, past the caryatids outside St Pancras Church and down Woburn Walk to Burton Street. Drunk as I was myself, the idea that he thought I had been judging him sickened me. His belligerence set us facing one another on opposite sides of a chasm, the scant bridge there had been between us dangling in it.

Four

Living in London had always been a problem. I'd slept on couches, rented bedsits and squatted, from Kensal Green to Kingston-upon-Thames. Though a friend and I had once managed to get hold of what was called a 'hard-to-let' council flat on the Isle of Dogs, council housing was out of the question. Since the Seventies, government subsidies to local authorities for housing had taken a battering. It had fallen to housing associations to take up the job of providing accommodation for people like me, if you could get on their books.

My arrival at No. 32 Burton Street had been six weeks shy of the passing, in October 1980, of the Housing Act and the implementation of the Right to Buy scheme. The writing was on the wall for housing associations like Shortlife Community Housing, the housing association to which the occupants of No. 32 paid rent. SCH, as the association was known, administered much of the housing stock the Borough of Camden was not able to maintain due to lack of subsidy, particularly round King's Cross, and notably the forbidding Victorian tenements on the nearby Hillview Estate.

Over the course of the next few months, a couple of the girls moved out, as, apparently, did the Beards.

One afternoon, Jem came to see me in my cubicle. He had been working off his rent arrears at the SCH offices. He had come across an empty rent book and filled it out on my behalf. He told the housing association that I had asked him to bring my own arrears up to date. He professed puzzlement that my tenant's file wasn't to be found in their records. He handed me the completed rent book with the name James Fernleagh on the front. I owed him £4.

A week or two later we were all woken up at eight in the morning by pounding on the front door. Men in suits and hard hats strode up and down the staircase. It was due to the building work on the rest of the street, they informed us, that the front wall of our house was beginning to drift away and was in imminent danger of bringing the rest of the house down round our ears. A guy from SCH came round to summon us to a meeting to decide our fate.

Shane, Jem, Cath Cinnamon and I met in the bare back room of SCH's offices. We sat around the Formica-topped table and waited to see what would happen. Though efforts would be made to accommodate everyone in time, as it turned out there were just two single-occupancy flats available, one on Mornington Crescent at the foot of Camden High Street, the other on Gray's Inn Road. Two of us were going to have to think of something else.

We sat frozen with irresolution. I was scared that the discrepancy in my status as tenant with SCH would be brought to light and that I would be sent back to Teddington. Jem took charge.

'Well,' he said, 'I think Cath should have one of the flats. I can stay with someone.' He turned to Shane. 'And you have friends.'

'What?' Shane appealed to Jem in disbelief. 'He gets a fucking flat? Him?'

'He's in your band,' Jem said. 'You brought him here.'

'Yeah, well,' Shane said. 'But where am I going to go?'

'You know people,' Jem said.

To Shane's chagrin, I was given the flat on Mornington Crescent. I moved into it that night. The morning revealed a living room dominated by a curvilinear, art-deco window with a view over the gardens of the houses in the crescent, and in the distance, beyond the main line from Euston and the housing blocks on Albany Street, the Snowdon Aviary at Regent's Park Zoo. Shane stayed on a friend's floor for a few weeks. He rarely missed an opportunity to vent his rancour over my good luck. It was only when a flat became available on Cromer Street, above a corner shop, a few doors down from the SCH offices, that he seemed to give up his resentment.

·✠·

Of the Nips' managers, it was Howard who did the lion's share of the work. I hardly came across John. Now and again he would show up at rehearsal. Howard, on the other hand, tirelessly orbited, on a distant ellipse, whatever brokers of power in the music business he could find and dedicated himself to the dogged maintenance of relationships with people who begrudged him what little they gave him.

Shane's notoriety before I joined the Nips had attracted the attention of Paul Weller from the Jam. Weller had produced a demo of the Nips' 'Happy Song' and 'Nobody to Love'. When the Vapors – protégés of Bruce Foxton, the Jam's bass player – had a hit with a song called 'Turning Japanese', it goaded Howard into the belief that Weller might be persuaded to become the Nips' protégeur. For a while though, the best that Howard could come up with was Shane's, my and Howard's inclusion – though even that was never assured – on the Jam's guest list when they played in London.

Eventually, the spoils of Howard's war of attrition with John Weller, Paul's dad, stretched to a couple of gigs supporting the

Jam, at Queen's Hall in Leeds and the Music Machine on Camden High Street. At Queen's Hall, other than the fifty or so fans who sprinted across the empty hall once the doors opened to secure their places along the barriers for the Jam, we played to a sparse audience. We were first on the bill, before a group called the Piranhas.

For our support slot at the Music Machine, to John Weller's anger, we wore pyjamas and nighties and forced our new drummer Jon Moss, who had recently replaced Terry Smith, to wear a negligée.

During our set, I looked across at Shanne over on the left side of the stage. She was by now five months pregnant. Her bass seesawed over her distended stomach. I became despondent about what was going to happen at the end of her pregnancy.

By dint of tireless ingratiation, Howard finally managed to schedule us to record for Paul Weller's Respond label in the New Year. Shane had let me know that, due to her pregnancy, Shanne would not be recording. To me, to work with Paul Weller was an opportunity too good to miss. It seemed a simple matter of my offering to play bass and getting it done. I made the mistake of ringing Shanne with my idea.

'You're not playing the bass on anything,' she said. 'You're not in the band.'

I put the phone down and spent a glum weekend with a stinking cold in my freezing flat. The sun hardly seemed to rise above the horizon before it began to sink beneath the rooftops, beaming viscid orange light into the bamboo screens I had found and had hung at the windows. I was miserable. Everything had gone to shit again.

In the New Year I got a job with Camden Council Election Office, going from address to address - Saffron Hill to Somerstown, Highgate to Holborn - chasing up residents who hadn't returned electoral registration forms. In the afternoons, I'd bring the completed forms back to the offices on Judd Street and then drop round at Shane's new flat on Cromer Street.

I touched the bare wires together that sprouted out of his front door jamb. A bell tinkled aloft in his rooms. I stepped back out into the road, so he could see me from the window at the top of the stairs. Up above, the window opened and he put his head out.

'What?' And then he'd see me standing there in the street, say, 'Oh,' and retract his head. I'd have to wait a while longer until his head appeared again. He worked his arm out and awkwardly released a key into the air. It jingled on the pavement somewhere. I let myself in, pushing open the door against the tide of mail behind it and up the grimy stairs.

There was just the one room. The door opened onto a wooden table and a couple of chairs, beyond which the windows gave onto the Holy Cross Church and the housing estates across the street. In the corner of the room stood a bar of maritime theme, with gunwales and portholes. Across from the bar was his bed: a mattress on the floor across the hearth, the fireplace closed off by a four-bar electric fire mounted on plasterboard. There was a portrait of Brendan Behan on the wall. There were bin bags everywhere containing his belongings, or rubbish – I couldn't tell which – heaped up along the walls behind the brown vinyl-covered armchair. The bathroom was a horrid affair. The bath was mounded high with more black bin bags. He had me make tea for us. The kitchen was a galley with flooring of mustard-coloured vinyl. It had a gas hob, an old kettle and a supposedly stainless-steel sink. On the draining board were scattered the filthiest tea mugs. They were encrusted with tannin on the inside and befouled with something on the outside that made water bead. There was no hot water to wash the mugs with, no detergent, no scouring sponge or even a brush. I brought the tea through to set on his bare wood table and gingerly went about drinking it.

We spent hours talking – or rather, he spent hours talking to me, about the hostage-taking in Iran, Rupert Murdoch's recent acquisition of *The Times*, Bobby Sands's hunger strike, but then veered off onto subjects as far apart as *Finnegans Wake*, the Khmer Rouge and the buxomness of the women depicted on cans of Tennent's lager. The connections Shane made left me with the feeling that I was lost in some potholing expedition. His meaning seemed forever to slip like water through the narrow-est of chinks, into a neighbouring chamber whose reverberations scattered all its sense.

Shane had been to the library. A book about ancient Rome had put him in a lather about hedonism, wanton cruelty, tyranny and the proximity of death, not to mention ancient Roman fash-ion, which frothed him up too, with its flowing togas, leather and studs.

The Nips' other manager, John Hasler, Shanne's husband, had recently proposed Shane and myself get a band together. The New Romantics were *au courant* at the time. As opposed to New

Romantics, our band would be neo-decadent. Shane was delirious to have noticed that Roman *haute couture* was an avenue which had not yet been explored by such bands as Spandau Ballet and Visage. If we were going to get a band together, Shane had earmarked the toga for himself, and wanted me to know that he had set aside the gladiator's outfit for me.

He snapped through the pages at his table with the book on his filthy knee to show me the draped contours and laurelled temples of some patrician or other, slapping the page flat with his hand, cackling at the voluptuousness and the androgyny.

He smote the leaves of the book until he found a picture of a gladiator, wearing a leather loincloth, a shoulder piece, a net over the other arm and carrying a trident. I was sceptical, but prey to Shane's enthusiasm. I couldn't prevent myself rather liking the daft image he conjured up, of myself on stage in loincloth and with a casting-net.

'It's well *sexy!*' he said. He brought his face close to mine, hissing with lasciviousness. I could see the blackened joints at the base of his dental caps.

'I don't think so,' I said.

'Nah!' he said, emptying his face of leering prurience and replacing it with an expression of goofy abnegation, his mouth dropping, his eyebrows ascending.

'I mean, you'd look – good! With a guitar? Wearing that gear? I mean,' he said. 'Come on!'

I humoured him. I didn't want to test what I hoped was his irony too far in case he was actually serious. I wanted to give the outfit and the whole idea of gearing myself out in Roman attire, along with the matter of pandering to what seemed Shane's ambivalent sexuality, the thumbs down. I was more interested to hear about the music a band dressed up from the first century might play.

'Cretan music!' he said. Shane's inspiration seemed to have come from Shanne Hasler, who, since disbanding the Nips had apparently been trying to put a band together to play music from the Aegean Islands.

He clattered about in a pile of tapes on the counter of his bar and shoved one into a battered tape player. The music that came out, played on what sounded like a violin and a bouzouki, was sinuous, made of endlessly repeated motifs. It reminded me of the examples of pre-Western, minimalist and gamelan music that had been required listening at college. I told him I found it a bit on the boring, repetitive side.

'That's the *whole point!*' he said. Slapping his book of Roman culture on his knee, he cited the fact that *Finnegans Wake* had already started by the time you opened it and seemed not likely to finish any time soon after you closed it. It was cyclical, without beginning and endless, like Cretan music.

'Like Irish music,' I said.

'Well,' Shane said, 'Irish music's like fucking Arabic music, innit?'

Five

The job for Camden Council ended and I signed on Social Security. I started getting the *Melody Maker* again and went off to the odd audition. Before long, I found myself in a band called the Giants. They played soul music. We recorded a single produced by Pete Watts and Dale Griffin, the bassist and drummer for Mott the Hoople. I had been a fan in the Seventies. A school friend and I had lamented their vault to fame when they released 'All the Young Dudes' in 1972.

I spent the rest of the year playing occasional gigs with the Giants, rehearsing in the bass player's living room in Carshalton, clattering at my typewriter in my flat. That summer I spent the afternoons up on the roof with my back against the lift's sheave-house and with the help of the Compact Edition of the *Oxford English Dictionary* read Joyce's *Ulysses* from cover to cover.

In November, Jon Moss, handsome with guarded, dark eyes, came to visit me. He brought with him a demo-tape of the band he had joined after the Nips ended, called Culture Club. They wanted to replace the guitarist. My cassette player was broken, so we went down to sit in the dark of his car, which was parked in a side street round the corner from my block of flats. We listened, tapping our feet. I became aware of a guy walking up the pavement at the same time as I realised that our foot-tapping was rocking the car. It occurred to me that the guy might be forgiven for misconstruing what we were doing.

When the song finished, I said if they got rid of their guitarist, I'd play with his band. Moss said he'd ring me.

»✠«

After Christmas, Howard Cohen started taking me out to see a band called Dolly Mixture, at the Marquee, the Starlight Room, the Venue in Victoria. Dolly Mixture's second single with Paul Weller's Respond label was due for release in March. At the end of February, the band was to start a tour with other acts on the label. In his seemingly chronic endeavour to get close to the Weller family, Howard toiled to win at least Dolly Mixture's tolerance. He hardly missed an opportunity to invite me out to see them.

Dolly Mixture was an all-girl group who favoured frocks, berets, striped tights and Dr Martens. There were three of them: Rachel, prim but with flame-red feathered hair, played guitar; Hester pounded the drums with an injured ferocity; Debsey played bass, her mascara'd eyes lucent, scanning the space above the audience. Debsey and Rachel shared lead vocals, but I loved Debsey's voice. I adored its plainness and its nasality which imbued the songs she sang with an unselfconscious irony.

Debsey was lovely, with pale skin, raven hair and a flick of freckles across the bridge of her nose. She was full of accents, with an ironic sense of her own refinement. We flirted with one another. One night, after one of Dolly Mixture's shows, as the cab containing us and some of Dolly Mixture's entourage dropped me off outside my block of flats, Debsey and I fleetingly touched hands through the open window. After one of her gigs at Dingwalls, a few weeks later, she came back to my flat. I didn't hear from her for a week and a half, until she came to knock on my door. By closing time in the local pub she had become my girlfriend.

In the first week of our relationship, when we weren't in my flat – drinking tea, talking, reading books – we went on walks through the West End. She would wave her slender arm to point out some detail of cornice under the eaves of the buildings in Berkeley Square. In Regent's Park, she widened her nostrils and narrowed her eyes in rapture at the roses in Queen Mary's Gardens.

She was particular to the point of fastidiousness. When it came to making her breakfast in the mornings, she taught me how to prod toast straight out of the toaster, to prevent it turning stiff like cardboard. She would bring to my attention the fact that I had not spread the butter and the marmalade to the very edges.

Dolly Mixture had started up in Cambridge, where Debsey's parents had been to university and where her grandmother still lived. Debsey now lived with her parents in the top two storeys of a Georgian terraced house on Liverpool Road, Islington. Her father worked in public relations somewhere on City Road. At the weekends, he played piano for The Water Rats, the Victorian music hall at the Pindar of Wakefield on Gray's Inn Road. Her mother had been in theatre. She was a formidable woman, sensitive to the point of injury.

Dolly Mixture had already released a couple of singles. The first had been for Chrysalis Records – a cover of the Shirelles' hit 'Baby It's You'. She and her band hated their version of it. The fact that Chrysalis had chosen it as their début single, intending to market Dolly Mixture as a teen girl group, depressed Debsey to the point of suffocation. Their next two releases had been recordings of their own songs, both released on Paul Weller's Respond Records and both produced by the Damned's Captain Sensible and Paul Gray.

We had been going out a week, when Debsey went away on the '82 and Responding Tour. I had a meagre idea of what life was like on the road. I had no idea where in the country she was or where she was going next. Though she wrote to me, her letters contained scant descriptions of the cities she was in, the venues she played. No sooner had she returned home it seemed than, in April, she went away to a studio in Kent to sing backing vocals with Dolly Mixture for Captain Sensible's solo album, the single from which was a version of Rodgers and Hammerstein's 'Happy Talk'. I didn't see Debsey for days, sometimes weeks at a time.

⚜

On my way to and from rehearsals with the Giants, or, when the Giants folded, to and from auditions, I'd often find myself in King's Cross. Shane's flat was a short walk from the station.

Nothing much had changed in the year since I'd last seen him. The detritus of bottles, books and bags had further encroached on the floor space. An enormous, broken colour television stood tilted by the wall. Again, he had me make tea. In the course of our conversation, Shane extolled the wonders of the DeLorean car and cackled over the fact that a team of scrap-metal dealers had hoisted the Argentinian flag on an island under British sovereignty in the South Atlantic.

We talked, too, about Howard Cohen's plans to re-form the Nips. Howard Cohen had lately been to see someone at Polydor Records, whose response had been that it would be a nuisance.

'But a *good* nuisance,' Howard had said.

Shane and I barely touched on the subject.

'If I was going to do anything, I'd want to do fucking Cretan music,' he said. 'If I was going to start another band I'd call it the New Republicans.' He released a wheezing laugh.

We went out to get drunk in one of the couple of pubs in the locality he hadn't been barred from. When the pub closed we staggered back up his staircase with a carry-out. I found a tin whistle on the windowsill. I asked him if he minded me playing it. He shrugged and sat heavily on the bentwood chair at his table. He shook out a cigarette and lit it. I took the whistle and sat down on his mattress with my back against the wall.

I'd recently taken a record of Irish music out of the library on Camden High Street. It was called *Tin Whistles*, by Paddy Moloney and Sean Potts. I had spent a couple of afternoons lifting the needle on and off the record, learning what sounded like the easiest melody on it, an air called 'Jimmy Mo Mhíle Stór'.

Shane's whistle was a dingy nickel one. Despite the crusted tidemark on the blue mouthpiece which I couldn't wipe off on my sleeve, I put it to my lips to play. The instant I did, Shane was up out of his seat, dancing.

I struggled to get the tune right while he danced down the room, shuffling mostly, but taking a little skip from time to time. His arms flopped by his sides, one hand holding his can of lager. Not a lot of the melody joined together well, though I did manage a slide or two and to tap the empty holes of the whistle to make a vibrato which I'd learnt from listening to Moloney and Potts's record.

He capered round his room with his back to me in his rumpled black trousers, tall. When he turned round to skip back up the room the focus had gone from his eyes, not so much out of drunkenness but because he seemed to be in another world, ancient and immemorial, lost in the familiarity of the tune despite my clumsy playing. I fancied he had found temporary respite not just from the squalor of his flat, the confusion of London, but from his stubborn restlessness too. For ten minutes I blew into the whistle and covered the holes as best I could, and in the right order, while Shane paddled the floorboards, staring at his feet.

He happened to tuck one shoe behind the other. He twirled clumsily, staggered to the side and stopped.

'I'm too fucking drunk,' he said. I stopped playing. He slumped down on the mattress next to me.

'But don't stop,' he said. 'Don't stop. It's fucking good to hear that shit.'

I played some more, both of us sitting shoulder to shoulder on his mattress, feet on the floor, knees up, Shane's arms balanced on his knees, but 'Jimmy Mo Mhíle Stór' was the only tune I knew and it quickly became tedious to go round and round it. I put the whistle down. We sat in silence. I was about to make my apologies to leave for the walk home up St Pancras Road when he said:

'Do you think I drink too much?'

Despite witnessing his dispatch of two Black Zombies at Dingwalls, followed by our lurching, rancorous journey back to Burton Street, I hadn't given it much thought. I avoided saying yes. Besides, I wanted more from him than I would have got if I had.

'Do you think you do?' I said.

'I can't get to sleep without a couple of tins of Tennent's.'

I couldn't say it sounded particularly bad, but there was something about his confession that he drank alone which drew me up. It obviously concerned him. I had assumed that all his drinking was done in company and that he'd go back to his flat, exhausted after a day's round, as I saw it, of carrying sail from pub to club.

'Well,' I found myself saying, knowing that I was missing the point, 'if you can't get to sleep.'

'But I see things,' he said. 'You know, see things.'

'Like DTs?' I said, fascinated. I hadn't met anyone who had had DTs.

'I dunno,' he said. 'Yeah, I suppose.'

I expected Shane to wheeze out a laugh of self-deprecation – the cackle which blew even the dimmest ember of irony into combustion. That night, though, he sounded scared. He told me that his mind kept going round and round at night and he couldn't stop it.

I felt bad for his restlessness. He seemed carried by a relentless current which never just deposited him on the beach of his flat on Cromer Street, but sucked him back and rolled him up and down there too. It was an energy I envied, though it scared me.

⊕

I lost interest in going to auditions. I was short of money too. I sold my guitar and my amp. The guy who bought it pointed out that because the screw holes in the body didn't match up with those in the scratch plate, the guitar wasn't an original Telecaster. With the amp thrown in, I took as much as I'd originally paid for the guitar. I was angry to have deluded myself.

I saw Debsey intermittently. In June, Sensible's 'Happy Talk' had spent two weeks at No. 1. Its success and that of its follow-up, 'Wot!', swept Dolly Mixture into a cycle of promotion. She spent a lot of the time away filming videos, making appearances on *Top of the Pops* and doing Dolly Mixture's own gigs.

Each morning I obeyed the sign I'd stuck on my bedroom wall which read: 'GET UP'. I made tea. I had an ex-office IBM typewriter. It was a brute and ten times the weight of the Olivetti I had been pecking away on in my cubicle at No. 32 Burton Street. I jammed the table into the corner against the momentum of the carriage return. With *Roget's Thesaurus* and the *Oxford English Dictionary* on the table next to me, my mug of tea, smoke twisting from a cigarette balanced on the edge of my ashtray, I hammered at the keyboard. In the afternoons I'd read or cycle round the city. In the evenings, I'd go out drinking with Howard and maybe Shane, or stay in and listen to the radio.

45

Once a week I went to a writing workshop at the City Literary Institute in Holborn.

On an afternoon at the end of August, Debsey was away in Norwich with Sensible. Between the thwacks of my IBM, I became aware of a knocking on the door.

I opened to Jem. He had had no idea which flat was mine and had eventually been directed to it by the sound of the typewriter at the end of my hallway.

He was carrying a plastic carrier bag with him. He put it down in the living room. I hadn't seen him in the year and a half since we had been evicted from the house on Burton Street. At first it was awkward welcoming him into my living room, until it occurred to me that Jem had helped me get the flat in the first place. I showed him round.

While I made a cup of tea in the galley kitchen, he leant on the door jamb and told me that he had been playing music with Shane, both of them on guitar, with Shane singing. They had been busking in Finsbury Park tube station and had auditioned, unsuccessfully, for a pitch at the newly refurbished Covent Garden Market. I asked him what kind of music.

'Well, it's quite interesting really,' he said, with almost professorial detachment. 'It's folk music, but then sort of punky.'

He left the kitchen and went into the living room. In a moment or two he came back with the plastic carrier bag.

'I've brought this,' he said. 'Shane thought he remembered that you could play the piano.'

He wiggled a white-painted accordion out.

'We want you to learn how to play it,' he said.

I was dismissive about the idea of being in a band again. I was writing now. I had a flat to myself. I was twenty-seven. Nonetheless, I thought playing the accordion with Jem and Shane might be a welcome distraction.

'If it gets in the way of my writing . . .' I said. He said he understood.

'Only,' he added, 'in a couple of weeks, we have a gig.'

'Oh,' I said.

He left my flat with a handshake. I went off to clear up the tea things. I listened to his tread down the corridor.

It needed straps. The only thing to hand was my dad's old scholars' tie which I knotted round the metal fittings. I hoisted it up. It was lighter than I expected. I laughed at the gimcrackery of it, the fact that it was made mostly of wood and cardboard and held together by pins. It was basically a harmonica with keys attached. Opening the bellows revealed gold, bookbinders' edging, white cardboard, tucks of amber leather where the cardboard folded and the bright metal corners of the vanes. The grille was brazen filigree with tarnished wire cloth underneath. I loved the tawdry pearloid plastic of the keys. I made a five-finger chord and dragged it open. The sound was luscious. It had the sonority of a mouth organ deepened by the wood and the bellows. It was succulent with vibration as the double voicing of the reeds got going, a slight dissonance undulating between them as the air passed through. That afternoon, the presentiment of a common destiny passed between the accordion and me.

Six

Shane cackled at the formality with which Jem and I reintroduced ourselves at our practice the following week. Because both of us came from 'oop nawth', as Shane liked to put it, he delighted in imagining there was some latent rivalry between us.

I felt a kinship with Jem from the beginning. For a start, our initials coincided and, based on a lenient geography, and despite my brother's chestnut that anyone who lived south of Stockport was a Cockney, we did both think of ourselves as 'northerners'. Jem was from Stoke-on-Trent. I was from suburban Manchester. Both of us were products of a distinctly middle-class upbringing. Jem's grammar school education mirrored my boarding school one. Though my father was the son of a provincial industry captain, and Jem's dad the son of Bessarabian Jews who set up shop in Chapel Market in Islington, our fathers were both domineering men with a deal of influence. Jem's father was a university professor. Mine was the managing director of a building company in the North West. Yet another intersection in my and Jem's Venn diagram consisted of the fact that Jem's mum happened to be acquainted, through the Cheshire Liberal Party, with my Aunty Pat.

To show off what I'd accomplished in the week since Jem had come round to my flat, I pulled the accordion out of the laundry bag, hoisted it up, worked the straps over my shoulders and played for both of them. I'd figured out the chords of 'Abide with

Me,' with a churchy accompaniment of rising thirds on the bass buttons.

'See? I told you!' Shane said to Jem. 'He's a fucking genius.'

I loved music and reckoned myself good at it. I didn't have perfect pitch but I could hear harmonic ratios and interference beats. I knew from O-Level Physics about the propagation of sound, longitudinal waves, rarefaction and compression, about resonance and reverberation. I enjoyed knowing about Pythagorean intervals and the properties of a vibrating string. There wasn't an instrument I couldn't get something out of. When it came to learning the accordion, I had an idea how I wanted it to sound.

We started on a couple of the songs Jem and Shane had been working on. They were simple enough, though Shane's clumsiness with the guitar confused me at first. He stopped and started, his fingers clamping down on first one chord, then another. 'Streams of Whiskey' – a song Shane had written – had just three chords which followed a fairly obvious progression. 'The Old Main Drag' – another of Shane's – was a different matter, forever revolving round the tonic in a pattern that at first I couldn't get. The last song we tried, written by Brendan Behan, was called 'The Auld Triangle.' It contained an awkward shift from A seventh to a C which flummoxed my fingers on the bass buttons.

When I made simple arpeggios of the chords of 'Streams of Whiskey,' Shane cried out, 'Yeah, yeah! Alpine!'

At the end of the night, as I stowed the accordion back in the plastic bag, Shane asked me if I was into being in a band.

'Sure,' I said. 'But if it's going to take up too much time I'm going to have to knock it on the head.'

'Why?' he asked.

'I'm writing a book,' I said. Shane patted the tabletop, thinking. 'Yeah, well, we're all writing books,' he said.

49

Shane had a tape he and Jem had recorded so that I could learn the songs at home. He slid it off the top of the table to hand it to me, but spent the next few moments tapping and tapping the cassette tape, first on the heel of his hand, then on his knee, wafting it between his mucky fingers. When he finally handed it over to me, it was with a gesture of such flippancy that I instantly knew how proud he was of the songs on it.

There were twelve songs, including a couple of instrumentals. They had such titles as 'The Clobberer', 'The Battle of Brisbane', 'Connemara Let's Go', 'Poor Paddy on the Railway', 'The Humours of Whiskey', 'Kitty', 'The Dark Streets of London' and 'The Boys from the County Hell'. The recording was full of stops and starts. Both Shane and Jem sounded self-conscious, to the point of inaudibility on Jem's part, and peremptoriness on Shane's. Shane's singing was different from what I had been used to in the Nips. He no longer delivered the words with derision towards whoever might be listening, but with a sneer in the direction of his presumption to record the songs in the first place.

The next week we rehearsed with the whole band, which turned out to be just ourselves – and John Hasler. Hasler apparently had been the original drummer for the Invaders, the band which had eventually become Madness. Knowing Hasler's history with Shane, it puzzled me that he should be in our group. We met in the public bar in the Norfolk Arms, a tiny room with a painted Victorian fireplace and mantelshelf. It had been a while since I'd seen John's boyish face, his fair hair reminiscent of Tintin. I nodded a greeting. He nodded back. We had a couple of pints and then went up to the flat Jem now shared with a guy called Rick in Whidborne Buildings.

Hillview Estate – the four late-Victorian tenement blocks of Midhope, Lucas and Whidborne Buildings, East and West – was SCH's flagship. Hillview Estate as a whole must have been home to three hundred people or more. The buildings dominated Cromer Street from the Boot public house to the council estates on the far side of Loxham Street. They exuded an abiding and embattled sense of community and seemed to be a repository of Camden's counterculture.

The walls of Whidborne Buildings were streaked white with effluent from the waste-water hoppers high up the wall. Drab curtains hung in a couple of the windows, blankets in a couple more. A solitary window box provided a feeble flicker of colour.

An archway opened into the central well, a dingy cistern over-looked by the ranks of grimy windows and the landings on the stairwells, each railed across with iron. A polychromatic section of wall brightened the murk a little. A bin dump lurked under corrugated iron at one end of the courtyard. Bicycles were tethered at the other, by the stone steps up to Cromer Street.

Jem and Rick Trevan lived at No. 142. It was a tenebrous flat, though vivid swatches of fabric hanging over the walls relieved the dinginess. The table in Jem's room was strewn with stuff – tiny plastic trumpets, pens, moneyboxes, key rings, tin cans, photographs of the clock of St Pancras Station and a stack of battery-operated clock movements. Leaning against the wall, there was a painting of a figure, naked, curled over with its arse in the air and a bunch of flowers sprouting out between its but-tocks. As we went down the corridor to the back bedroom where we were going to rehearse, we passed another room. Under a lamp, furiously pressing out snakeskin badges from a machine with a lever, sat Jem's rangy, ginger-haired flatmate, Rick Trevan.

'Wotcha,' he said.

In the back bedroom John set up by the window. I squeezed up against the wall, behind the chest of drawers. Jem stood in the middle of the room. Shane stood up near the door, out of the light.

With the exception of Shane, we were all learning our instruments from scratch. Though Jem, I knew from living in Burton Street, could play guitar, the banjo was new to him. I watched him as he played. His eyes were sightless with concentration. His lips grimaced spasmodically in time to the chord changes. His mouth would form a taut line across his face, relax into a silent 'oooh', then abruptly suck in a snatch of air.

John Hasler bent over the two drums he had – for simplicity's sake a tom-tom and a snare. When he went about hitting them, he drew his face into an expression of judiciousness.

Shane clutched his guitar pick in his fist and scrubbed at the strings, angling his head this way and that. The fingers of his left hand would grope about looking for the next chord. By the time his fingers had found it, the chord had often passed and they had to move on in search of the next one. When he sang, he lifted his head up and closed his eyes. He'd suck in air between his teeth and wet his flaking lips from time to time. In the slow songs his voice was sonorous and heartfelt. In the fast ones, it was derisive.

I had difficulty remembering which song was which. I had practised up in my flat, pacing about my front room, listening to Shane and Jem's tape, going over the songs, trying to get them to stick. They wouldn't. Because they all seemed to start in G or D, I ended up not being able to tell them apart. I wouldn't know what the song was until it started.

After the first rehearsal, we didn't get together for a week. I practised against my tape up in my flat. As the date came closer, we rehearsed a couple of consecutive nights. The weekend before the gig, we spent both Saturday and Sunday in Rick Trevan's cramped back bedroom.

The gig Jem had told me about when he'd come to my flat was cancelled. A guy called Justin Ward who lived in Stanley Buildings – another SCH property between St Pancras and King's Cross stations – replaced it with a gig at the Pindar of Wakefield on Gray's Inn Road – more or less at the end of Shane's street – for the 5th October. Jem had found someone to do the sound for us – a musician called Darryl Hunt whom both Shane and Jem knew from around King's Cross.

For the gig at the Pindar of Wakefield, Shane had invited his friend Spider to play with us. I didn't know what instrument he played. I didn't want to ask. I had met Spider when I was living at No. 32 Burton Street. I had come in after work to find Shane in the kitchen with a guy wearing a black windjammer and jeans, whose hair was dyed the colour of soot and buzzed into a box shape. I had nothing better to do, so I had sat in the filthy armchair and let myself be introduced. It wasn't long before Spider and Shane started hurling insults at one another. The oaths were so barbarous that I knew they were pretending, but the vileness that came out of Spider's mouth was prodigious, and Shane's contumely, protean. I laughed, uneasily. In the end Shane had served up a show-stopper of such grossness that it had reduced Spider to helpless guffawing.

We met up with Spider in the Norfolk Arms after one of our rehearsals. Again, Spider and Shane vied with one another, the pair of them trading cruelties, quotations and quips until they collapsed into helpless cackling. I was amazed at the references the two of them made – the ones I thought I recognised, at least: Shakespeare, Joyce, Flann O'Brien, Beckett. Spider, it seemed, had a virtually eidetic memory. His facility to quote, often at length, from books, films, television programmes was staggering and more often than not hilarious. His knowledge of history and geography seemed encyclopedic.

'If we're doing a gig,' Spider said, 'we need a name.'

'The Men They Couldn't Hang,' Shane said.

'The Noisy Boysies,' Spider said.

'The Black Velvet Underground.'

'Pogue Mahone,' said Spider.

'Pogue Mahone! Ye-es! Fuck! Yeah!' Shane said, slapping his head with the palm of his hand.

' "Pogue mahone! Acushla machree! It's destroyed we are from this day! It's destroyed we are surely!" ' Spider said. 'It's from *Ulysses*. It means kiss my arse. Pogue Mahone!'

'Pogue Mahone!' Shane said.

Before going down to the Pindar of Wakefield, with the exception of Spider whom we were going to meet there, we convened at Jem's flat. We had all agreed to wear suits and shirts with buttons. When Shane came in, late, he stood in the hallway-cum-living room and took muster. He wore a black suit with narrow lapels and tapered trousers. He looked us all up and down. He scratched his head above his ear. His eyebrows plicated his forehead as if he was surprised not to catch someone out.

We had all our instruments ready. They stood in the hallway in their cases. It was a short walk down Cromer Street to the Pindar of Wakefield. We were nervous. Just as we were about to leave, Shane stopped us.

'Wait! Wait! Wait!' he shouted. He had a hole in his shoe, on the upper, where the leather had split and the white of his sock was showing through. John went down to the corner shop for a bottle of Kiwi scuff cover. Shane hoisted his shoe up onto the seat of the chair, stretched his arms clear of the sleeves of his tight jacket, to apply the sponge to the sock showing in the hole. The way we presented ourselves, I knew then, was going to come up in the future.

We descended the stairs. Instrument cases in hand, we walked down the dark street to the Pindar of Wakefield, four abreast, blocking off the road, in my mind's eye like the Wild Bunch, our shadows cast behind us, fanning out over the surface of Cromer Street. We were pared down to essentials: suits, shirts with buttons, shoes, black instrument cases. Spider met us in a leather jacket and jeans, and with a stripe of red dye in his hair.

The moment we started to play, I could feel myself losing grip of the purposefulness I had grimly enjoyed as we walked down Cromer Street. The shock of standing up in front of a small horde of the occupants of Hillview Estate and a couple of friends who had made the journey up from Kingston-upon-Thames – not to mention Debsey's family who were all sitting in the far corner – shook every last melody and song structure from my mind. I had to shout out for Jem to remind me how most of the songs began.

I was surprised how well Spider knew the songs. It turned out that he and Shane were already in a band called the Millwall Chainsaws, both of them singing. They had played a gig at Richard Strange's club Cabaret Futura. They had played Irish songs and as a joke had called themselves – I remembered Shane mentioning to me – the New Republicans, another band name Spider had come up with. British squaddies in the audience that night had pelted them with chips.

Anchored by the microphone and its stand to the side of the stage, I was grateful to be on the periphery one moment, the next, hot with embarrassment to wear so conspicuous an instrument as an accordion. When it came to playing, I found myself caught up with the intricacy of it, conscious of the angle my arms needed to adopt for the height of the keys, the angle my head had to strike both to see and to hear what I was doing, making sure that the grille of the accordion stayed close to the microphone. Everything was going on, literally, under my nose.

I heard Shane's guitar-playing to be much more erratic than in rehearsal. John's drumming seemed full of false starts and reiterations. By far the greatest disturbance was Spider.

The occasion of our first gig had clearly gone to his head. It seemed to have transformed him into a ranting, anachronistic ersatz punk, snarling a succession of grotesquely affected ejaculations of what sounded like punk slogans and otherwise screaming his head off.

The only calmative influence was Jem, who stood next to me, four-square, dependable, though cautious and aloof. I looked across at him. He was staring agape out into the crowd.

Beyond him stood Shane, singing, his eyes half-closed. Whether or not he knew it, he had set the microphone at such a height to require him to sing up and out. It implied a larger audience than the one we had. His charisma was undeniable. His carriage, his contours, the attitude he copped, from which he did not break, were simultaneously authentic and artful.

Seven

After our first gig, helped by Shane's renown not just in the music world but in and around Hillview Estate, shows came up: at the 101 Club on Clapham Road, the 100 Club on Oxford Street and the offer of a residency at the Pindar of Wakefield. Shamed by his performance earlier in the month, Spider had started teaching himself to play the tin whistle. There was a pressing need to rehearse.

I turned up at the Norfolk Arms. We had been forewarned that Shane had found us a bass player, an Irish girl he'd met at a club and who had stridden into the record shop he worked in, offering to play bass. As I came through from the bar with my pint, she was in the vault, leaning against the mantelpiece. She was a lank, lean, surly, black-jacketed waif, her hair backcombed into black candyfloss which she twisted around her barrow-boy gloved fingers, encouraging a jet skein to fall over her shy but febrile eyes. She was beautiful.

'You must be Cait the bass player,' I said.

'No,' she answered – in the loveliest of voices, soft and singing, with a trace of an Irish accent. 'I'm just Cait.'

There was an atmosphere of sang-froid in the parlour of the Norfolk Arms, a watchful embarrassment among us which caused us to regard our new bass player askance. I wondered if she was conscious that Shane might have breezed her into the band because he fancied her. I didn't really care who joined the band. My attitude, as I had reminded Shane and Jem and Spider, was that I was writing a novel and that if the band threatened to obstruct its progress I would quit. My lack of commitment seemed to afford me some charity towards Cait.

'I can't believe this,' she said, covering her mouth with her fingertips. Indicating Shane, she said: 'I've been a fan of this cunt for years.'

'How old are you?' I asked.

'Seventeen,' she said. The previous Tuesday had been my twenty-eighth birthday. I felt sorry for her, and at the same time relieved. In a couple of weeks, when Shane tired of her, I assumed she would be gone.

Up in Rick Trevan's back room, the situation was awkward. It turned out that Cait hadn't much idea how to play bass. Shane took her under his wing. With a solicitousness that was comical, he tried to teach her the bass notes for the songs. The process soon fell foul of his ineptitude and Cait became even more confused as to what she was supposed to do. Jem was no help. I wondered if Shane's foisting on us a girl he had picked up at a club in the past week prevented Jem from stepping up to assist. I ended up teaching Cait the notes to the songs, lifting my eyebrows at the approach of a chord change, and, if she missed it, pulling harder on the accordion to bring her back into line.

At the end of the rehearsal, we went back down to the Norfolk Arms for closing time. We stood around by the fireplace. I found myself talking with Cait. As if to remind me and everyone around her of her age, her punk ethos and her status as the only girl in the group, something I said caused her to punch me in the stomach, so unexpectedly and with such force that the blow sent me to my knees.

The first gig she played with us was with King Kurt at the 101 Club. At rehearsals during the week, she stood on the bed, her head up in the ceiling corner, and smacked the notes out on her bass, driving the pick onto the strings, her pale fingers stretching for the next note. There was a want of caution about her that made me embarrassed on her account, but which nonetheless fascinated me.

On stage, too, she played her bass with swagger. We hadn't wanted to go on after King Kurt but lost the toss. King Kurt had a reputation for mess. When it came time for our set, the plastic sheeting which covered the backline amps was dribbling with flour-paste and the stage littered with rabbit and chicken entrails. Cait stood tall, her head erect, her hair black, stiffened with backcombing. She swung the neck of her bass back and forth and alternately shot out looks of malevolence into the half-empty room or down onto the mat of giblets and paste on the floor.

We finished our set. Most of the audience left. I had packed away my accordion and was standing at the back of the room with a drink when Cait came up to the centre microphone. To the delight of a couple of guys who were still sitting at a table at the front, Cait propped her hand onto her waist and launched into a couple of Irish rebel songs. Though it wandered sharp, her voice was lovely. It had a natural, sultry vibrato – I struggled to place where I might have heard it before, until it came to me that it was in Marilyn Monroe's 'Diamonds Are a Girl's Best Friend'. The vibrato and the intonation of Cait's voice was innocent and unaffected, and her eyes dusky and insolent with the adolescent embarrassment of knowing how well she could sing, and how much she craved the attention. When she finished singing, the two guys at the table down the front fell to whistling and shouting. Cait threw up two fingers in their direction and sashayed up the room.

With gigs coming up we tried to rehearse every other night. Shane's attendance was unpredictable. One weekend, we learnt that he'd gone off to his parents' house in Tunbridge Wells to get his laundry done. As it had been in the Nips, the condition he was in when he did manage to make it to rehearsal was unpredictable too. He was either drunk and argumentative, or meek and apologetic. I knew Jem to have visited him to talk about what we were supposed to be doing, how important rehearsals were. The effects of his exhortations were short-lived, but I had the feeling Jem would prevail.

Spider's attendance at rehearsal was just as unreliable. When he showed up, he ranted at length about scrapes he'd got himself into. He pitched into debates with Shane about someone or other they knew, somewhere or other they had been, which had had some comical dénouement or other. Frequently he'd give out about his girlfriend Anya, a brittle girl I'd come across a couple of times. Jem had also let Spider know how unacceptable his performance at the Pindar of Wakefield had been, how much he had disapproved of his absence at rehearsals.

Shane and Spider delayed count-ins and interrupted them when they were under way, by eruptions of coughing fits and laryngeal explosions from Shane. Their sallies seemed to go on for ever. I folded my hands on the top of the accordion and waited for them to finish, ready to balance my roll-up on the edge of the ashtray if it looked like we were going to begin a song.

Occasionally Spider would argue, and inexhaustibly, about how fast a particular song should be or should have been.

'Drivel without a pause,' I said.

'Oh!' Spider said, in mock injury.

When he got round to playing, Spider snapped his leg to the beat and played with his eyes closed, elbows out wide. He was a fidgety player. For glissandi, he slid his ring finger over a hole on his whistle up to the second knuckle and lifted it off with the precision of a tea-taster. He was fearless when it came to taking on such ornaments as I'd heard on the Potts and Moloney record, though they sometimes ended in warbles. Vibrato and intonation were elusive. After a song, he would flick the whistle as if to clear an obstruction from the mouthpiece.

'Fuck!' he'd say.

The other instrument Spider played was a metal beer tray which he bashed against his head.

'It's a traditional Irish instrument,' Shane explained.

'What are we doing?' Spider beseeched once, looking to be on the verge of stamping his feet, his whistle clenched in his fist, tendons showing white under the skin of his wrist.

'We're knocking on the door of silence and awaiting an answer,' I said.

One evening, Shane was so late that we sent Spider to go and find him. Spider came back empty-handed and volunteered to sing in Shane's place. He knew the words to all the songs we were doing. We had been working on 'The Auld Triangle.' Spider closed his eyes and sang the entirety of it in a key several steps distant from the one in which we were playing it.

We said nothing. We didn't look at one another. None of us had the courage to stop playing and suggest getting on with one of the instrumentals we could better have spent our time practising.

Jem was dogged and patient. He stood squarely in the room, his feet at ten to two, his sleeves rolled up, the banjo hanging from his symmetrically angled shoulders. The chaos in the room glanced off him like arrows against a testudo, as he moved inexorably forward to get the next song done.

I lent Shane my guitar. The one he had, he'd either lost or it had been stolen. Whenever he picked mine up to play, I winced. It wasn't a particularly good or expensive guitar, but since selling my Telecaster it was the only one I had. He made a bear garden of putting the guitar on, distracted as he was by his cigarette smouldering in the ashtray or by his can of Tennent's, working the strap over his shoulder, pulling on the cigarette, dropping his guitar pick, not realising that the strap had become detached from its button on the bottom of the guitar and letting the instrument fall, to slam it between his arm and his thigh to stop it dropping to the ground. Whenever he set it down, he was incapable of doing so without banging it against the chair that was in the room or against the chest of drawers.

After a couple of weeks, Shane brought my guitar to rehearsal with a V-shaped hole in the front of it.

'My door fell on it!' he said.

'Your door fell on it?'

'My door doesn't have any fucking hinges!' he spat. 'Yeah?' he added, in such a way that I felt foolish to have expected it to.

At rehearsals and at gigs I was the one to tune everything. I gestured to Jem to bring his drone string into alignment, either by means of the palm of my hand uppermost, edging him up, or palm downmost, urging him down, then, the closer he got to bringing the strings in unison, making a pincer of my fingers, closing the gap between my fingertips, then slicing the air to signify that the banjo was in tune. Shane was worse. He twisted the machine-heads with savage wrenches, raising the out-of-tune string past accordance and then, after I had shouted, 'Down! Down!', screwing the machine-heads in the opposite direction. With a deal of begrudging fuss Shane gave up the guitar for me to tune.

Cait wanted no help when it came to tuning her bass. She tuned it only when it was absolutely necessary – and with an obduracy that suffered no interruption.

Spider's tuning was complicated. Hot water needed running over the mouthpiece to soften the glue which held it to the tube before we could twist it free. Spider would blow a few notes, look at me defencelessly, twist the mouthpiece and blow again. The note was never true, but we'd fix it afterwards with gaffer tape anyway.

As rehearsals went on, Shane seemed convinced that C and F and G were all the chords you needed to make music. Relative minors he didn't know. It was rare that we came across one. Now and again a melody would jar against the chord structure he brought to bear on it. I suggested an alternative chord progression.

'What!?' he cried. 'No! It doesn't go like that!'

We went round the song again and again. Each time the problematic section came up, the chords ground against the melody. I couldn't keep my mouth shut any longer.

'If we went from F to G here,' I said, 'instead of G to F.'

He tried it out, scrubbing through the chords, with his head down, bent over the guitar, staring at his fingers. He looked up angrily.

'Yeah!' he said. 'Yeah! It's *supposed* to go that way!'

Maybe it was the fact that she was the only girl, the youngest and the most recent addition to the band which conferred on Cait a right to cut crap. Maybe it was the disparity between her and our ages which gave her the licence to disdain us as pusillanimous when it came to the matter of decision-making, of taking the bull by the horns.

John's lack of talent had come up in conversation, but that was only ever as far as we got, only ever as far as we wanted to go. We were reluctant to swinge.

Just as we'd turned up at rehearsal one afternoon, without

warning, Cait lit into John with a ferocity that made us blench.

'I don't understand what the fuck you're doing in this fucking band,' she said. 'You can't play for shit. Why don't you just fuck off?'

John looked at us, from one to the other.

'Go on, fuck off!' Cait said.

John looked at her with a panicked smile of disbelief, then, cowed and beaten, he left.

We stood around in the room for a moment or two in horror at what she'd done. Spider broke the silence with a sputter of laughter, his hand covering his mouth, his forehead pleated in disbelief. We all laughed, not so much at John's pathetic figure skulking out of Rick Trevan's flat, but from embarrassment at the intimacy Cait seemed to have forced on us by her violence and impulsiveness.

It crossed my mind that Cait's fury at John – the man who had deprived Shane of his virtual namesake in the Nips – might have been evidence of her wanting to prove her love for Shane. Up until that moment, there had been scant indication of Cait's feelings. She and Shane turned up at rehearsals independently of one another. At no time was I aware of any familiarity, private joke or secret look that passed between them.

Shane must have had some idea of Cait's feelings for him. In the days following, he told me a joke: a woman's paramour had become so besotted that, when she confessed to being bothered to distraction by her lapdog, saying, 'Oh, sometimes I do wish that damn dog were dead!', her suitor took the dog away and shot it. After the telling, Shane wheezed himself empty of air.

We set about finding another drummer. There was a guy Shane and Jem knew who lived in Whidborne Buildings but who played in another band and had said he wasn't interested. We tried a couple of other drummers. Neither of them lasted more than an afternoon or evening. None of them understood what we were doing and none of us seemed to be able to put what it was we wanted into words. One of these drummers played a gig with us at Dingwalls the January following John Hasler's sacking. The drummer was so inept, the gig so bad, that it ended with Jem driving his forehead against the wall in frustration.

We hunkered down with the aim of pre-empting what seemed to be drummers' partiality for unnecessary dynamics and being seated when they played. I loved the idea that we all stood to play and that a drummer should stand too and carry a stick in each hand with a drum for each – a floor-tom and a snare. The set-up connoted a quick getaway, implied nomadism. I relished the picture of us all having carried our gear down to our first gig at the Pindar of Wakefield.

For a few weeks we moved our rehearsals to the flat of a friend of Shane's near Marble Arch. At Cathy MacMillan's flat we set about simplifying the drum patterns to a matter of hitting a floor-tom on the onbeat, and the snare drum on the off – the marching beat, 2/2, the polka. We recorded the songs on cassette, to present to the next candidate for the job of drummer.

In March 1983, Andrew Ranken, the guy in Whidborne Buildings whom Jem and Shane had badgered to join the group, threw over his other band, the Operation, which, with his Fine Art degree course at Goldsmiths College, had been the reason he gave to Jem and Shane for his unavailability, and came to drum with us.

He brought his own drums: a turquoise cocktail drum – deep and booming – and snare drum. He tolerated us prohibiting him from sitting down to play. His presence was one of smouldering power. He stood at his drums with bare forearms. His hands were strong and they gripped the drumsticks with the thumb aligned and the stick snug in the heel of his hand. His fingernails were brutally smooth and hard. When he played, his body bent over the drums but his head stayed erect, his lips pressed together. Despite his face's forbidding, granite-hewn, lurkingly angry aspect, beneath his stern eyebrows Andrew's eyes were vulnerable, accentuated by dense eyelashes.

That he had been difficult to get, but had finally relented and turned up with his gear, seemed to imbue Andrew with a prerogative that was difficult to put your finger on. It depressed me whenever Andrew said he wasn't available for a rehearsal or a gig. It wasn't just because I had discovered a passion for what we were doing and a place in it, but mostly because his commitments reminded me that the novel I was supposed to be writing was dying of neglect.

Eight

Jem supplemented his income by teaching maths and photography to juvenile delinquents at a centre in Deptford and by selling clocks up at Camden Market. He made the clocks himself by slotting a picture of St Pancras Station clock tower into a plastic photograph frame and mounting a battery-operated movement to the back.

Shane worked in a record shop called Rocks Off on Hanway Street, an alleyway which ran between Tottenham Court Road and Oxford Street. Rocks Off was the sister shop to Rock On on Kentish Town Road. Both shops had been founded by Ted Carroll, who, after giving up his job as Thin Lizzy's manager, went on to sell records from a stall near Portobello Road Market, expanding at first to premises in Soho and then to Camden. Carroll ran the Camden shop. Rocks Off was run by a couple of Belfast men called Stan Brennan and Phil Gaston.

Brennan seemed to follow a more or less Camden model: he had crisp hair done in short back and sides, clear plastic Liberty glasses, jeans and windbreaker. Phil Gaston was a gangly man, goofy, with a liquid Belfast accent and crooked teeth. They came to all our gigs.

Spider, I was told, had a job selling cars. I didn't know what Cait did.

I'd had a couple of jobs – my sweeping job at the equipment repair shop in Soho and the refurbishment of a club on Charing

Cross Road – but since my job for the electoral register ended I had been signing on. I had besides a private income. Livid at the amount of tax the family had had to pay on my grandfather's death in 1971, my father, in the past couple of years, in order to avoid death duties, had divided what equity he held in the family's building company between me and my brothers. The biannual dividend from the shares – sometimes up to £500 – along with whatever wages I happened to earn from the haphazard employment I had and the pittance I got from the DHSS, allowed me to live without the anxiety everyone else I knew suffered.

After our eviction from No. 32 Burton Street, and while living in the flat in Whidborne Buildings with Rick Trevan, Jem had been writing letters to Camden Council in an attempt to get himself rehoused. To begin with, the letters were formal requests to the council to recognise his eviction and consequent homelessness, in the hope of gaining priority in the council's points system. At the beginning of 1983, I came across him filling out an application form, in which he cited cramped conditions and a medical condition – neurosis – evident by his tiny scribbling in the top corner of the form. SCH was stretched to the limit. It had been over two years since the passing of the Housing Act. Homelessness in London was rampant.

On Valentine's Day, Jem came to rehearsal to announce that his girlfriend Marcia was pregnant and that they were going to get married.

Jem and Marcia had met at a training course for teachers of English as a Foreign Language. Marcia was beautiful. She had full, dark hair and fiercely dark, expressive eyebrows. Her small and purposeful mouth, glazed by custom with carmine lipstick, was drawn into an aristocratic pucker.

In conversation with Marcia, her grey-blue eyes fixed you with a stare which, while outwardly curious, seemed simultaneously trained inwards. A memory or a thought process would detain her attention for a moment or two and cloud her eyes, before the severity of her focus returned, drawing her eyebrows down in an expression that was often forbidding. Her disquisitions demanded full concentration, though I often struggled to track the arguments she made. In her distinctly blue-blooded accent, she'd suddenly ask me a question which, though I was sure it wasn't her intention, more often than not caught me out.

I congratulated Jem along with everyone else, but was stunned. That anyone should want to have a baby, the way we were all living in short-life accommodation and with little or no security of employment, amazed me.

What underlay my astonishment, though, was that I was jealous. Jem's announcement rendered his life compared to mine more adult, more a drama in which he was the protagonist. Jem was always taking things on and making things happen. I flailed around trying to get things done. Jem always seemed to have someone to meet, somewhere to go, things to do. I lived by myself in my flat, spending the mornings clattering on my typewriter and accomplishing pretty much nothing but a routine.

After his announcement, Jem renewed his efforts with Camden Council to get himself and Marcia – and the baby when he or she should arrive – somewhere to live. His pains eventually paid off with his and Marcia's move to a council flat on Wicklow Street, a crooked cobbled street between Gray's Inn Road and King's Cross Road.

On the 12th March, they were married in Chelsea. Their reception, at which Pogue Mahone was booked to play, was planned for the third week in May, at a wine bar off Gray's Inn Road.

I was envious of both of them. I was fairly sure I didn't want to get married, but the entire month of March – with a break to perform on a television appearance with Captain Sensible in France – Debsey had been on tour with Fun Boy Three, the group Neville Staples, Lynval Golding and Terry Hall had formed after leaving the Specials in March 1981.

Debsey's life was still full of prospects: tours, gigs, rehearsals, song-writing, meetings. I tried to redress the balance by spending the day pecking at my typewriter and ending it at either my writers' workshop, or, in the past couple of months, rehearsing with Shane, Jem, Spider, Cait and Andrew.

Pogue Mahone's weekly residency at the Pindar of Wakefield took place in April and May. Shane gave us all names. Andrew was The Clobberer, after one of the songs on the practice tape Shane and Jem had given me – and after a character in Flann O'Brien. Jem became known as Country Jem, by virtue of his predilection for country music. Cait was called Rocky. I was given the *nom de guerre* Maestro Jimmy Fearnley. Spider's name was already a soubriquet. Shane was just Shane.

Jem and Shane's friend Darryl could be depended on when it

came to helping us set up and mix the sound. The gigs were organised by a couple of girls called Fee and Sharon whose club on Wednesday nights went under the name 'Heywire!' After just a couple of weeks, our gigs at the pub had become raucous events, crowded and agog.

After one of them, as I threaded my way through the people to join Debsey, I saw Cait coming in the opposite direction. On her way past, she growled that she'd seen Shane go into the toilets with Spider's girlfriend Anya. Such was Shane's capriciousness that there were many more reasons to go to the toilets with Spider's girlfriend than the obvious one. I thought nothing of it. Besides, I had seen so little evidence of intimacy between Cait and Shane that I assumed their relationship was over. It had been six months since Cait had fired John Hasler.

A week later, the night before Jem and Marcia's wedding reception, we met to rehearse at Rick Trevan's flat. We waited for Cait, for a long time. While we waited, it turned out that after the gig the previous week at the Pindar, Spider, Cait and Shane had gone down to the Pakenham Arms on Calthorpe Street where an altercation had resulted in Cait walking out in high dudgeon.

Shane sent Spider to get her from the guesthouse she had recently moved into.

'At least get her to come to the fucking gig tomorrow,' Shane said. 'Yeah?'

Half an hour later Spider was back.

'She's not coming,' he said. 'And she doesn't want to do the gig.'

Shane clawed his face.

'Oh God!' he said. 'What did you say to her?'

'She just said she didn't want anything more to do with it. She wanted to know if you'd finished with her.'

'I asked, "What did *you* say to *her*?" ' Shane said.

'Well,' Spider said, 'I said the chances were that that was what you wanted.'

'You said *what*?' Shane said, his eyes wide in disbelief. He raked his hair with his fingers and slapped his forehead in desperation. 'You fucking idiot! You fucking idiot! I told you to go round there to get her to do the gig. I didn't tell you to bring up her fucking love life!'

'So, it's my fault, is it?'

'You fucking bastard!'

'Fuck you!' Spider said. 'You're her fucking *boyfriend*,' he sneered.

'Fuck off,' Shane said.

There was a chair in the back bedroom. He sat heavily on it and pulled a few times on a cigarette, wiped his nose, blew the smoke out.

'We need a fucking bass player,' he said. He turned to Spider. With his voice full of accusation he added: 'All of a sudden!'

Sidelined by the exigencies of Jem's wedding reception, Cait was forgotten. Andrew knew of someone who might be able to take over playing bass for the one gig. He went off to use the phone but came back shaking his head.

I knew two bass players. One of them was Debsey, but she was my girlfriend. The other bass player I knew was Shanne Hasler, who had now resumed her maiden name, Bradley. The instant it occurred to me, before I could shut the thought away, a broad smile appeared on Shane's face.

'I know someone who would do it,' he leered.

'Oh, no,' I said. 'She's not going to be doing it. I don't want her in the group.'

'Not even for one gig?'

'Not even for one gig. I don't bear grudges or anything,' I lied.

72

'But, if she's going to play, you're going to have to look for another accordionist.'

'Well,' Spider said, 'we've been thinking . . .'

I was glad of the joke. I knew before it came out of my mouth that to say such a thing was rash, but I had learnt that if you needed to stop Shane in his tracks, not a chink of light should show through the wall of your resolve.

Shane's jaw dropped into jowls. His eyes widened with surprise. After a couple of seconds, he clopped his tongue against the roof of his mouth and nodded. I didn't care if his gesture was a signal of his capitulation or the deferment of a coming conflict.

The matter was dropped. Jem played bass. We rehearsed until closing time. Down in the Norfolk Arms, we set aside whatever problems Shane and Cait might have had and put our heads together as to how to get Cait to come to Jem and Marcia's reception to play.

We scheduled visits to her guesthouse for the following day. First, Jem would go across. A couple of hours later I would drop by. In the afternoon, closer to the time we were due to turn up for a sound check, Shane was to visit. We hoped by then he would be able to mend whatever damage had been done and bring her to Smithy's Wine Bar.

The entrance to the Jesmond Dene guesthouse was a black, sun-matted doorway seemingly hidden on a stretch of Argyle Street. The manager told me that the girl on the second floor had had a couple of visitors that morning, but that she wasn't in. I went round to Jem and Marcia's new flat on Wicklow Street. He told me that when he'd been over to the guesthouse he had had the same result. We puzzled about who the other visitor might have been.

Time was getting tight. We had to get the gear from Rick Trevan's flat. We forgot about Cait. If she wasn't in, she wasn't in.

There wasn't much else we could do about it. She knew about the reception. We imagined she'd just turn up. Before we left, he showed me an airing cupboard full of new towels.

'Wedding presents,' he said. 'The money would have been good.'

We were setting up our gear when Shane came in. He'd been to the Jesmond Dene, as agreed. Cait had been there the whole time.

'She's taken some pills,' he said.

We wanted to know how many and what kind.

'How the fuck would I know! Some fucking pills!' he said. 'She's cross-eyed and limp.'

'Oh fuck,' Spider said.

'And I'm not going back there,' Shane said. 'She's vicious.'

The guesthouse manager opened the front door to Jem and me.

'Your friend is sleeping,' he said. 'She has asked not to be disturbed.'

'We're her friends,' Jem said. 'We need to look in on her.' The man shook his head and took us up the stairs.

The door to Cait's diminutive room stood open. It was surprisingly tidy. A small, light-blue suitcase, zipped closed, stood on the top of the empty wardrobe. The net curtains at the windows were drawn to. Cait lay on the bed curled up under a coat she had pulled over her head. She was wearing her boots. The disorder of her black hair sprouted out of the coat collar.

'Hiya, Cait!' we called as we went in. Jem crouched next to the bed.

'We've come to visit you!' he shouted cheerily.

Cait's mouth slowly formed the words, 'Go away.'

'We only just got here,' I said.

'What do you want to sleep in the middle of the afternoon for?'

Jem shouted. 'Why are you so sleepy? Have you had anything to eat today?'

I wanted him to take charge the way he took charge of Shane's unreliability, the way he had taken Spider to task about his performance at our first gig at the Pindar of Wakefield, the way he did things like get married and sort out gigs for us to play. I wanted to be able to rely on him, but he was going about it all wrong.

'Sleep,' Cait murmured into the pillow.

'We can't let you go to sleep,' I said. 'Sit up and talk to us.'

I worked my hands under her shoulders and tried to pull her up. She was heavy. She opened her eyes for a brief moment. Her pupils were dilated and sightless. She whined and struggled to lie down again. I gave up. She flopped back down.

'Come out for a walk with us,' Jem said heartily. 'Come round to my flat and have something to eat!'

'Leave,' she managed to say, scarcely moving her lips and in a voice so weak that it barely engaged her vocal cords. 'Want to sleep,' she breathed.

The feebleness of her voice together with the fact that she had dispensed with personal pronouns gave me the feeling that she was faking. When I tried to pull her coat off her shoulders she shivered elaborately.

Jem and I talked over Cait's body on the bed. To call for an ambulance seemed an overreaction. I volunteered to go down to one of the phones at King's Cross and find a local doctor.

Outside it was beginning to get dark. The sky was purple. King's Cross seemed a bleak and dirty place. At one of the public phones I rang the first doctor's number I came across in the Yellow Pages. There was no answer. I pressed off the ringing tone, lifted on the dialling tone and rang 999.

When I got back to the guesthouse, Jem had managed to get

Cait to tell him that she had taken twenty-five sleeping pills that morning, and that she had downed more later. We waited for a while. I saw that she was holding something in her hand, cradled close to her throat. I gently pulled from her a crumpled and damp souvenir picture, within a border of green plaitwork, of St Patrick. I returned it to her fingers, which closed around it and drew it back under her chin.

A couple of paramedics came, a man and a woman. The man took Cait's pulse. The woman tried to shine a pencil-light into Cait's eyes.

'Open your eyes,' the woman paramedic said to Cait.

'No,' Cait said. 'What for?'

'For me,' she said. She shone the light into Cait's eyes.

'Ow!' Cait said.

'She'll live,' the woman paramedic said. 'But we're going to take her to the hospital and clean her out. It'll not be pleasant.' She left the room.

'One of you want to come with her?' the man said. I said something about both of us having to go somewhere.

'That's all right,' he said. 'You don't have to come.'

I was relieved not to have to go down to the hospital. I didn't want any more to do with Cait. The woman came back with a carry-chair and a red blanket. They lifted Cait off the bed and put her in it. Cait curled up, shivering.

'Anyone?' the woman said.

'I'll go,' Jem said. 'It's fine,' he said to me. 'I'll see you later.'

I listened to the thump of the carry-chair on the treads and reproved myself for not going with him. I heard the street door close.

I looked round for some sort of note. I took down Cait's suitcase from the top of the wardrobe. It was packed with excessive neatness. On the top was a copy of *Ulysses* and *Confessions of an Irish Rebel* by Brendan Behan and a couple of pullovers – a greeny-black short-sleeved one I'd seen her wear and a powder-blue one which I hadn't, and which seemed to belong to a Cait I didn't know. There was a slip of paper. I unfolded it.

> *Shane 98 Cromer Street WC1*
> *You can do what you want with stuff.*

I closed up the suitcase and put it back on top of the wardrobe and went across to Smithy's Wine Bar. It was beginning to get dark. When I got there, Spider, Shane and Andrew wanted to know where Jem was.

'And it's his fucking wedding reception!' they said.

People had started to turn up. They had turned lights on in the wine bar. Debsey was standing with Marcia, wearing a lavender-coloured frock. Stricken, she looked from me to Marcia. Marcia stood with a glass of champagne, clutching her elbows.

'Generous to a fault,' Marcia said with a sweep of her hand. Before long, Jem came in from the street. He hadn't much to tell us. The ambulance had drawn into Casualty at University College Hospital. Cait had been wheeled out of sight.

When it came time for our performance, we got up on the stage at the end of the room and picked up our instruments. Jem took up the bass. Shane clanged a chord on the guitar and sniffed into the microphone.

'We haven't got a bass player,' he said. 'She's dead.'

⁜

Before a doctor could come to treat her, Cait discharged herself and went home. It wasn't until three weeks had gone by that we all met again for rehearsal. There was no mention of the episode.

I wondered if the swagger with which she came into the room might have been intended to pre-empt enquiry. I stole looks at her now and again, half expecting to catch her in a moment of ruefulness, but she stood in her customary position on the bed in the corner, next to the window, inscrutable. I looked out for a sheepish solicitude towards Cait from Shane, but his behaviour was unchanged, as he made a buffoonery of balancing his smoking cigarette on the saucer on the chest of drawers, struggling into the strap of the guitar, sniffing, assembling his fingers on the fretboard, thwacking a chord.

'Awright?' he said.

Nine

In July I had to move from Mornington Crescent. SCH gave me a top-floor flat in a Victorian dwelling between the bottom of Royal College Street and the Hospital for Tropical Diseases. An arched entryway led into a courtyard. A curtain here and there blew out through an open window in the heat. My new flat was dark and cramped. A small kitchen overlooked the central courtyard.

Debsey's family helped me move in. Her dad drove us round to the house belonging to a couple in Crouch End who were selling a bed for £40. Her mum took me up to the PDSA in Islington to look for furniture. Debsey came to help me paint the flat.

It had been over a year since the successes of Captain Sensible's 'Happy Talk' and 'Wot!' The following autumn Dolly Mixture had provided backing vocals for Sensible's less successful second solo record, *The Power of Love*. On their own label, Debsey, Rachel and Hester had released a retrospective double album of all their demos. The LPs, called *Demonstration Tapes*, came in a white cardboard sleeve. One afternoon on the floor of her parents' living room, I had helped Debsey stamp and number a pile of them and handed them to her to sign. The double album included the last single the group had released – a wistful, rose-tinted, valedictory single called 'Remember This'.

On a promotional trip to Europe that summer, in the Belgian harbour town of Ostend, Sensible and Dolly Mixture's guitarist Rachel started a relationship. It broke the once steadfast triangle of the three girls' friendship.

Debsey wanted pink for the bedroom of my new flat.

'I'm going to want something to lift my mood in the mornings,' Debsey said, adding, 'if I'm going to be staying with you.'

It was a warm day at the end of August that Jem, Shane, Cait, Spider, Andrew and I went up to the studio Justin Ward had built in his flat – in reality the spare room, carpeted from floor to ceiling. It was the second time, in fact, that we had been to his studio. A couple of weeks after our first gig at the Pindar of Wakefield, we had gone up to his flat in Stanley Buildings to record 'Streams of Whiskey', 'Poor Paddy on the Railway' and Eric Bogle's 'And the Band Played Waltzing Matilda', but had come away with a cassette tape with half the stereo missing. We knew we could give a good account of the rehearsing we'd been doing, the songs we'd been playing out live, and besides, we now had Andrew playing drums.

Spider came up with an instrumental called 'The Repeal of the Licensing Laws'. 'Connemara Let's Go' had been inspired by the Cretan music Shane had played to me when I had dropped in on him at his flat after the Nips had collapsed. It had only two chords, C and A minor, under a nullifyingly repetitive loop of melody.

'Greenland Whale Fisheries' was our version of a traditional sea shanty. It opened with a tune Jem had been learning from a teach-yourself book on bluegrass banjo. In the middle, released by a 'Yaaaah!' from Shane, Jem reiterated the melody, with Andrew welting the drums and Cait pounding on her bass.

We knew what we were doing. The effort we had put into rehearsing showed. We had a drummer who was judicious, and spare, restricted as he was to standing up to play just a snare and his cocktail drum.

When we had first started, though he practised and practised, Jem's playing had seemed rigid and free of dynamic, as he learnt by rote the patterns his fingers had to form to accomplish his boomalackas, bum-ditties, clawhammers, drop thumbs, or whatever he was working on. Now, his playing was unflinchingly precise. The semiquavers of the banjo and the accordion synchronised. Where Spider's whistle-playing had been erratic and dislocated, it was now more or less crisp and focused.

Though Shane's guitar-playing resisted improvement, his singing was without match. After a false start or two – a bout of lavish phlegm-evacuation or an attack of the necessity to light a cigarette and draw lungfuls of smoke from it – Shane planted his huge feet on the ground, drove his hands into his pockets, closed his eyes, opened his mouth and sang out.

On a break we went up to the roof. We stood leaning on the ledge by the rusted railings in the lee of the teetering chimney pots, the pointing loosened and crumbling, to look down on the rear of St Pancras Station: the arching roof, the glinting rails which twisted and crossed one another through stands of willowherb and between mounds of iodine-coloured cinder, piles of insulators and rusting track, the concrete sheds with all the windows put out. I loved London and loved being part of something that was so much a part of the city.

We thought we needed backing vocals. I had been a boy chorister. I tried to come up with harmonies, but the songs ran so fast that the melodies escaped me. I couldn't keep up. What harmonies I managed to come up with only made the songs sound overwrought. We argued round the table in Justin's kitchen.

'Harmony vocals are what are *expected*,' Jem said. 'I think we should just drop the whole thing.'

The only backing vocals that worked were unison voices. Spider and Shane took them up on 'Greenland Whale Fisheries' and in the horror-stricken antiphony on 'Connemara Let's Go', with Jem throwing in 'down in the ground where the dead men go' in the cycle of choruses. Cait braved a harmony on 'Streams of Whiskey', but her voice wandered, lost, behind everyone else's. We said nothing. Behind the pretence of assisting Justin at his desk, I hid my embarrassment at my Manchester accent.

In the pub, Shane started tapping on the surface of one of the tables with the bottom of his pint glass of snakebite.

'Spider should sing,' he said.

'You're the front man,' we said.

'I'm not the front man!' Shane screeched. He turned his glass round and round on the table, staring at it.

'It was never about *me* being the front man! I always wanted *him* to be the front man!' he said, pointing at Spider. 'He's better-looking than me, for one thing. I never wanted to be the singer. We were always supposed to not just have the one singer! It was always supposed to be all of us singing.'

'But you're the singer.'

His eyes grew wide with disbelief that we didn't understand.

'I mean,' he said, 'Jem could sing something! And Cait!'

Cait had been singing lead vocals with a group our roadie and soundman Darryl had put together with his friend Dave Scott, called Pride Of The Cross. I'd seen them a couple of times at the Pindar of Wakefield. The congruity of Cait's voice to songs like Peggy Lee's 'Don't Smoke in Bed' and 'Is That All There Is?' was astonishing.

'Andrew's got a beautiful voice,' Spider said.

'Yeah!' Shane said, slapping the tabletop with his hands. 'Andrew!'

For the sake of Shane's emotional even keel and hoping that

in time he would come round, we acquiesced. We distributed songs between us. A couple of them became part of the set, as we went from the Hope and Anchor in Islington, to the Bull and Gate in Kentish Town, to the Greyhound on Fulham Palace Road.

Jem, as Country Jem Finer, sang 'Me and Bobby McGee'.

Buhsted fladdin baddon rewj, wadin furrer train,
Feelin nurly faded as mah jeens.

We gave Cait the Velvet Underground's 'All Tomorrow's Parties', and Shane came up with Crystal Gayle's 'Don't It Make My Brown Eyes Blue'. She sang both songs beautifully in her Marilyn Monroe voice. She towered at the microphone, her dyed-black, backcombed hair falling over half her face.

Spider occasionally sang 'Hot Dogs with Everything', a song of Shane's the Nips used to play. He continued to trade vocals with Shane on 'Connemara Let's Go'. Despite Andrew's deep, rich, bass voice and the fact that he sang blues in his other group, a song was never chosen for Andrew to sing.

For me, Shane chose 'The Green Green Grass of Home'. The only version I knew was Tom Jones's. Because my dad liked such singers as Tom Jones, Engelbert Humperdinck, Matt Monro and Tony Christie, I took the song for maggoty nostalgia and not one that dealt with the last hours of a prisoner on death row, nor did I recognise that Shane was trying to make a point about guilt and penitence, that death is never distant and that life is not what you think. I had no idea what it was really about, but turned up at a sound check at the Hope and Anchor knowing that he was going to ask me to sing it.

'James!' Shane shouted when the time came.

I came up to the microphone with my accordion. The song

started with up-down strumming from Shane, arpeggios from Jem, Cait picking out fifths on the bass, tom-tom and side stick from Andrew, a chord on the accordion. I put my mouth to the microphone.

> *The ohld hohm town lukes the sehm*
> *As Ah step down frum the trehn*

All of a sudden the room was full of my voice, the Manchester accent, full of the way I didn't actually understand the song.

'Nah. Nah. Nah. Nah,' Shane said, shaking his head, walking across to the centre microphone as if he thought I would not want to step away from it. 'This isn't a good idea.'

⛛

When I had first signed on for social security, I had not provided any details of the dividends from my shares in the family con-struction company, so, when I got a letter from the DHSS, informing me of a visit from one of its agents, in terror of pro-ceedings, I signed off.

Though my rent was low, what was left of the last half-yearly dividend was not enough to live on until the next payment. The money from Pogue Mahone's gigs was a pittance. I took myself to Tottenham Court Road tube station, Oxford Circus and the long corridor to the museums at South Kensington, to busk. I performed songs I could play both the melody and the bass but-tons for on the accordion: 'Lily Marlene', 'The Third Man Theme', 'Around the World in 80 Days', 'The Spell' waltz from *Sleeping Beauty*, the theme from *Limelight*.

A guy came up to me at a bend in the corridor at Tottenham Court Road.

'Can ye play "The Sash"?' he said. He had an accent from Northern Ireland. I didn't know what 'The Sash' was. I laughed. 'Play "The Sash"!' he said again. 'Go on, play *the fucking Sash!*' He stood in front of me waving his arms about.

'*Sure I'm an Ulster Orangeman, from Erin's isle I came,*' he sang. 'Go on!' he said. 'Play it!'

I wanted him to go away. The only Irish tune I'd learnt both the bass buttons and the melody for was 'Peggy Gordon'. We'd been doing it at gigs. I played him that.

'Fuck you,' he said and walked off.

At the end of my pitches, I'd pack up, go back to the flat and count out my money. The way I was living, going out most nights, no longer getting social security, what I earned from busking wasn't enough.

Shane got wind of the home visit from the DHSS. He cackled at my setback and the idea of moral laxity on my part.

'You cunt!' he said.

I had expected Jem to disapprove both of my comparative affluence and of the moral hypocrisy of dole-dodging. Instead, he offered to put it to the couple whose house he was painting that he needed help with the job. He would let me know. He said nothing about his own impecuniousness and the fact that in a matter of weeks he and Marcia would have another mouth to feed.

Within a few days he invited me to come and work with him. Though he couldn't tell me how long the job was going to last, his employers seemed to have plenty of money and changed their minds all the time about what it was they wanted done. The wage would be £40 a week, cash. It was about as much as I ever earned on any job. After inveigling me onto the books at SCH, this was the second time Jem had bailed me out.

We spent the rest of the year working together, first at the bay-fronted house of Jem's friends in Drayton Park, followed by a Victorian terraced house in Barnsbury belonging to another of what seemed to be Jem's patrons. Our employers provided all the materials – brushes, rollers, paint, sandpaper, everything – and left us in the house by ourselves. They seldom came back before we had cleaned up our brushes and gone home.

We painted as well as we could. No one seemed too bothered by the fact that we weren't painters, nor that by the end of the week there wasn't much to show for the hours we put in.

As we went back and forth from the roller tray to our section of wall, or bent towards our respective window or door frame or stood out on the back patio with our cups of tea, Jem and I talked. We were bemused by what seemed the timeliness of what Pogue Mahone was doing. The release in 1982 of Dexys Midnight Runners' *Too-Rye-Ay* seemed to have spawned all manner of bands across London playing with acoustic instruments – violins, banjos and accordions. There were skiffle bands playing home-made music with tea-chest basses, washboards and zob sticks. There were country bands with western shirts, bolo ties, cowboy hats and beehives playing upright basses and acoustic guitars. There were amalgams of the two in the form of bands like the Boothill Foot-Tappers, Hackney Five-O and the Shillelagh Sisters – not to mention the Skiff Skats for whom John Hasler now played washboard, and the Men They Couldn't Hang, whose name we gave them and for whom Shanne Bradley played bass. Though we scorned the banality of what was going on in the charts, we liked the pentatonic expansiveness of Big Country's 'In a Big Country', which had been released in May.

We talked about music – chords and modes, scales, tunings. We talked about what we could do – gigs, the music we could play, the way we could play it. We talked about making an album, recording and releasing it ourselves.

When we'd finished talking, we went back to our jobs and listened to the radio. In September, Culture Club's 'Karma Chameleon' was at No. 1 in the charts. I told Jem about Jon Moss and me listening to Culture Club's demo-tape in his car in the street outside my flat in Mornington Crescent.

'You were meant for better things,' Jem said.

When Marcia's pregnancy came to term, Jem left me to work by myself. On the 9th October 1983 – my twenty-ninth birthday – Marcia gave birth to a daughter, Ella Jean, at Middlesex Hospital. Marcia had issued an edict that there were to be no visitors. I bought flowers in Fitzrovia and turned up in the maternity ward. To see the tiny thing in her Perspex bassinet, I wondered what on earth we were all doing.

»✠«

Pogue Mahone were playing gigs every week, radiating from our home turf of the Pindar of Wakefield, to the Irish Centre in Kentish Town, the Empire Rooms on Tottenham Court Road, the Wag Club, the Bull and Gate in Kentish Town, Dingwalls, the Hope and Anchor, and at the end of November, an acoustic gig crammed into the corner of a room near Charing Cross Road as part of the London Film Festival. We never wrote out a set list. Without warning, Shane's crotchetiness would drive him to shelve whatever song he took a dislike to. At the Sir George Robey at Finsbury Park we argued wantonly between songs. Cait kicked beer glasses across the stage. Jem's face, usually mild with equanimity, became distorted with fury. The crowd in front of us, packed to the bar at the back, pounded the stage. I saw a guy open his hand on the shards of a beer glass in front of him, oblivious to what he was doing. We could do little but wait for Shane to start the next song.

·✠·

We took up meeting on a more or less regular basis at the Pindar of Wakefield. We talked about recording. We thought the format of an EP best suited for what we were doing. Shane said he had someone to produce it, a guy called Philip Chevron whom he knew, who worked at Rock On records in Camden. Chevron came to meet us at the Pindar. He was a diminutive guy with pink, pocked cheeks. A spume of sand-coloured hair tumbled on the top of his head. He had a tapering face, a narrow mouth with a slight twist in it and a fleshy, almost conical nose. He looked entrepreneurial in a camel overcoat. He nodded at what we had to say and touched his lips with a crooked knuckle.

In the end, it was Stan Brennan, Shane's boss at Rocks Off records on Hanway Street, who took us to Elephant Recording Studios in Wapping to record, not an EP but 'The Dark Streets of London', backed by 'And the Band Played Waltzing Matilda'.

Elephant Studios were on Wapping High Street, in the basement of one of the warehouses. It was a dingy and airless place with hessian wall-covering and an uneven floor with fibre carpeting. We were greeted by Graham Sharpe, the studio owner, who went around in a corduroy flat cap and a cravat and seemed never to leave the place. He had a cot in the office. He seemed to be in a chronic state of surprise to encounter anyone at all on the premises.

In spite of recording 'The Dark Streets of London' as a single with Stan Brennan, we spent a Sunday towards the end of February shooting a video of the version of 'Streams of Whiskey' we had recorded at Justin Ward's living-room studio. One of us knew a director who lived nearby. He was called Richard Elgard but went under the name of Video Rick. In the week, we storyboarded in the Pakenham Arms. The production – a camera, cassette player, ourselves and our instruments – started out at the bin dump at the far end of the courtyard in Whidborne Buildings, followed by a drained stretch of Regent's Canal up York Way where we set up a couple of deckchairs on a reeking beach of detritus. Jem and Shane, in a pastiche of Wham!'s 'Club Tropicana', stripped down to blue boxer shorts and red Y-fronts and mimed to a verse, each with a glass of cider, the bottle balanced between them in the chaos of lumber and rubbish in the freezing cold.

A couple of days later, after a sound check at the Wag Club on Wardour Street, I went up to Debsey's parents' flat on Liverpool Road to kill some time before our gig at eleven. The family was watching the television. Debsey's mum peered occasionally over the top of her bifocals from her students' homework. Debsey's dad leant uncomfortably in his armchair, a stiff leg thrust out. We thought Debsey's young sister had gone to bed. The door opened. We all looked behind us. Caroline sometimes walked in her sleep. Debsey's mum got up to guide her back upstairs.

'The house is on fire,' Caroline said.

'Yes, I know,' Debsey's mum said. 'Oh good Lord!' she added.

We gathered at the foot of the stairs to see flames coursing under the ceiling of the landing above. I went up with a bucket of water which I ended up pitching uselessly across the floor. I closed as many doors as I could and came back down.

We stood out on the street waiting for the fire brigade to come. When it drew up, four or five men in whistling yellow trews ran from the tender carrying a hose. They crashed in through the front door and we listened to the muffled crepitations coming from inside and watched the flames in the windows of the upper floor flicker down. I had to leave to go back to the Wag Club.

I went to visit Debsey's family the following day. The doors I'd closed had caused the fire to surge up the stairwell and char the attic where her brother sometimes stayed. Debsey's room had been spared, but was uninhabitable. For ten days the painters and decorators worked on the Wykes' flat. Debsey came to stay with me. During the day she had things to do, but in the evenings she brought a toothbrush, a couple of books, a change of tights.

London Weekend Television, for an instalment of their series on pop culture called *South of Watford*, came to film us at the Fridge in Brixton and to interview Shane at the Pindar of Wakefield. Hosted by Ben Elton, the programme would be devoted to what was being called the 'alternative country' music scene in London and would feature the Boothill Foot-Tappers and the Shillelagh Sisters.

In March we opened for the Clash at Brixton Academy. I was elated. The Clash had been one of my favourite bands. When I was living at home, earning the money for my Telecaster, the top floor of my parents' house of a Friday night pounded to 'Janie Jones', 'White Riot', 'I'm So Bored with the USA' and '48 Hours', as my brother and I got ready to go out after work. Once I'd bought my guitar and had gone back down to London I had been to see the Clash at the Music Machine. I had turned up from work in my suit. I left the gig drenched and all the money in my pockets stuck together. The Clash we supported at Brixton Academy, though, was what was known as the Clash Mark Two. Topper Headon had been let go after the Clash had recorded *Combat Rock* in 1982 and Mick Jones in the autumn of the following year. The Clash Mark Two was a darker, more virile incarnation.

We played outside London for the first time, in Longleat, at the wedding reception of someone Shane knew, after a forty-minute stop to play at a festival on an athletics field near Ladbroke Grove. In the afternoon the festival site was an expanse of orange gravel, empty but for a handful of friends from my school who showed up to linger by some barriers at the far edge of the field. Up at the front barriers, Scottish John, a road-sweeper fan of ours, stood with his forearms draped over the rail waiting for us to begin. When we did, Scottish John exploded into a flurry of paroxysms, sideways punches and capering.

Afterwards, we packed up and drove out of London in the Transit van we'd hired, to Shane's friends' wedding reception. We were required to play two sets. We argued in the interval about how to stretch out the limited material we knew. Shane started to put forward songs I took to be Irish folk standards. None of us had any idea how to play even the ones we'd heard of. Shane clawed his face in incredulity.

On the three-hour drive back to London we sat where we could find space in the back of the van with the gear. Corks banged against the roof of the van from the case of champagne we had stolen and hidden near the base of a tree in the gardens outside the reception marquee.

For St Patrick's Day, Jem rented a bus to drive us, and whoever wanted to come along too, up to Wolverhampton to play the Students' Union at the Polytechnic. He photocopied a map from the

A–Z, highlighting where to pick up the bus, the parking bay next to King's Cross Station. Forty people showed up. On the way back from Wolverhampton the toilets overflowed and drenched our equipment.

A couple of days later we travelled to Oxford to play at the Jericho Tavern. The stage was a dais against the wall. The audience sat on chairs upholstered in burgundy velour and brass nails. After each song, they applauded briefly and then waited, listening to every discussion we had as to what song to play next, our voices even at the level of whispers audible throughout the room.

We had a return gig at the 100 Club on Oxford Street. We met outside Shane's flat. Jem and Cait and Andrew were standing under his windows on the corner. It was pleasant enough to wait in the sunshine of an October afternoon.

Spider came up ruffling his hair and apologising for being late. We said not to worry. Spider told us that he and Shane had been at the Electric Ballroom the night before.

'And then I lost him,' Spider said.

We waited a while longer. We started to worry too. Time was getting on.

'I hope he's all right,' Spider said.

Shane eventually came up from the direction of Judd Street. The side of his face was swollen and his left eye closed with fluid.

'What happened to you?' we said.

'That looks like it hurts,' Spider said. Shane sniffed, his hands in his pockets. It was hard to pull on a cigarette because of the shape of his mouth and he had to work to get suction. It turned out that the night before a couple of guys at the Electric Ballroom had kicked him around the toilets.

'Like a fucking rag doll,' he said. He kept touching his mouth where the stump of one of his teeth was missing a dental cap. He slurred his words and avoided our eyes.

'Must have said something to cause offence,' he said and wheezed a laugh, but carefully and with minimal effort. I found myself laughing too.

'James,' Jem murmured. He turned to Shane.

'Do you think you can do the gig?' he asked him. Shane shrugged.

'Give it a go,' he said.

He was worse off than we knew. He held onto the mike stand for support. His eyes closed, he teetered back and forth, but tall and with the mike up high. He blundered through the songs he could remember. He forgot words but sang on, letting his mistakes go, if he was aware of them. In between songs, he stood waiting for the next, as if bracing for a renewed ordeal.

When he began to stagger, Stan Brennan shouted to take him off. Jem went across to him. They exchanged a couple of words, Shane bending his head down to Jem. I saw Shane nod. Spider came across to put his arm round Shane's shoulders and lead him to a seat by the side of the stage. We played what we could without him, but our spirit was gone and we finished after five or six songs.

'He's got the constitution of a fucking mountain goat,' I said to Cait afterwards.

'He'll make old bones,' she replied.

✤

'The Dark Streets of London' and 'And the Band Played Waltzing Matilda' came out in a limited release of 234 copies, with a white label, in a white sleeve, and a sticker with a picture of a harp on it and the words '*póg mo thóin*' – Irish for pogue mahone.

After the record's release David 'Kid' Jensen, the Canadian DJ, friend and foil of John Peel, started to play it on Radio 1. Our prow jibed distinctly seaward.

At the end of the following week, *South of Watford* was broadcast. I phoned my parents to tell them. I settled down to watch. Shane's interview with Ben Elton in the bar of the Pindar of Wakefield was a tour de force and made light of the editorial weighting of the show in favour of the Shillelagh Sisters and the Skiff Skats, because Chas Smash, a member of Madness, was in it. Shane sat insolently on a stool, leaning on the bar. He wiped his nose with a finger, stirred his eye, scratched his jaw, pulled lungfuls of smoke, paused to lift his pint to his mouth, flicked ash and otherwise bent shapeless the preconceptions I had, not just about folk music, what was called countrybilly and even the Clash – whom he labelled as 'dinosaurs' – but also about how you were supposed to behave on television. I was mortified about what my father's response would be. The following day he rang me up.

'Your singer's a moron, I'm afraid,' he said. 'Do yourself the service of finding another career, or at least another group. Because if you hitch your fortunes to that man, you're sunk.'

Ten

We sat crowded together in the front parlour of the Pindar of Wakefield. By custom, Shane sat in one of the straight-backed chairs opposite the velvet seats in the bay window. He was a difficult person to sit next to. He couldn't sit still and would lean across his neighbour to address a point with his neighbour-but-one-or-two.

One of the items on the agenda was the matter of what clothes we should wear on stage and for the photo sessions that were beginning to come up.

'Like the Kray twins!' Shane was saying. He had brought with him a book about London gangsters. It was open to the page of a photograph of Reggie and Ronnie Kray. Shane stabbed it.

'Sharp! I mean! Fuck!' he said.

The photograph depicted the twins striding, in gleaming shoes, away from a block of flats. Each wore a lightly checked, boxy jacket with narrow lapels. Reggie looked into the camera, jacket open, black tie. Ronnie frowned off, one jacket button done up, pale tie, slightly patterned.

'Know what I mean?' he said, brushing an imaginary fleck from the photograph.

With the number of gigs we were doing and money more or less regularly coming in, we could afford to buy new suits. We talked about opening a joint bank account and buying new instruments too.

We wanted to get Shane a twelve-string. We thought it would generally fill out the sound. Better still, it suited the metreless accompaniment we had discovered, where chords shifted one to the other according to the dictates of Shane's singing. Andrew rolled on the tom-tom, Cait rumbled on the bass, Jem turned arpeggios on the banjo, I held down the chords, Shane scrubbed, Spider followed the vocal melody line. We could make the accompaniment murmur, underpinning Shane's voice in a dream-like whisper. The jangling sonorities of a twelve-string we knew would best suit what we'd found.

The meeting turned to the matter of who we could get to roadie, who we could get to do the sound, who to make T-shirts and badges and who to sell them, and who we could get to manage us.

The roadie and sound-engineer part was easy. In the past couple of months, since our first dates at the Pindar of Wakefield, Darryl Hunt had simply taken over the various jobs of mixing our sound, humping our gear and driving us to gigs. Darryl was a doyen of SCH. He lived in Gray's Inn Buildings on the corner of Rosebery Avenue and was an aficionado of local events.

He was a musician himself and with a veneer of celebrity about him, having founded a band called Plummet Airlines when he was a student of Fine Arts at Nottingham School of Art. Plummet Airlines had been among the first bands to release with Stiff Records in 1976. His girlfriend Julie had already taken up the publication of a fanzine. She took up making and selling T-shirts.

When it came to a manager the candidate seemed obvious. Stan Brennan had taken on the entire production of 'Dark Streets of London' and had managed to get it played on Radio 1. He seemed reasonably well situated when it came to the particular echelons of the music business we worked in. He was a nice guy,

96

if a little earnest. He seemed to care for Shane with a solicitude that was almost parental.

Most of the gigs we had been getting, so far, had come by way of a combination of Shane's notoriety and Jem's doggedness. Jem had become the person whom the music press had begun to seek out for interviews and to arrange photo sessions. It was Jem who had finalised the contract to record our first radio session for John Peel on the 10th April at the BBC's Maida Vale studios. Though we seemed to be doing well enough without a manager, Jem and Shane appealed to the rest of us to step up to help. I suffered a panic of irresolution when it came to organising anything. Though I dreaded the responsibility, I took on the booking of a gig at the Ritzy in Brixton.

Furnished with a new banjo for Jem, a new bass amp for Cait and a twelve-string guitar for Shane, we turned up at the bar across from the BBC studios on Delaware Road. There was a dartboard and, through the windows draped in creeper at the back, a small sunlit lawn. We crowded one of the tables in the corner by the window to wait for Cait.

When she turned up she climbed over us with her pint of cider, standing on the wooden bench in crêpe-soled shoes and voluminous black trousers before plumping down in the middle of us.

'All right lads?' she said. 'Look at this place! The BB fucking C!'

She sat with her forearms on the table. When she drank she banged the glass down on the table and wiped her mouth on the back of a fingerless leather glove.

'What the fuck!' she said.

We sat round the scuffed table, drinking. None of us went across the road to find out where and when we were needed. With a sad and wide-eyed face, his mouth protruding, it was Jem who pricked our consciences to drink up.

When we finally trooped out of the bar, we were all drunk, but Cait more than anyone, her inebriation intensifying her scorn of the BBC as the repository of Englishness, a despised flagship of the British Empire, the pre-eminent organ of Irish repression. A subterranean passageway went from the bar under the road and into a labyrinthine system of corridors. It took us a while to find Studio 4.

We took our instruments from their cases and set up the drums. An engineer stationed the amps and microphones and cables about the room. Our allotted producer turned out to be Dale Griffin, Mott the Hoople's drummer. He knew Shane and me through Howard Cohen. He remembered the recording I'd done with the Giants, which he and Pete Watts had produced. Griffin was an earnest, seasoned sort of man, tow of hair, deviated of septum, hunched of shoulder, denim of jacket.

Once we started running through the first song, it was obvious that Cait was too drunk both to play bass and to realise it. We beseeched her to hand her instrument over to someone else. She became irascible and pugnacious.

Griffin summoned a couple of us into the control room. We left Cait plonking notes in the studio. Griffin suggested we just forget about the session, that we pack everything up and go home. Over a pot of tea up in the canteen, Jem and I persuaded him to continue, provided we could get her out of the studio and have someone else play bass.

When we got back, Cait put up a great fight. Jem and I took a leg each, Andrew her arms, and we lifted her out of the studio. As we wrestled her past the control room, I saw Griffin staring with as much unconcern as he could muster at the ranks of knobs on his mixing desk. On our way down the serpentine corridors, Cait's long body writhed and snapped like a landed eel. She jammed her brothel-creepers against pretty much each door jamb or pipe along the way, jarring our progress to an exit.

'Fuckers!' she shouted.

Kid Jensen had been playing 'Dark Streets of London' regularly on his evening programme on Radio 1. When a producer from BBC Radio Scotland informed Broadcasting House that each time Jensen uttered the words 'pogue mahone', he was saying 'kiss my arse' to any Gaelic listener tuning in, Jensen blithely swapped to calling us the Pogues. Another Radio 1 DJ, Mike Read, famous for - on air - having taken off Frankie Goes To Hollywood's 'Relax' and proclaiming it obscene, castigated us for our choice of name and refused to play our record. We were hot to protest at being banned, hoping for a publicity coup of some sort, but Jem urged pragmatism.

'I'd rather they just played the record,' he said. We went along with Kid Jensen and called ourselves the Pogues.

With the purpose of securing us a record deal, Brennan took us into a demo studio in West Kensington where we recorded almost sufficient material for an album. Along with 'The Repeal of the Licensing Laws', 'Greenland Whale Fisheries' and 'Connemara Let's Go', all of which had been included on the tape we took away from Justin Ward's flat, we recorded traditional songs we'd been playing live – 'The Rocky Road to Dublin' and 'Kitty' – and a parcel of songs Shane had written – 'Transmetropolitan', 'The Boys from the County Hell', 'Sea Shanty', and an instrumental, 'The Battle of Brisbane'. When we'd done, Brennan told us he would let us know when he'd finished mixing. I chafed against being banished from the studio.

'Broth,' he said, with a defensive tilt to his head. 'Cooks.'

After a week or so he met us in a pub and handed each of us a cassette copy. He had had fun with some of the songs. 'Connemara Let's Go' now had a driving backbeat.

In another couple of weeks, he met us to announce that Stiff Records wanted to sign us. As long as Jem understood what the meanings of such things as options, advances, recoupment and territories were, I wasn't worried. My elation at the prospect of a record company giving us a contract to make an album – perhaps two, possibly three – eclipsed the concerns I had at my lack of familiarity with the terminology.

Brennan was in high feather when we went down to Chiswick to sign with Dave Robinson. It was a bright spring morning. We filed through the offices with our guide, Jamie, a benevolent if opaque guy dressed in black windjammer, jeans and crêpe-soled shoes and with de rigueur buzzed back and sides. The offices were open-plan, filled with light, with white-painted walls, carpeted ramps, slabs of handrail and an interior balcony or two with tubular iron railings. There were dry-erase whiteboards everywhere. One of them charted the performance of Stiff's record releases: the Belle Stars, Madness, Yello, the Gibson Brothers, Tracy Ullman, the Passion Puppets.

'You're going to be going up on that board,' Jamie said. Up until that moment I had been content to think we weren't much more than a product of our locality, of the sisterhood of grim tenement buildings on Cromer Street, and the Norfolk Arms, the Boot and the Pindar of Wakefield. The accumulation of our record being played on Radio 1, the *South of Watford* documentary, the John Peel session – and now the fact that our name was going up on the project board at Stiff Records – meant the expansion of our milieu to include the whole of London, and maybe the nation itself. The perspective which opened up made me reel.

We followed Jamie up one of the grey-carpeted ramps and out to a sunlit patio bounded by a parapet and wooden lattice. Up a couple of steps there were blinding-white tables, Dave Robinson and champagne.

Dave Robinson was a guy with a footballer's haircut standing with his arms folded across his chest, in a blue blazer, white shirt and faded jeans. He had fleshy eyelids which shaded his eyes. We stood in the sunlight and listened as he, Jamie and Brennan reiterated how great the band was and how great the relationship with the record company was going to be. In return we let them know, in the language of in-jokes, barbs and bravado, that we weren't to be fucked with.

Along with the drink, the occasion went to Cait's head. She took the opportunity throughout the short meeting to blurt a series of infelicitous remarks which I was sure she intended to ironise the relationship between a record company and its artists. She alluded continually to such tropes as the biting of

hands that fed and to selling out. I squirmed with embarrassment at her overfamiliarity with people we had just met and
wished she'd shut up. It was to Shane, however, that Robinson
and Brennan and Jamie referred. They knew it was Shane who
defined the company spirit, the ethos. His sense of irony was
iron-clad. He scorned everything, no matter what it was, and
with a facility that was winning.

Afterwards, I walked round Chiswick in the soft summery
wind looking at the houses and trees. I was not so drunk as to
doubt my excitement to be in a band, my thrill at the prospect of
making a record, and my impatience for a date to start.

⋆✠⋆

It took us a couple of sessions at Elephant Studios, of a couple of
weeks each time, to complete the record. We had already done
the work in Rick Trevan's back bedroom and in the course of
nine months of regular gigs. The banjo and the accordion were
inextricable, our arpeggios striving to link to Shane's up-and-
down strumming on his twelve-string and underpinned by the
one-two, one-two of Andrew's cocktail drum and snare. Andrew
played with his shirtsleeves rolled up, his body stooped over
the drums, his head bent back. Cait swung her bass. Spider's
leg snapped back and forth, his head tilted to the side, then he
would draw the whistle to his mouth, his long fingers overdoing
the notes, sliding and trilling. In the middle of the room stood
Shane, tall, the microphone hoisted high, so high that he sang up
and out with his eyes half-closed, his twelve-string guitar across
him, welting it with downstrokes, gripping down on the chords
with swollen knuckles.

When it came to recording the guide tracks, as we all played
through the songs hoping to capture a decent bass and drum

102

track, Shane thrashed along as best he could, but derailment was never distant. When it came to his re-recording the guitar in a booth, his metre was erratic and his grip less than sure. When the velocity of the songs cast Shane adrift or when his ham-handedness threatened to mar the ethereality of the accompaniment to 'The Auld Triangle', I played the guitar. I loved to play the guitar.

I loved to come up with overdubs too. I sawed at double-stops on the violin for the choruses of 'Transmetropolitan'. A bottleneck provided a wolf-whistlish hook in the chorus of 'The Boys from the County Hell'.

As the recording began to come to a close, we all piled in on overdubs. For the end of 'The Battle of Brisbane' we went out to a concrete stairwell and hurled a cymbal down it. To replicate the beer tray on 'Waxie's Dargle', which sounded puny in the studio, we laid into an anvil we had got from somewhere. For good measure we took a microphone into the toilets to record the flush. On one of the last days of recording, Shane and I stood in one of the booths, he shaking a handful of goat-bells, I a string of hooves, for the clanking and clopping sounds at the beginning of 'Connemara Let's Go', which Brennan, scorning its obtuseness, had renamed 'Down in the Ground Where the Dead Men Go'.

The Pogues were good at screaming. At the end of 'Down in the Ground Where the Dead Men Go', the screams piled up on top of one another over the growing cacophony at the end of the song. Shane and Spider were no slouches when it came to blood-curdling screams. Shane howled until his eyes watered. A quiver shook Spider's entire body when he voided his lungs. When Cait came up to the microphone though, Shane and Spider's howls seemed to merely echo in the hills, where her screams vaulted the peaks, reaming the air, carrying with them, seemingly, every injustice visited on the Irish since the twelfth century, and more besides.

I paid no heed to Brennan's admonishments about band members sitting in on the process of mixing. I went down to the studio every day, and took a place on the lumpy sofa in the control room behind the backs of the engineers, Nick Robbins and Craig Thompson, and Brennan. I thought that at least one of the band should come down to the studio to oversee the mixing of our first record. After Brennan's production of the demo we made with him, I harboured a mild distrust of his abilities at the mixing desk. I didn't have much else to do besides. Whenever I said anything, Brennan would lean backwards to address me over his shoulder and then return to hog the mixing desk.

We made 'Transmetropolitan' the first song on the record. Of all the songs, it was our mission statement. The brave and expository major couplets of the whistle and accordion melody built up to a fanfare, heralding what should have been the explosion of Shane's voice into the verse.

I loved Shane's kaleidoscopic lyrics – the street names, names of cafés, pubs, hostels. Valtaro's was a café on Cartwright Gardens, round the corner from Leigh Street. Arlington House was a hostel round the corner from my block of flats in Camden and, at one time, Brendan Behan's home. The Scottish Stores was a pub in the lee of King's Cross Station. Mill Lane veered between Shoot Up Hill and West End Lane in West Hampstead.

'What the fuck is so beautiful about Mill Lane?' Spider said when we gathered on the lumpy sofa in the control room to listen back.

'I live round the corner from Mill Lane,' Andrew said. 'It's beautiful.'

It was a generous and degenerate song. It brought us all together, in our second-hand suits, lumberjack shirts, Fred Perrys, with our outdated instruments. It pressed us to march across

London, following Shane, like the children following the Pied Piper out of Hamelin.

It was the same with 'Streams of Whiskey'. It made me want to follow Shane wherever he went. Like no other song I'd ever heard it made me want to drink, and drink like Shane drank. I wanted to go down to the Chelsea too – wherever that pub was – and walk in on my feet, but leave there on my back. I loved the recklessness and the bitter joy of the song – a fantasy in which Shane put himself beyond everything, beyond control, beyond authority, and which situated him almost mythologically in a place that seemed to share coordinates with Big Rock Candy Mountain, Cockaigne and Tír na nÓg – or it placed him inescapably in hell and more irretrievably than anyone could know.

When the record was finished, we went to Rick Trevan's flat in Whidborne Buildings to celebrate not just the completion of the record but also our tour of the United Kingdom and Ireland supporting Elvis Costello and the Attractions in the autumn. In the middle of recording there had been a rumour that Costello had seen us play at the Diorama in Regent's Park. By the time the record was finished the offer was firm.

Brennan's pride in the record was apparent in the way he tried to mute it. Sitting uncomfortably on the arm of one of the chairs with his hands clasped together, Brennan tried to give a celebratory recap of the project. It wasn't long, though, before Shane and Spider and Cait had moved on and were laughing about something as they sat on the couch. Brennan leant down from his perch towards me. He'd had a couple of drinks.

'You're going to make serious dosh,' he said. 'You know that, don't you?'

I couldn't prevent my head filling with images of Mediterranean villas, stately homes, compounds in Brentwood, runway-side seats in Bryant Park, boarding ladders at Cannes. I looked round at Rick Trevan's flat, at the bare pillars, the grey, paint-splattered industrial carpet, the grubby beige material thrown over the couch, and at Shane and Spider and Cait sitting on it. At that point Shane erupted at something Spider said, clasping his brown fingers to his forehead and twisting his face towards him. Spit bubbled in his nose and needed to be wiped with the back of his hand. Spider was slumped in the sofa, giggling into his chest.

'You think?' I said.

'I know,' Brennan said.

'I dunno,' I said.

'You will,' Brennan said. 'You should start planning,' he went on. 'Some people buy a house. Some people invest.' He looked at me expectantly.

'I'd buy a narrow boat,' I said.

'Oh yes!' Andrew said. 'We'll all want narrow boats!'

Brennan wiped his face and looked dolefully across at Shane.

⚜

Debsey and I went up to the Yorkshire Dales. In the Sixties, my parents had bought a grim, rain-lashed cottage on the other side of the M6 from Kendal. The week Debsey and I chose, it rained every day – and every day Debsey was obliged to make contact with Rachel and Hester, to see what was going on for Dolly Mixture in London.

There was no telephone in the cottage. We had to make the quarter-mile walk up the valley to the public telephone box. I stood on the road outside, opposite the dilapidated farm build-ings, a ruined Saab in the mired courtyard, geese honking in a neighbouring field, waiting as Debsey pushed her money into the slot and a finger into her ear to get news from London.

After a while, she set the receiver on the cradle and pushed

106

the door open. We trudged against the wind back down to the house. The slanting rain drifted in sheets up the valley, stinging our cheeks and burning our hands. It seemed bent on lashing her with the pointlessness of her hopes for her career. I pitied her for her musical vocation. Its unwillingness to cough up the slightest reward made her miserable. What must have made her more miserable was that, without much effort on my part, Pogue Mahone was reviving mine.

Though it had been Jem who had superintended the arrangements and signed the contract for our near-calamitous session for John Peel in April, the BBC contacted Brennan to arrange the payment of our fee. At the beginning of May the BBC called me at home to set up another session, this time for our shield-bearer Kid Jensen's show. Despite my giving them Jem's address and phone number, Jensen's producer sent the contract to Brennan at Rocks Off records.

We thought Brennan was joking when he asked for ten per cent commission on the fee for both sessions when we met him in a pub on Wardour Street.

'Fuck off out of it!' Cait said. Shane stared, mute, while she set on Brennan with unmitigated venom. Jem, struggling to conceal his resentment, refused even the slightest cut of any of the money.

Brennan warned us of record companies' and venues' unwillingness to conduct negotiations with any band if it didn't have a representative.

'Go and get your own sessions,' he said, and left the pub.

⊹

With the money coming in from gigs along with the advance from Stiff Records, we opened a bank account at the Royal Bank of Scotland in King's Cross. I cycled down to the bank every Wednesday to pick up £900 in an envelope and then back up the pavement to our table in the Pindar of Wakefield where I handed out our £150 each. In the course of one of these meetings, the question came up as to what we were going to call our record. We looked at Shane. He tilted his head as if the answer was obvious.

'*Red Roses for Me*,' he said.

The following Wednesday when I came into the pub, Shane was sitting with his hand clapped to his face and staring with wildness in his eyes.

'Yes!' he hissed. 'Yes! Yes!'

'What?' we all said.

'Duster coats!' Shane said. 'Spider just come up with duster coats! From *The Long Riders!*'

We looked at him for a moment or two.

'The *L-o-n-g R-i-d-e-r-s!*' Shane repeated, stretching out the vowels as if we were deaf or stupid. As if pricked by remorse he added: 'You know?'

The duster coats Spider and Shane were talking about were

108

the long riding coats worn by the Keaches, Carradines and Guests, playing the Jameses, Youngers and Fords, in Walter Hill's film about the James Gang. Those who had seen the film thought it was a good idea.

From the recording advance we had in the bank, we had a set of them made by a couple of girls Darryl knew. We went up to their workshop on York Way. The coats were of grey linen with a velvet collar and cuffs with a buttoned tab. They were close to floor-length and had a cantle pleat. The coats conjured up our walk down the road from Shane's flat to our first gig at the Pindar of Wakefield, carrying our instruments, our shadows behind us spreading over the surface of the street.

While we tried them on, Shane and Spider traded quotes from the film. Spider cocked an imaginary six-shooter, sneered malevolently and emptied it in the direction of my chest.

' "You think about that," ' Spider said, in an exaggerated Missouri accent, ' "on your way to HAYELL!" '

He blew the smoke from the barrel and reholstered.

Eleven

We had been trying to rouse Shane from his second-floor flat for easily half an hour. We'd touched together the wires sticking out of the frame of his front door. We'd shouted up. In the end I reached in through the railings of the Holy Cross Church, scooped up a handful of gravel and threw it across Shane's windows. He snatched open the casement and stuck his head out.

'ALL FUCKING RIGHT!'

Another half an hour later Shane came down swinging a filthy bag which clanked with bottles. We slid the door of the van open for him and made room.

'All right?' he said.

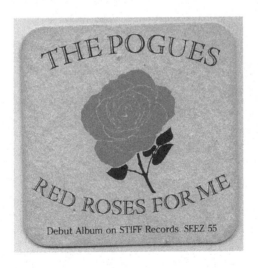

THE POGUES

RED ROSES FOR ME

Debut Album on STIFF Records. SEEZ 55

It was the last week of September. We were on our way to the first gig of our tour supporting Elvis Costello and the Attractions. Our first single with Stiff Records, 'The Boys from the County Hell', was about to come out, though we had had to stomach the record company's insistence that we edit out half of Jem's banjo introduction. We had our own merchandise: a T-shirt and a beer mat with a line from the song – 'Lend me ten pounds and I'll buy you a drink' – on the back; a miniature bar mirror; a lacquered shillelagh.

⊹

The first gig was in Belfast. Our gear had gone ahead in one of Costello's trucks. Darryl had rented a passenger van – a white Iveco Daily with, unaccountably, an orange stripe down the side. We had three hundred miles to drive to Holyhead to catch the ferry. Darryl was anxious about the time.

As we set off Darryl pushed a tape into the van's machine. A banjo and an accordion warbling with musette tuning started to play a jig backed by clicking spoons and a country bass-line. Cait, as soon as she heard the introduction, knew what it was.

'Brendan!' she shouted.

> *I'm a páidín*
> *From Tullabhadín*

I didn't know what a *páidín* was, nor where Tullabhadín might be found. The singer was a guy called Brendan Shine. I didn't know anything about him either. From the ironic fuss Cait made about the song I supposed he might be the Irish counterpart to Rolf Harris. His phrasing was heavy with elaborate *h*'s before many of the syllables. All the *a* vowels were exaggeratedly flattened. The song was a kind of personal ad: Fifty-year-old

111

man, called Dan, 'with money and acres of land', enjoys music and 'the craic', seeks 'a honey' with 'a bit of money'.

In the past couple of years, I'd heard the word 'craic' a lot, the words 'awful' and 'mighty' as emphasis, and the substitution of 'my' by 'me', too. As I listened to the song, the phrase 'sure I'm your man' started to annoy the fuck out of me.

When it came to saying anything at all about the Irish, I hadn't a leg to stand on. My experience of the Irish was scant. My English upbringing resulted in my regarding them as, at best, figures of fun or, at worst, in the climate of the Troubles, agents of death and destruction. The little experience of Irish people I had, had come from working on building sites with men my father called 'navvies', whom he dismissed as feckless, universally stupid and, more often than not, drunk. Otherwise, what I knew about the Irish and Ireland had come mostly from books. At school I'd read Wilde, Shaw, Beckett and Yeats and had struggled with the fact that the former two weren't English. On one of my visits to Shane's flat on Cromer Street, he had lent me a couple of Flann O'Brien's books, *The Best of Myles* and *An Béal Bocht,* and told me to read *The Third Policeman* and *At Swim-Two-Birds.*

In the books, the comical archetype of the Irish seemed only to confirm my father's judgement of them, until I came to see that the butt of the joke was not actually the Irish themselves, but people like my dad who were too witless to get it.

'That song degrades the Irish,' I said when the song had finished, hoping to typify the sententious northerner to the same degree that Brendan Shine's Dan typified the rural Irishman.

Spider honked in disbelief. Shane and Cait told me to fuck off. Jem simply sighed, 'James.'

As hard as Darryl drove to make up for our late departure, when the ferry terminal at Holyhead came into view we saw, out beyond the grey rim of the Irish Sea, the mauve smudge of smoke from the stack of the ferry we were supposed to have been on. We said nothing about how we had had to wait outside Shane's flat. Instead Darryl left us in the van and hurried across to the terminal. In fifteen minutes he was back with the news that we could use our Sealink tickets on a B&I ferry leaving in forty minutes.

I'd never been to Ireland before. I had never been on tour before. I went up on deck and leant on the rail to await the spasm of the screws starting. As the ferry cleared the breakwater and the lighthouse, salty hair-stiffening blasts gusted off the Irish Sea. In the stern, the Welsh coast narrowed to a dark thread, slubbed with hills.

In Belfast, helicopters floated clattering against the vivid bracken of the Black Mountain rising up beyond the fringes of the city. Armoured Land Rovers with louvred steel windows and mesh aprons crept through the streets. Security cameras craned from the corner of every building.

Our route from the ferry terminal took us through neighbourhoods of coloured kerbstones and painted gable-ends. The red, white and blue, the Protestant Red Hands of Ulster, the St George's Crosses, the initials UVF gave way to depictions of Bobby Sands, men in black balaclavas and the Ulster, Munster, Connaught and Leinster flags. Shane was in a ferment about driving through a Nationalist area in a vehicle not just with British licence plates, but also one with a broad orange stripe down the side.

'Let's get out of here,' Shane said. 'We'll get killed.'

'Don't be daft,' I said.

'What? What!?' he screeched. 'What the fuck do you know? You English cunt!'

In the van on the way up to Holyhead, Shane had pointed out that the colours of my lumberjack shirt were those of the Union Jack. I hadn't given much thought to it when I'd got dressed that

113

morning. It was one of only two shirts I had. The other was white.

'And your accent,' he had said.

'What about my accent?'

'What you mean what about your accent!?' Shane said. 'The squaddies, in Belfast – *the occupying force* – are all guys from fucking Yorkshire and Lancashire. They hear an accent like yours in – in West Belfast – you're fucking well *dead*!'

'They'll kneecap you down an alleyway,' Spider said.

Darryl nosed the van through the security checkpoint of the Europa Hotel, according to Andrew the most bombed hotel in Europe. The concrete and glass frontage was severe, angled into a shallow chevron. The hotel was surrounded by razor-wire.

The following day we had an interview and photo shoot for an English music paper in the Crown Liquor Saloon opposite the hotel.

'Just keep your fucking voice down,' Shane said to me as we left the security gate and crossed the road. 'If anyone asks you what religion you are,' Shane said, 'well – just don't talk to anybody.'

The Crown was an oppressively Victorian gin palace with stained-glass windows, a tiled floor and a moulded ceiling the colour of blood. After the interview we fell into talking with a couple of men who wanted to know who we were, what we were famous for. So much had Shane's protectiveness got to me that I dreaded them asking about me. I kept my mouth shut and made sure to keep my coat closed up to my neck for fear they would see the red, white and blue of my shirt. Whatever social adeptness I thought I had, deserted me.

We showed up at the Ulster Hall around the time we'd been told to and mustered our gear in the centre of the floor of the auditorium. The hall was huge, with a balustraded balcony, huge windows and chandeliers. Behind the stage towered the ranks of pipes of an organ. We sat around waiting for our turn to go up onto the stage to do our sound check while Costello did his. We disdained his prerogative as the headliner, the time he took over his sound check commensurate with his sense of self-importance.

I'd been taken to see Costello at the Nashville Rooms on Cromwell Road in London in 1977. When he came out onto the stage, the pigeon-toed testy nerd in Buddy Holly glasses, wearing jeans with deep turn-ups, turned into an apoplectic scourge – agitated, impatient, spleenful. His veins swelled at his temples and a ridge formed down the centre of his forehead.

At his sound check at the Ulster Hall, Costello looked like just another guy in blazer, jeans and specs making a living. We scoffed at his puffery when he went back to his hotel after he'd finished.

When it came to our sound check, we were confused as to how it was all supposed to work. There was a chaos of cables and boxes and activity. Space seemed reluctantly to be made for us. Darryl wheeled out our gear and arranged it around the stage, liaising with whomever of Costello's crew he could get to lend a hand. We got our instruments out and then stood around waiting to be told what to do. The feeling that we were a nuisance was made worse by the implicit requirement to be grateful to Costello for bringing us on the road in the first place, and to his crew for bringing our gear on the truck.

Despite all the gigs he'd done, Shane had never come to understand that the guy behind the desk in the wings controlled the sound on stage. Shane directed all his requirements to the front-of-house engineer in his barriered pen in the auditorium. He was a fat, balding guy with a red face whom everybody called the Bishop.

'Don't talk to *me*!' the Bishop laughed from the desk, inviting

115

his crew to laugh at us too. 'Talk to *your* guy!' he shouted. He waded out of his enclosure crying out 'Dinner!' and wafted his crew towards backstage, leaving only a guy called Flakey to look after us. Flakey was our guy and we drank up his kindness as he nodded us through our instrument checks from his desk.

Wearing our cherished duster coats, we strode out onto the stage in front of half an acre of faces, upturned at the front but thinning out abruptly the further away they stretched from the stage lights. We crashed through our short set. The half-hour we had been allotted hurtled past, strewn with such crises as Jem snagging on the introduction to 'Boys from the County Hell', my left hand failing to keep up with the rhythm of 'Dingle Regatta' on the accordion buttons. The hall boomed with reverberation. Spider bent a beer tray in half against his head. As the end of the chorus of 'Streams of Whiskey' came up we all stepped back from the line of microphones as one, to play the instrumental section. And then it was over and we went back to our dressing room, laughing. We wrenched off our duster coats, complained about how little beer there was to drink and went out to find a pub.

⋅✠⋅

The next show was in Galway. Darryl drove with his arm resting confidently in the open window, his hair blown by the wind, occasionally swapping hands to pat the passenger seat next to him to confirm that he had everything he needed – tapes, papers, maps, fags. Jem sat with the Office on the seat next to him. The Office was a Crawford's shortbread tin. It contained a notebook, a pencil, receipts and all the money we had – a meagre float from Stiff Records as tour support, to which we would add the £50 a night we were being paid to play on Costello's tour. Shane sat looking devoutly out of the window at the Irish countryside. Overgrown yellow-flecked hedges crowded lush fields. An estuary, still as a mirror, reflected reed banks and swans. Plaits of ivy strangled stands of twisted oaks.

We drove through towns with such names as Gubaveeney, Corraquigly, Sheskinacurry, Drumshanbo, Ballinaboy, Knocknafushoga, Cloonsheeva. Andrew repeated them in his liquid *basso profundo* as the van passed the signs. Without disdain of my ignorance, Shane told me about the Anglicisation of Ireland, dating from the earliest plantations in the 1500s, and the renaming of villages. At best, he told me, the Irish place names were translated into English. Failing translation, they swapped syllable for syllable, phoneme for phoneme, Gaelic for English. If the conglomerations of surds and diphthongs stumped them, or if they just felt like it, they gave the town a new name altogether.

I was ashamed to know so little. My upbringing seemed to doom me never to know enough. I had been a dunce at history at school. In the rubble of my comprehension of English history stood a pillar maintaining that Oliver Cromwell had single-handedly invented parliamentary government by means of vanquishing the foppish and florid, and above all Catholic, Charles I. Before forty-eight hours had elapsed in the minivan in Shane's company – and in Spider's and Darryl's, neither of whom was a slouch when it came to history – I discovered Cromwell to be a murderer who laid waste to a town called Drogheda in 1649, killing 3,500 of its inhabitants, before going on to do the same in Wexford. I hadn't known about this other side of the Lord Protector. My oblivion seemed tantamount to condonement. Privately, I claimed immunity from my inherited responsibility for Cromwell's binge-killing by the fact that, when I came across his death mask on a trip to Warwick Castle when I was fourteen, I thought he looked like a shithead.

When we got to Galway we were told that one of our flight cases had been left in Belfast. Costello's crew had brought instead a case belonging to the Ulster Orchestra. It was full of woodwind. The Attractions lent us some of their equipment – a bass for Cait and one of Costello's acoustic guitars for Shane. The Attractions didn't have a banjo. The crew offered Jem a turquoise electric guitar from Costello's collection. During the gig, if he didn't know the chords, Jem turned the volume off and strummed away as if he did.

Each day we listened to Darryl's tape, over and over. We never tired of hearing the Jolly Beggarmen, the Dubliners and the Clancy Brothers and Tommy Makem. They sang hearty songs, which were full of appetite, thirst and lust and which generally ended up in a fight. Though beer and whiskey flew, noses got broken and gobs belted, though shillelagh law became all the rage, nobody really got hurt. In 'Finnegan's Wake', the corpse even came back to life.

We listened to reels and jigs and slides, played for the most part by the Bothy Band whose melodies hurtled round in a seemingly endless train of notes. The uilleann pipes, flute, fiddle and whistle locked together, though now and again one would brim over the others with a brief line of harmony. Against the acoustic guitar which slung the rhythm forward, the bucolic and Arcadian sound of the flute brought to mind a country of fields and tilth

118

and hills and livestock. When the uilleann pipes struck up, the sound conjured flights of waterfowl, rushes, water and clouds. The bouzouki fanned the fen with an almost Mediterranean wind. The fiddle struck in and superimposed imagery that was American, hoisting up shameless harmonies.

The Bothy Band meshed with our van journey as we passed lakes and rising fell-flanks. The landscape was rough, overgrown and brutal. Spider lifted his face and crowed to the ceiling of the van.

On our way to Dublin we sang along with the Dubliners.

> *And we're all off to Dublin in the green, in the green*
> *Where the helmets glisten in the sun*
> *Where the bayonets flash and the rifles crash*
> *To the rattle of a Thompson gun.*

We drove down O'Connell Street on our way to our hotel on Ormond Quay. Shane pointed out the bullet holes in the fluted columns in front of the Post Office, from the Easter Rising in 1916.

'*Oifig an Phoist*,' Andrew said in stentorian tones.

'Oi'm figgan poissed too!' Spider said.

At the National Stadium, the corridor and dressing rooms were hushed. Costello, we were told, had come down with laryngitis and was going to pull the gig. We rolled our eyes ceilingward and shrank into our dressing room – a cubicle with a heater up on the wall – to wait and see what was going to happen next.

Shane had been complaining about his throat. We never let him pull out of a gig. It became a regular occurrence to see him buckling over in the dressing room, coughing explosively in an effort to hawk up whatever the obstruction was. Increasingly, he resorted to jets of Chloraseptic which he would get as close to his vocal cords as possible by craning his head forward to the nozzle. He extended his neck as if to protect his filthy clothes. After thumbing the doings down, he doubled over, retching and gagging. When he'd finished and wiped his nose the length of his forearm, blinking and teary, he looked woundedly across at us, as if the victim of an affront. We implored him to rest his voice, but it was never long before he started up shouting with Spider, trading outrages, braying with laughter, before we went up on stage.

In the end, when word came that Costello had changed his mind and the gig was going to go ahead, we derided him for his capriciousness.

We left the fields and abundant hedgerows of Ireland for the combed stubble of English hayfields. We stopped at roadside pubs and off-licences and loaded up with beer and whiskey. I sat with my knees up on the back of the seat in front. The open window of the minivan blew tears into my eyes. The autumn sunlight shone across the fields, gilding the hedgerows and the trees. I clutched a bottle of duty-free Powers by the neck, tasting the fields and peat-water in it. We hooted at the ructions at Tim Finnegan's wake. We hollered at the braiding of the pipes and the fiddle and the flute. We huzzahed when Andrew had learnt the words to the Clancy Brothers' and Tommy Makem's 'Courtin' in the Kitchen', singing, in his tremulous bass voice, chin down, Adam's apple low:

> *Come single belle and beau*
> *Unto me now pay attention*
> *Don't ever fall in love*
> *For it's the Devil's own invention*

There were a couple of occasions which threatened us with expulsion from the tour. Fed up with the Bishop's ill-treatment, we ambushed him in a corridor on his way to catering and backed him up against the wall. I was scared we might have overdone it. He was tiny. His belligerence evaporated. His cries of 'Dinner!' ended.

In St Austell, on his way back from the beach, Jem filled the pockets of his duster coat with sand. He cut a tiny hole in each pocket to let it trickle out while he was playing. He had hoped to leave two tidy mounds to mark where he had been standing. After the usual commotion of the changeover between our set and Costello's, Steve Nieve, the Attractions' keyboard player, was furious to find the sand had gritted his organ pedals.

It was a couple of weeks before Guy Fawkes Night that we spent the morning drinking Centenary and Bismarck port in Yates's Wine Lodge in Nottingham. Spider and I bought a bottle each for the drive. By the time we got to the University, we'd loaded up with Brock's bangers from a newsagent's and I was villainously drunk. Spider and I sowed the bangers about the room. After threats of expulsion, at the Hammersmith Palais we eventually came clean to the promoters about the scorch-marks we left behind. We had to shell out £40 from the Crawford's shortbread tin.

It became obvious that there was something going on between Cait and Costello. She had started to call Costello 'Brian' when they passed one another backstage or if they should come across one another in catering. In return, he had begun to call her 'Beryl.'

It had made us laugh to give ourselves the names of characters from 'The Bash Street Kids' in *The Beano*. Jem was Biffo the Bear, Spider Roger the Dodger. I was Lord Snooty. Shane was Plug. We had chosen Minnie the Minx for Cait, but Elvis's choice of Beryl – from Beryl the Peril, a character in *The Topper* – was the one she wanted to stick.

'Who the fuck is Brian?' we asked. Cait giggled girlishly and covered her mouth. 'He's Brian – the snail!' she said. 'From *The Magic Roundabout*! He's all cute and defenceless and everything.'

Underlying the banality, there was a needfulness about her which looked like it wouldn't tolerate mockery.

A hazard in the glancing flirtation between Brian and Beryl came with the arrival of Bebe Buell, model and Playmate, with whom Costello, separated from his wife, had been having what had been described in the papers as a 'tempestuous' affair. She showed up at the Apollo in Oxford. I came in from the minibus after Costello's show, to see Buell and Costello in the hotel bar. They were sitting on stools on the far side of the room away from the rest of the Attractions and crew. Costello was in his suit, leaning with one arm on the bar. She wore a knitted beret. There was an atmosphere of exclusivity and implicit danger about the place.

The following day at Portsmouth Guildhall, a change seemed to have come over Cait. Displaced from Elvis's court, she rejoined us, wanting to be one of the boys again and full of an exile's self-righteousness. Up in our dressing room after the gig, she began to hurl empties out of the window. They exploded on the ground where Costello's crew was loading out. When we heard the sound of boots stamping up the stairs and loud shouts, Cait knocked off the bottom of a bottle of wine against the wall. She brandished what was left by the neck and waited for whoever was coming up the stairs. Before they got to our dressing room, Andrew managed to wrestle the broken bottle from her and hid it behind his back.

A couple of roadies and a driver appeared puffing and indignant in the doorway. We faced them down with a unanimous and impregnable denial that we knew what the fuck they were talking about.

The wheel of Costello and Cait's relationship soon recovered from the poked stick of Bebe Buell's appearance. I came across Brian and Beryl in the lobby of the hotel in Leeds before going out to the University for our show. The two of them sat in intimately uncomfortable positions, knees, thighs, elbows, shoulders touching, a notebook open somehow on Costello's lap. When I sat in the armchair opposite, Costello looked across at me, lofting the quizzical eyebrows above his heavy-rimmed glasses framing tired but serene eyes.

Between Leeds and Newcastle we had a day off. We took our time setting out. It was already the afternoon by the time we pulled up for lunch at the Three Horse Shoes in Boroughbridge and filed into the pinched front parlour for beer and steak and kidney pie.

By the time we left, it was dark and we were drunk. We bought carry-out for the drive to Newcastle. The pints seemed to have loosened Andrew's face and cast his eyebrows adrift. Shane hobbled to the sliding door.

Once we were on our way, on a whim, Darryl ducked off the A1 and into the North Yorkshire Moors. Through the windows, but for the headlights frosting the road ahead, the sections of dry-stone wall and the verge of heath, it was pitch dark.

In the van in the blackness, Shane muttered something about feeling shit.

'You drink too much!' Andrew shouted, laughing at the back of Shane's head. 'If you gave up drinking! Or at least moderated it a bit!'

Shane sat with his arms folded across his stomach, his face turned to the window.

The month of touring had been hard on all of us but harder on Shane. We hadn't slept much, sometimes three to a room, in bed-and-breakfasts. We'd all been drinking a lot, staying out. The hours Shane kept, though, were yet more adrift. Though the tour production laid on catering, we were lucky to get any food. Shane hardly seemed to eat anything but kaolin and morphine, which formed a crust around his mouth and caked the front of his coat. Every day Shane brought a bag clanking with bottles onto the minivan.

His throat was already a chronic grievance. Now his guts were troubling him. His carriage had become careful and hunched in protection of his ailing stomach. On some days, his defenceless eyes stared out from the pallor of his face.

'Oh, I do worry about him,' my mother had said after our show in Manchester. 'If I could only have him for a while, if I could have him home, and give him a good meal, and a bed, just for a while.'

Her eyes had filled with tears which she tried to blink away.

In the van, we all started to chide him.

'No fucking wonder your voice's shot and your stomach's ruined.'

'We worry about you!' Spider shouted. 'Can't you see?'

'Fuck off!' Shane said.

'Stop the bus!' Jem yelled. 'Stop the bus. I can't stand this any more. It's all just so fucking stupid. Let me off.'

'We're in the middle of the moors,' Darryl said.

'I don't care!' Jem said. 'I'm getting off. Stop the fucking bus.'

Darryl drew up by the roadside. We remonstrated with Jem in the doorway, but he wrenched the sliding door closed behind him and disappeared.

A couple of moments later, Spider clambered down the bus and climbed out.

'I'm getting off too!' Spider said. He vanished into the darkness.

'Oh fuck,' Darryl said.

We sat there for a minute not knowing what to do. Shane sniffed and brought a bottle to his mouth. Darryl started up, drove down the road, rounded a corner and pulled in to the side a quarter of a mile further on. He shut down the engine. I got out.

'It's okay,' I said. 'I'm not going to run off.'

The moor tops were barely visible under the night sky. There was an orange dinge above Middlesbrough beyond the horizon to the north. Until Darryl set the hazard lights going to let them both see where the van was, the separate masses of Andrew's anger, Shane's intransigence and Spider and Jem's disappearances combined and intensified in the pitch dark until I thought my head would crack.

Spider came scrambling up the bank, out of breath. Ten minutes later, there was a knock on the side of the van. We slid the door open. Jem got in.

'And in a tradition that was to become time-honoured,' Spider said, 'they rejoined the group.' Shane wheezed with mirth. We drove the rest of the way to Newcastle in silence.

Though Costello was going on to play a couple of shows in London at the Dominion Theatre, our last gig of the tour was in Norwich at the University of East Anglia. After his shows in London Costello was going out on another tour of the British Isles, with T-Bone Burnett. After that, he was leaving for Europe. Cait was skittish.

She burst into our dressing room. She had a can of shaving foam and a razor. She wrenched the taps open at one of the basins and started to shave her head, upward from the nape of her neck and her ears.

'What the fuck are you doing?' Spider asked.

'What's it look like?'

When she'd finished, a crown of dark hair sprouted from a disc on the top of her head. The rest of her scalp was white, flecked here and there with pink foam and covered in nicks from the razor.

'You're not fucking going on stage looking like that,' we said.

'Why not?' she said.

'Because it looks fucking stupid,' Shane said.

Someone threw her a towel to wrap her head with.

'Really?' she said.

'Fuck yeah.'

'Fuck yez all,' she said. 'You're a bunch of cunts.'

She wrapped her head with the towel like a turban, her black hair sticking out of a hole in the top. When she had gone, a silence descended on the room.

'Well,' Spider said, 'he's not going to forget her in a hurry.'

After the show, the road manager came to invite us to Costello's dressing room. There was an awkward air of festivity. Costello climbed up to play the piano which stood on the dais. Cait sat morose and sullen on the upholstered ledge with her head in the towel turban. We drank the Attractions' beer and laughed. Then the Attractions and Costello had to head off. Their bus was waiting.

'We should do something together,' Costello said breezily as he made his way out of the room.

'Yeah,' we all said, but knew he didn't mean it.

'You're all coming to the Dominion?' he said, looking at us over the top of his Buddy Holly glasses. 'You're all on the list.'

We sat on the minibus waiting for Cait. When she was in, she sat with her coat about her, her knees up, her dark eyes staring sideways out of the window. Darryl pulled out of the car park. On the way back to London I nursed a half-bottle of Powers in my lap and watched the pulse of the motorway lights on the road through the windows.

It was around two in the morning as I walked up from where

Darryl dropped us all off outside Shane's flat, up Midland Road by the side of St Pancras Station and along the body repair shops in the arches under the railway, my bag over my shoulder. I clasped the front of my coat across my stomach against the cold. I had never been so tired, dulled by the sustained crush of other human beings, concussed by the confusion of their demands, blunted by the cycle of sleep, travel, sound check, show, sleep, travel, sound check, show. At the same time I was aware of the certainty, dense and hard, that the crucible of Darryl's Iveco Daily had fused us all together and permanently, with the makings of the next record among the tracks on Darryl's tape.

Twelve

In the Boot on Cromer Street, Jem leant on the table and started to draw a finger through the beer on the tabletop. He protruded his lips.

'I've been meaning to say something,' he said. He stared at his finger in the beer. We all looked at him. His eyes were wide and sad. His eyebrows lifted wrinkles into his forehead.

'I can't do this any more,' he said.

'Can't do what?' The thought that he was going to leave the band horrified me.

'I can't do this – this,' he faltered. His eyes became so wide that his pupils floated free of his eyelids. 'I can't do – basically,' he continued, 'what I think a manager should be doing.'

During our tour with Costello it had befallen Jem to organise the itinerary, buy the ferry tickets, book hotels, settle bills, wrangle the money we were due from Costello's production and try to balance our accounts. In the van, he would sit with his knees up against the back of the seat in front with the Office open in his lap, tapping his teeth with a pencil. At the end of each week, when we returned to London for Costello's weekly residency at the Hammersmith Palais, Jem had gone round to Stiff Records to ask for more money.

To add to his tribulations, a couple of weeks after we had returned from the tour, he told us that Marcia was pregnant again. Their second baby was due in May.

He lifted his eyes to gaze forlornly at all of us. He complained that the responsibility he took for liaising with the record company, for decisions concerning where, when and for how much we played, anywhere, was too much for him. Stan Brennan had been right: increasingly the companies we attempted to do business with were reluctant to conduct negotiations with any one of us.

'But it's not just that,' he said. 'Eventually, eventually, it's going to make me into your enemy. I'm not prepared to set myself up for that. I want to be a member of the band again.'

I was riven with guilt to think we had deserted him. The one gig I'd set up at the Ritzy in Brixton seemed a paltry contribution.

'We need to get a manager,' he said.

The prospect dismayed me. I trusted Jem with our affairs and I hated the idea of bringing anyone else into our adventure. The hiring of a manager – with all the imagery of briefcases, blazers and thinning hair – I feared would scuttle the story of our transition from disparate bunch of strangers into something more or less resembling a unit, with an identifiable ethos. But I felt so badly for Jem that I did not contest.

Shane came up with a guy from Dublin called Frank Murray. Murray apparently had been Kirsty MacColl's manager and had tour-managed Thin Lizzy. We arranged to meet him in the Windsor Castle on Parkway in Camden. It was early in the day and the place smelled of cigarettes and Brasso. We sat around with pints and waited.

When Murray came in he bore an unsurprising resemblance to Dave Robinson. As anticipated, he was wearing a blue sports coat, jeans and loafers. His hair was cut in a generic George Orwell style, but wavy. He sat down on one of the stools across from our table with his legs apart, elbows planted on each thigh, a twist of hair needing pushing back. He looked vulnerable despite the thinness of his mouth and the dark plush which shaded his jaw.

We were unruly a bit, to make an impression and because it was expected. We took the piss out of him too, to break the ice and to show him that we weren't going to be walked over. He rebuffed our teasing by means of an airy outline of his capabilities, our expectations and the music business, then got up and left.

There wasn't much to review, other than the guy himself and his offer to take us on for twenty per cent, for a trial period. It had hardly taken up any of our time at all. We had a manager and we hadn't even to sign a contract.

The following week, we met him again in the Boot after a rehearsal to talk about the plans he had.

'Just give me two years of your life,' he said. 'That's all I ask. Just two years.'

I pictured us in a couple of years as an established musical entity enjoying deserved esteem, making records regularly. We would each be a musician of repute. We would each have side projects: record production, collaborations, film scores. I would be able to balance my musical and writing careers. I would be living in my own house, if not my own narrow boat.

Frank's management company was called Hill 16 Ltd. Frank was proud of the name, so called after one of the terraces in Croke Park, the GAA stadium in Dublin. The story was that Hill 16 – originally a mound at the north end of the ground – got its name from the 1916 Easter Rising, the rubble from which had gone to build the terrace.

Up Kentish Town Road from Hill 16 Ltd's offices was a pub called the Devonshire Arms. After the Pindar of Wakefield, and lately the Boot, the Dev as it was known started to become our watering hole.

Gigs began to come in. We played the Cricketers Arms near

the Oval in London. We went up to Digbeth Civic Hall near Birmingham. We drove out in the minivan to the Labour Club in Newport, to play a gig in solidarity with the National Union of Mineworkers, the miners' strike already in its ninth month.

On the 31st December we played at the ICA on the Mall, as part of Harp Lager's ICA Rock Week. As the end of 1984 had been approaching I had made Debsey a card to welcome the New Year. It depicted a window opening up towards a blue sky, fluffy with clouds. I wanted it to come across as a statement of hope for the year to come. My career with the Pogues was taking off. Debsey's seemed to have all but stalled.

Debsey's last project with Hester and Rachel had been in April, around the time the Pogues had recorded our first session for John Peel. Dolly Mixture had spent a couple of weeks recording an EP at a home studio in Suffolk. It consisted mostly of instrumental parlour pieces, with Rachel playing the cello and Debsey the piano. *The Fireside EP*, as it was called, had been released a month or so before the Pogues went into the studio to record *Red Roses for Me*. Since then, Dolly Mixture had been away with Captain Sensible for scattershot television engagements in such places as Stratford, Bristol and Hull. At an appearance at Alton Towers Debsey found out that Sensible and Rachel were due to have a baby.

Debsey did not attend our New Year's Eve show at the ICA. After the gig, I walked the three miles through the West End and up Rosebery Avenue to Islington to drop the card into her parents' letter-box on Liverpool Road.

In the first week of the New Year, Frank flew us up to Newcastle for a live performance on the Tyne Tees Television music show *The Tube*, hosted by Paula Yates and Jools Holland – our first appearance on a bona fide pop programme. On the plane he gave us details of a tour he had booked of Ireland, with a couple of dates up north and one in Scotland, due to start at the beginning of February. After that he had plans for a couple of St Patrick's Night shows in London, followed by our first tour of Europe and Scandinavia.

Not long after, I got a phone call from Jem. The weeks away from his family on the Costello tour had been hard on him, made plain by his flight from our minivan on the North Yorkshire Moors. Now Marcia was five months pregnant and Ella a baby of fifteen months. The advance from Stiff Records and the fees from the gigs we were doing were only bringing in £150 a week. It was probably more than any of us had ever earned, but hardly enough for a new family.

'I haven't spoken to anyone else about this,' he said. 'I wanted to talk to you first.' His tone was so measured and gritty that my heart sank.

'You all right?' I said.

'No,' he said. 'Not really.' There was a long pause. 'I really feel I have to leave the group.'

'Oh dear,' I said.

Without Jem's nous the band would just collapse. None of us had the canniness to make the decisions that seemed to come so easily to Jem. None of us had his mental alacrity, his energy or his pertinacity when it came to dealing with Shane. None of us had the acumen or the moral stamina to deal with the likes of Dave Robinson and maybe Frank Murray.

It occurred to me that Jem might have rung me to challenge me to argue him down. I knew the approaching weeks of absence from his family would aggravate his circumstances at home. I was shamelessly indifferent to them and not afraid to imply that his defection would amount to a betrayal of what had become our brotherhood. I asked him not to quit.

'And don't get me wrong,' I added, 'but what the fuck else are you going to do?'

'Let me talk to Marcia,' he said in the end.

When Jem showed up at the next gig, neither of us referred to our conversation.

The gig was a return to the Cricketers Arms near the Oval cricket ground. Frank had set up a slew of interviews after the sound check, in advance of what was described in our fanzine as our 'Irish mini-tour' in February. Frank distributed us throughout the blue-panelled rooms and ushered in a journalist for each of us.

I admired the ease with which Shane both sent up and relished the process of self-publicising. Jem had a knack for synthesising and giving a context to what we were doing. Spider was mischievous, unpredictable, funny and personable.

It was rare that I was asked to do an interview. My eagerness to come up with something printable tended to produce ponderous and over-earnest commonplaces. Besides, I had little idea about our context – in Irish music, folk music or in pop music in general. I found it difficult to formulate an opinion about what we thought we were doing beyond the matter of playing music with people and trying to get on with them.

The first string of Frank's gigs took us to Reading University, the Blue Note in Derby, Queen Margaret College Students' Union in Glasgow and the Paradise Club in Preston, where no sooner had we started playing than the crowd swarmed the stage. In frustration, Andrew delivered a crack to someone's head with his drumsticks.

In a couple of days we were back in London and Debsey finally moved out of her parents' place, into a housing association property on Wharton Street round the corner from where Jem and Marcia lived. Debsey and Marcia had become firm friends. Part of me regretted her not moving in with me, but Debsey wanted her independence. Before we left for Ireland, I went to see her new room. Her window overlooked the street which rose from King's Cross Road. A door from her kitchenette opened onto a small balcony over the front door. Debsey sat me on her bed and had me listen to the Smiths' 'How Soon Is Now?' over and over while she ironed in the doorway.

Before our flight to Belfast for the Irish section of the tour Shane drank himself into a dither. Spooked by the door of the metal detector, he tried to shimmy his way round the side of it. The security officer ushered him through. When the engines powered up and the plane thrust forward, Cait shrieked and pummelled the back of my seat with a volley of kicks.

From Belfast we drove across the Six Counties to Letterkenny. After our show in a local pub, a spotty kid came to sit next to me at the bar. His accent was hard to decipher and he was drunk. I was about to finish my pint of Smithwick's and put the glass down empty as a signal that I was going to move on, but I ended up listening to him. He spoke more to the surface of the bar than to me. All his life, he said, he had been waiting for someone like Shane to come along.

'He's just like me,' he said. 'Well, not like me. People like me. The people who live here. Anywhere, really. Those other wankers. In bands, whatever bands. Don't have the fucking time for them. They don't have the time for people like us. But MacGowan, he's like us. He's a man of the people. It's like he knows, you know? How's he know about me? He's clever, like. You got to be clever to write songs the way he does. But that clever that he knows about people like me? He's the man. You know what I mean?'

After Letterkenny we drove two hundred miles to Carlow, a market town an hour south of Dublin. It was dark when we arrived and the streetlights cast a wintry yellow light on the drab parade of businesses and bars along Tullow Street. In the bar of the Royal Hotel I had a whiskey and red and watched an earwig crawl up one of the porcelain beer pumps. Before our show at the Ritz Ballroom we went to a bar called Archbald's. It was raucous with our fans. A phalanx surrounded Shane and Spider and started to ply the two of them with questions. The determination and eagerness of the interrogation seemed focused on preventing Spider and Shane from making their excuses and peeling off. One after the other, lads jostled to get a question in before the others.

My attention was drawn to an argument on the other side of the bar. A guy wearing a leather jacket was quarrelling with another guy, pretty much dressed identically. The guy's eyes were glassy and his face was contorted with drink as he fought to moderate his reactions by constant flicks of his head as if he were trying to dislodge the impulse to shunt his interlocutor to the wall and give him a pounding. The thought that he was likely to show up in our audience at the ballroom down the street made my heart sink.

We walked out on stage. The ballroom was not much more than a large saloon, sparely furnished with a fruit machine near the steamed-up windows at the back, and a bare chimney-breast and mantel in the wall near me. A boisterous, drunk, predominantly male audience pressed against the flimsy barrier.

Things went well at first. The opening song, 'Streams of Whiskey', seemed to act like an astringent on the crowd of men, convulsing the throng, sending shoulder against shoulder, elbow against elbow, hip against hip, buttocks against groin. I winced to see a windjammered body collide obliquely with a neighbour, elbows high enough to catch a cheek.

From my vantage point by the side of the stage, I loved to watch the line of us step up to the microphones, as one, to sing the chorus and then to step back for the instrumental section.

Shane scrubbed his guitar, head down. Cait, her hair recently dyed red, the collar of her duster coat up, scribed an arc with the neck of her bass. Spider, the only one remaining at his mike, twitched his leg. Jem stood looking out with the detachment of a maître d'hôtel, his lips pursing and puffing from the concentration of playing. Angled away from the crowd, fag in my mouth more often than not, blinking against the smoke, I bent over the accordion and stamped my heel.

A quarter of the way through the set, alerted by a rumbling in the audience, punctuated by shouts and a girl's angry scream, I looked up from my fingers to see frantic shoving going on in the middle of the crowd. The guy I'd seen in Archbald's, his face pink and distorted with the effort, lunged, arms straight, palms up, into another guy who in a valiant but ridiculous attempt to both keep his balance and to fend the guy off was windmilling his arms. People stepped back to get out of the way but others came striding in, clambering to get through. They pulled at jackets, hands clawing and swiping, their legs in half-crouch. Some of them dragged arms free from the press and turned them into swinging fists arcing down into space or against someone's shoulder. The occasional sickening knuckle-blow glanced against an ear or someone's temple.

All the while we kept playing. The image came to mind of the bewhiskered piano player in a Western saloon pulling his hat down over his ears as the saloon explodes in gunfire and smoke, the tables go over and the ranks of bottles disintegrate into a cascade of liquor and shards. We didn't look at one another but gawped at the turmoil on the dance floor and kept going, thinking that the end of the song would bring the furore to an end.

Eventually we were able to finish the song, and with a flourish I hoped might come across as conclusive, but the fighting continued, the non-combatants flung to the edges of the dance floor, the participants going at it, deaf to anything else that was going on in the room. We stood there watching, Shane gawping at the tumult in front of him with an expression of bemusement on his face. I didn't have a clear plan when I stepped up to the microphone that Spider wasn't using.

'Quit fighting!' I found myself shouting. 'Quit it! Just stop the fucking fighting!'

My command did nothing. The squall lurched sideways as if the ballroom floor had tilted. Fists opened into claws grabbing for stability. Legs that a moment before had waded into the rumpus now capered backwards, trying to find a grip on the dance floor. The ruckus sent itself against the wall and along it into the corner. A couple of guys lost their balance altogether. When they hit the ground they tucked their knees up and covered their heads as the scrimmage appeared to bounce off the far wall and back towards us.

We stood and watched. Hostages to the chaos, there was nothing else we could do. I went around the stage in panic, appealing to everyone, anyone, to do something, vainly assuming that there was something we could do. Shane just shrugged. The fighting eventually ended with a couple of guys – one of them the guy from Archbald's – being dragged to either side, penned in by their mates and subjected to bellowed appeals to reason. There was panting and gasping and nodding of heads and hateful stares and eventually capitulation. The rest of the crowd started to return to press against the barriers. In a moment or two the combatants seemed to have vanished, absorbed by the rabble.

We played on without further incident. I played on without enthusiasm. I couldn't help thinking that beneath society's superstructure of civility and mutuality was a basement writhing with blind and inchoate urges.

'The fucking cunts!' I said when we were able to finish and go backstage. 'What a bunch of fucking cunts! We're supposed to be playing fucking music out there. It's supposed to be entertainment! Christ!'

'Shut the fuck up,' Shane said. He scratched his nose, bored, and pulled on a cigarette.

'Fuck off Shane,' I said. 'That was just fucking debasing.' I appealed to the others, who looked just as depressed and stunned as I was. 'We can't allow that to happen again. We should have the lights go up, shine torches on them or something. We should leave the stage and only come back when . . .' I ran out of ideas just as Shane screamed:

'Oh, shut the fuck up with the fucking whingeing, you fucking faggot!'

His hands were gripping his face. His eyes slowly appeared from behind his brown fingers, staring dementedly at the floor. In a show of mastering his fury he spread his fingers in front of him, level to the ground. It took him a moment to get some sort of a grip on himself.

'Listen,' he said, as if he were talking to a child. 'Listen. They do what they do and nothing you can do or say makes any difference. People are – not just these people – *people*, you know – *people* just want to kill one another.'

'*People*,' he went on in a hoarse, supercilious whisper, 'are just *this much* away from murdering each other, this much away from raping one another, this much away from knifing, shooting, massacring, garrotting. It's fucking dog-eat-dog out there. It's fucking dog-eat-dog wherever you look. It's what they want to do and you got to let them get on with it because it means the fuckers are not likely to rape or knife or shoot or garrotte me or any of us. It's what they want to do and if it's what they want to do they're going to do it anyway no matter how much fucking whingeing and screeching and flapping you do. So shut up, stay away from my fucking microphone or anyone's microphone. They'll come and kill the fucking lot of us. They're just looking for an excuse. And shut the fuck up with your fucking debasement and all that shit – just play the fucking accordion and stay out of the way. That's what you're paid for.'

'And if only he could do *that* properly,' Spider sighed.

When I got back to the hotel, first back to the room I was sharing with Jem, I stood between the bed and the cheap dresser by the window and then crouched down to the ground, tucked myself into a ball and pounded my head with my fists. I couldn't understand how anyone could let himself become so bereft of responsibility for anything and yet write songs of such incisive beauty, full of chastening pity for the human condition.

Depending on whom we talked to, our gig at Trinity College in Dublin had been cancelled because of a protest at the University or because the Students' Union had bottled out of putting on our gig. Either way, the venue was changed to a club called McGonagle's on Anne Street for the following night. We had a day off. I drank whiskey and reds all afternoon in the hotel bar. It was dusk when I staggered up Grafton Street under a triumphal arch into St Stephen's Green. Willows draped the walkways and water birds shunted about. The road alongside the Royal Canal crawled with traffic. Reeds choked the canal. Somehow I ended up back in Grafton Street and drinking whiskey and red in Kehoe's with its moulded ceiling and bar dividers. McDaid's was crowded. I sat at a table with Jem and a couple of students. Jem laughed at how drunk I was. The tabletops were scrubbed oak. Every inch of wall was filled with framed pictures. The only one I recognised was James Joyce. People kept going on about Brendan Behan. A journalist from *Hot Press* magazine reckoned we could all breeze into a club called The Pink Elephant because of who we were. We squeezed arse to arse into cabs. The club was dowdy, concussive with music and full of people who knew of somewhere else to go.

The next day, I took the DART out to Howth. I looked out over the estuary – the flashings of the Poolbeg power station chimneys, the distant lattices of cranes under the dappled sky. I climbed up Howth Head, my shoes crunching on the granular quartz on the paths. Up on the top, I breathed in lungfuls of salt air blowing off the sea out of the mist. I wanted to go home. I dreaded McGonagle's.

A line of punks squirmed forward against the chests of the bouncers along the front of the stage, behind them a crush of puce faces and wet hair. The first song, 'Greenland Whale Fisheries', seemed to send a charge through the crowd. In one mass, they jumped, staggered backwards and rushed forwards, pitched side-ways. Heads shook, bodies cavorted. Here and there shoulders twisted to free an arm, but to my relief only to wave or let loll over someone's shoulder. Though I stared down the keyboard of the accordion, I watched the audience, bracing for a repeat of the gig in Carlow. Now and again a bouncer rammed the pistons of his forearms into the crowd to push them away. Otherwise, nothing happened until we were clearing up after the set and people were leaving. The two bouncers in the middle of the apron, relaxing now that the compression had eased, let a kid through to collapse with his forearms on the stage and his head buried in them. Just as Jem came to the edge to pull the cables out of his DI box, the kid's arms opened up like a claw, wrapped around Jem's legs and star-ted to pull him off the stage. Jem shouted. The bouncers detached the kid and hauled him away.

Afterwards, in the dressing room, Spider shouted:

'See? Dublin loves us. It loves us so much it wanted to keep our banjo player!'

Thirteen

'You sick fuck!' Spider said. ' "Labelled parts one to three?" What sort of a twisted, fucked-up sort of mind comes up with lyrics like that?'

'Mine,' Shane said.

We had been rehearsing in the attic of Andrew's house, a Victorian white-painted bay that he and his long-time companion, Deborah Korner, shared in West Hampstead, a walk along the railway line from the station. The room we rehearsed in was under the roof and had a dormer window. It was a job getting us all in.

The first song we rehearsed was called 'Sally MacLennane' and was in jig-time, full of shouts of 'FAR AWAY!' and explosions of single stroke rolls on the drums. The melodies were so seamlessly Irish that I was surprised to find out that the song wasn't traditional. The words of the chorus brought to mind the ceremony I knew Shane indulged in, when he would gather his bosom friends in one of the bars at Euston railway station to see him off on the boat train to Holyhead for the ferry to Dun Laoghaire.

Another of the songs Shane brought in was a waltz, in C, called 'A Pair of Brown Eyes'. There was a delicacy about the chord progression I hadn't heard in Shane's writing before. A relative minor chord changed position from verse to verse. The harmonic structure of the chorus avoided resolution, going instead into a refrain of single notes, to be played on the banjo, stepping down in an aching reiteration of the chorus melody. A couple of verses and refrains later – finally resolving the melody of the chorus and underpinning the words – came a cadence so reminiscent of songs immemorially older than this one that it nearly brought tears to my eyes.

I tried to make sense of the lyrics I could hear – streams and rolling hills bearing with them images of water lilies and canals. After a couple of runs through, I started to become aware of an almost nightmarish kaleidoscope. As soon as I thought I had got used to the scene I'd happened on – a pub somewhere with a jukebox and an old man – a smash cut deposited me in a landscape worthy of Wilfred Owen, full of dismemberment, with arms and legs scattered all around.

As gruesome as the words were and as elusive as the meaning was, what I understood and felt for most of all was the guy at the end: Shane, I supposed, in the dawn, crawling and walking, talking to himself.

To our surprise, making good on what had seemed in the dressing room at East Anglia University a casual proposal of recording with us, at the beginning of 1985 Costello had let it be known he wanted to produce 'A Pair of Brown Eyes'. At the end of January, however, it was no longer Elvis Costello who sat waiting for us in the subterranean control room at Elephant Studios, but a guy he wanted to be called Declan Patrick MacManus. MacManus wore a black linen suit with a pork-pie hat tilted back. Though he still inclined his head to lift his eyes and brows over the top of them to view us, his glasses were no longer Holly but burgundy-tinted Lennon.

He sat on one of the swivel chairs with his arms on his knees peeling a pomelo. We sat on the lumpy couch in the control room, respectful, somewhat in awe, and listened to his account, told with an endearing diastematic lisp, of the recording of *Almost Blue*, the country record he had made in Nashville in 1981 with Billy Sherrill, the producer of George Jones and Tammy Wynette, who routinely brought a gun into the studio and had once emptied it into the mixing desk.

The recording was straightforward. We had rehearsed 'A Pair of Brown Eyes' over and over and had been playing it live since Christmas. A short snare roll brought in a straight C chord on the accordion with Jem playing an arpeggio, Shane strumming underneath. An accordion hook I'd lifted from Dermot O'Brien's 'Connemara Rose', one of the tracks on Darryl's tape, brought in Shane's voice. Costello had hired Colin Fairley to work alongside Elephant's engineer, Nick Robbins. Fairley had worked on Costello's *Punch the Clock* and knew how to execute 'radio-friendly' mixes.

Once the backing track was finished, Costello brought his musician/producer's attention to bear on the matter of overdubs. He had an idea to lift the chorus by means of a roll on the snare, to be answered, every measure but one, by a beat on a tambourine.

Andrew played the snare, Costello the tambourine. To listen back it was Costello's custom to lean on the far side of the mixing desk, an impish expression on his face, his arms up on the ledge and the brim of his hat tilted up.

'I hear mandolins,' he said. 'James?'

I sat across from Costello, our knees close to touching, both of us on swivel chairs in the control room. Each of us cradled a mandolin. His was a scroll-neck Gibson of some ancient provenance. Mine was the one we used on stage. We duplicated the banjo melody in the refrain, Costello taking a harmony above mine. We extended the tune downwards and, where the song was to fade out, played couplets in a style we both agreed was 'kind of Greek'. I was elated to submit to the tutelage of a musician I had revered for years, lofty with his approval, hot with embarrassment when I fucked up.

We broke from the studio for our gigs in Belfast, Letterkenny and Carlow. When we got back, we played a couple of gigs in Leeds and Nottingham. A grey-haired guy wearing a combat jacket buttoned up to his throat met us on the gravel driveway of the hotel in Nottingham. I assumed he'd come to fix the van, which had something wrong with it. The guy turned out to be a long-time friend of Frank's and the front-of-house sound-engineer for the bands Frank had managed in Dublin – Skid Row and Dr Strangely Strange. Paul Scully had crystalline-blue eyes in which flashed a mixture of benevolence, sensitivity and mischief. His arrival whittled Darryl's functions of general factotum down to those of roadie and driver.

If the recording of 'A Pair of Brown Eyes' and 'Sally MacLennane' was Costello's baptism by aspersion, after our shows in February he committed to full submersion by taking on the production of our second album. So completely had we come to like and trust Paul Scully that we asked him to engineer alongside Nick Robbins.

Most of the new songs we'd practised and practised either in Rick Trevan's back bedroom or at Andrew and Deborah's house, and many of them we had been playing live. 'And the Band Played Waltzing Matilda' and 'The Old Main Drag' we'd been playing for over a year. We had recorded the former the previous February with Stan Brennan. The latter dated back to my first rehearsals with Shane and Jem. Over the past couple of months we had been working not just on 'A Pair of Brown Eyes' and 'Sally MacLennane' – and on one by Phil Gaston, Brennan's partner at Rocks Off record shop, called 'Navigator' – but also on another two of Shane's newest songs: 'Billy's Bones', which referred to a traditional Irish anti-war song called 'Mrs

McGrath', and which borrowed the traditional Scottish melody 'Highland Laddie' for the introduction; and 'The Sick Bed of Cúchulainn', a song which seemed to tower above the others, lyrically and musically, from the start. The mandolin introduction was like the turning of the flimsiest of flyleaves to reveal a frontispiece of prodigious conceit: the figures of the Irish tenor John McCormack and his Austrian counterpart Richard Tauber in attendance at the bedside of, in Irish mythology, the equivalent to Achilles.

Costello would sit hunched on one of the wheeled swivel chairs contemplating the item of fruit he'd brought in from his local delicatessen, the sleeves of his black coat rolled up halfway. His fingers would turn the fruit he would never eat in his pudgy hands, all the while listening as the tape machine recorded. He would summon us into the control room to play back what we'd done. We would line up on the lumpy sofa or, if there wasn't room, perch on a radiator or lean against the wall and listen to the playback. Once we had arrived at consensus, we did repairs – a clunky dyssynchrony between the tom-tom and the bass, a flubbed note, a mishit. None of the songs was particularly problematic. Those we hadn't rehearsed much, we worked on in the studio: 'The Wild Cats of Kilkenny'; 'The Gentleman Soldier', yet another of the songs on Darryl's tape; 'Dirty Old Town', Ewan MacColl's song about Salford which we knew from the versions by the Spinners and the Dubliners.

Now and again, Costello would point out a structural problem. 'The Old Main Drag' in particular seemed to proceed verse after miserable verse, its protagonist suffering degradation after degradation until, with the final expiration of hope, it ended. Costello's solution was more the product of necessity than inspiration. In rehearsal, at the end of the song, a drone from a bass button on the accordion a fifth below the root note cut underneath the last line: 'For some money to take me from the old main drag'. By way of caesura Costello suggested we should similarly shift the key down a fifth for a couple of bars for a middle eight – appositely, we thought, after the mention in the lyrics of Tuinol. The respite was hardly a relief. The bass, banjo, guitar and tom-tom tolled fatefully over the low drone of the accordion until the horror resumed.

Excited to have stumbled on the idea of key changes, Costello took up the matter of modulation again with 'Dirty Old Town'. He cited Johnny Cash's 'I Walk the Line' which modulates down a fifth, two times in the song, to return the way it came to the original key of F. Giddy, Costello swept us along before him towards a similar structure. Costello played the guitar and Andrew the harmonica for the introduction in D. The verse with the full band came in a fifth lower, the melodies played on the whistle and, in preference over the accordion, on the mandolin. For the middle eight the key modulated another fifth downward, to return to G for the last verses. It was beautiful in its simplicity and almost noble in its provenance. I was proud to share with Costello his enthusiasm for such a construction and wished I had thought of it.

To complete the record Shane came up with the Scottish traditional song 'I'm a Man You Don't Meet Every Day', and volunteered Cait to sing it. The minatory cordiality of the song suited her. Spider's willingness to sing 'Jesse James' – the romantically fallacious biography of the murderer and train-robber – wasn't entirely inapposite either.

We used few session musicians. Tommy Keane and Henry Benagh came in to overdub, respectively, the uilleann pipes and fiddle on a couple of the tracks, notably 'Dirty Old Town'. Benagh was a bearded Tennessean. Keane was from Waterford. Both played up at a pub in Camden called The Good Mixer. When

Keane took up the pipes, such a look came over his face that you'd think he was blind. He worked the chanter, lifting it up and down off his thigh, staring sightlessly into space.

⊹

St Patrick's Day at the Clarendon Ballroom was a clamorous, tumultuous and deranged event. The hall seemed huge. It had ancient-looking fluted columns covered in peeling brown paint. A black curtain hanging from scaffolding separated backstage from the ballroom where I could hear conversations against the cacophony in the background. It was airless and hot. Fluorescent strips lit a concrete corridor lined with chip-frying machines and dented kitchen furniture.

Frank had brought his friend Phil Lynott to the gig. I tried to get a glimpse of him. I had been in my last year at school when the first incarnation of Thin Lizzy had released 'Whiskey in the Jar'. I had been more into the likes of Amon Düül, the Strawbs and Peter Hammill. The laddish glamorisation of sex, drink and violence of 'The Boys Are Back in Town', which a couple of my friends never seemed to have off their record players in 1976, hadn't interested me much. Nonetheless, I was fascinated by Lynott's presence and by the rumour he was going to come out and play with us.

I eventually managed to get a look at him. He was sitting on a metal table under the fluorescent light. Frank and a couple of other people were standing by. I mistook his slumping on the table leaning up against the wall for charismatic ennui. The fact was, he looked ill. His face was filmy and pallid, his eyes blank and watery. When we went on, Lynott stayed backstage. When we came off, our shirts stuck to our backs, faces running with sweat, he was gone.

Frank had read an interview with Alex Cox, the director of *Repo Man* which had come out the previous March and had been acclaimed for its punk energy and oppositional politics. On the strength of Cox describing our music as 'quite interesting,' Frank had apparently got in touch. In the week after our shows at the Clarendon Ballroom, Cox, who lived nearby, came out to see us at a gig at Liverpool Polytechnic. He was a gangly guy, lanky, dressed in a tan duster coat and eager to work with us. A couple of weeks later Frank hired him to film the video for 'A Pair of Brown Eyes', in which a literal pair of brown eyes in a paper bag becomes a metaphor for the blindness of society to a totalitarian state under Thatcher.

We resumed at Elephant Studios to do overdubs. We were sitting squashed together on the brown couch, behind Nick Robbins and Paul Scully who had replaced Colin Fairley. Costello stood on the far side of the mixing desk, the window to the studio behind him, his arms on the ledge, the grey pork-pie hat set at a junior reporter's angle, listening to playback through the speakers mounted in the wall behind.

At the end of the song, Costello stationed his destined-to-gouneaten pomelo or star fruit, persimmon or guava on top of the Yamaha speakers behind the far side of the mixing desk and stepped around in front of it. On the way, he picked up his guitar. He wafted a space for himself on one of the wheeled chairs. Robbins got up.

'I hear this,' he said. He took out a plectrum from his pocket and picked something out on the guitar – a line of notes, low down, ascending. He wheeled round to look at us all squished together on the corduroy couch.

'For the bridge up to the chorus,' he explained. His eyes came into view over the top of the rims of his glasses – not so much questioning as declarative.

We all nodded at Costello's idea. Sounds good, we said. Let's give it a try, we said. Swivelling back to the desk, he twirled a finger to indicate he wanted the tape rewound. He listened back to the section a couple of times, swizzling his finger once more, refining the line. He got up and floated the guitar over our heads, towards the door into the studio.

'Set me up,' he said.

Robbins and Scully followed him. Through the window I could see them station microphones, run wires, plug in things, deliver headphones, adjust, tweak a little and then leave.

I smarted at his *droit de seigneur* and became glum with myself for not coming up with something. I was always alert to the possibility of an overdub, not just to supplement a particular sequence or highlight a transition with a sonic frill, an *amuse-oreille*, but also to show off my ability with any instrument I laid my hands on. It should have been me out there, one of the band, the one who worked out all the chords to the songs, the musician in the band – as we had always joked but which I had always believed. I resented Costello's encroachment and I wondered if anyone else was aware how embarrassed for myself I was.

Later on in the afternoon when he'd recorded his overdub and everyone else was either round the pool table at the end of the corridor or had gone for something to eat, I overcame my restraint and put it to Costello that when it came to doing overdubs, didn't he think it should be one of the band to play them?

'Why?' he said.

'Because you're the producer,' I said. 'And we're the band.'

'You want to do overdubs?' he said. 'Here, take my guitar. There's mandolins, an autoharp. There's a pair of fucking maracas lying about. You've got an idea? Go and do your overdub. I had an idea and I went and I had them set me up and I did it. If it doesn't work, you can tell me. I'm not a child. I can take it.'

I wished I hadn't had the temerity to contest him, exposing my resentment towards him, and my jealousy. My failure to prevail seemed also to have exposed my abiding awe of him.

When we resumed to tackle another track, Costello took up his customary position on the far side of the mixing desk.

'Anyone of you wants to fly the idea of an overdub,' he said in his vaguely Scouse accent, 'be my guest. I'm trying to make a good record here. You've all probably got good ideas. Let's have them. But if I've got an idea, I'm going to go in there and try it out and if you don't like it we'll just move on.'

'James!' Spider said. 'What have you done now?'

Embarrassment coursed over my skin like fever. I wanted revenge on Costello but gave up expecting it to come in the form of plucking a sonic ornament from the air and taking it into the studio.

The recording continued amiably enough, and in Costello and Cait's case amorously enough. They were very much in love. Occasionally we found ourselves sitting in the control room waiting, as Costello took time with Cait in the studio, patching up a bass-line she'd fluffed. He stood close behind her – she almost a head taller than Costello – his arms encircling her, from which position he could guide her hands over the neck of her guitar and put her fingers on the correct fret. Now and again her shoulders wriggled with resistance.

At the beginning of the recording we all deferred to Costello as befitted his status and accomplishments. As the weeks passed, his presence in the studio became a more and more familiar one. We ceased to be curious about what kind of exotic fruit he'd picked up on the way to the studio and whether or not it happened to rhyme with his name. We had become used to his standing behind the mixing desk, bending over a guitar or a mandolin in the control room. The wonderment of being in the daily company of such a luminary wore off. In Shane's case it wore off sooner and more dramatically than in anyone else's.

One day Costello brought to the studio an Ovation Patriot Bicentennial acoustic guitar. It was blue – like a bluebottle – and one of the ugliest guitars I'd seen. It had the signature Ovation rounded fibreglass back which caused it to be forever sliding off my knee when I took it up to play one afternoon, and it had what were called the 'multi-sound hole epaulets' – the abstract, Seventies-style filigree near where the neck met the body. The sound that came out of it was by no means the acme of acoustics but in the course of our recording with Costello, the guitar, to Shane, seemed to attain hyperbolic importance.

Costello, like all of us, was in awe of Shane's talent, nervous of appearing not to understand him, shy of his irony, fearful of his temper. Costello, aware of Shane's covetousness of it, gave the guitar to him.

The guitar would not have been the only one Costello owned. I imagined the walls in Costello's flat in Holland Park to hang with all manner of vintage instruments – a couple of which he brought into the studio to play overdubs: an acoustic lap guitar with playing-card motifs up and down the fret board and a beautiful chocolate and tan J-series Gibson. Shane's inability to take care of anything would have precluded Costello from letting Shane even look at any of the guitars that really mattered to him.

Though the gift looked careless, I wondered if Costello hoped to rub Shane's nose in his distinction. It was as if the Ovation, too, was a means of distracting Shane, the way a parent jangles a bunch of keys to distract a child from the pain of fingers shut in a door. I suspected Costello of seeing how much Shane wanted to be in control, and of throwing a sop to Shane by letting him have his guitar.

In a week or two it seemed Shane thought the guitar possessed a mysterious power, as if it were not just the repository of all the songs Costello ever wrote, but a sacred charm to summon up songs as yet unwritten, hidden within Shane. The guitar never left Shane's side. It came to the studio with him every day, in a plastic bag. At the end of each day, it went back into the plastic bag and went home with him.

As the recording went on, the guitar seemed to become a talisman which somehow in Shane's mind stood for Costello himself. Shane's possession of the guitar appeared to have become protection against some sort of malevolent power he was beginning to convince himself exuded from Costello. As long as he had the guitar, he had Costello where he wanted him.

If Shane resented the way Costello was going about producing our record, it was difficult to tell. That he should covet Costello's crap guitar and keep it in constant sight should have alerted us that something was irking Shane. Shane's propensity for superstition didn't surprise me, but I had not been aware of how much it was a symptom of his lack of ability to say what was really on his mind. The bile that had been building in him only became obvious through the violence with which it erupted.

Costello happened to leave the room. As soon as he had, Shane levelled a kick at the Ovation Patriot Bicentennial as it leant against the arm of the sofa. Clumsy as he was, he did no damage to the guitar. It spun on its axis and ended up against the wall with a boing of strings. I was appalled not so much by the ferocity with which he laid into it, but by the fact that Shane seemed to have lost his marbles.

In fear of Costello's return to the control room and his probable puzzlement at Shane's behaviour and what it signified, we implored Shane to calm the fuck down, which he did, and as suddenly as his fury at the guitar, and at Costello himself, had flared up. At the end of the day, as usual, he bagged up the guitar and went home with it.

Fourteen

After our St Patrick's Day shows at the Clarendon Ballroom, with a sheepish bluffness, Frank had announced he had booked us a television appearance in Munich, together with a string of gigs in Germany. He had driven a hand into a pocket and rubbed his stubbly, red face. It was as if he expected resistance and was never prepared for the eventuality that we never offered any. At the beginning of May we would be going on a tour of Scandinavia too.

The birth of Jem and Marcia's second child was just two months away. With his staring, forehead-furrowed face, Jem said he would come to Munich for the television show, but would have to go home afterwards. Frank briskly put forward Philip Chevron to deputise. Chevron, it turned out, happened to be under Frank's management too.

Chevron had been the lead singer and songwriter with a Dublin band called the Radiators from Space. In the past couple of years, since we had first met him at the Pindar of Wakefield, he had produced the first single and a handful of tracks on the début album by the Men They Couldn't Hang and had worked with German chanteuse Agnes Bernelle, producing a collection of cabaret songs from the Weimar Republic. Chevron was a fan of ours. It was he who had brought Costello to see us play at the Diorama in Regent's Park, just as we were about to start to record *Red Roses for Me*.

Philip Chevron standing in for Jem was a daft idea from the

beginning. Philip was no banjo player. He played it like a guitar. Heavily, with a plectrum and with quivering fingers, he picked out arpeggios that were intended to mimic the forward and backward rolls which Jem had made second nature. I was surprised Chevron's fingers had the ability to hold the strings down. Everything about him was diminutive, from his shoulders down to his shoes.

It was our first trip abroad. I loved being in Germany, its trams and trees, the angled grids of windows, the rectangles of grass and warm spring sunlight. In each of our hotel rooms was a greeting from the hotel manager and a bottle of wine wrapped in noisy cellophane. I took the wine to indicate the elevation of our status.

After performing a forty-five-minute set for a programme called *Alabamahalle* at the Bayerischer Rundfunk studios, we were taken across the road for a tour of U-boat 96, the submarine in *Das Boot*. Its cramped confines, its strangulated bulkhead doors which required one to both raise foot and duck head to climb through, horrified and excited us. Bunches of brightly coloured plastic bananas hung in nets under the ceiling. They did little to offset the severity of the rivets and the iron plating.

Ludicrous as it was, we were incapable of not drawing parallels between *Das Boot* and the confinement of our minivan. We understood the film's German tag line: *Eine Reise ans Ende des Verstandes* – a journey to the edge of the mind. From that day *Das Boot* became a touchstone for our own experience of prolonged physical proximity magnified by the detachment that came with our particular brand of nomadism.

Jem flew back to London. We drove up into the Ruhrgebiet. After a couple of gigs, we crossed East Germany on the dilapidated transit road towards West Berlin. We bought vodka from an Intershop. There was a picture of a bison on the label, a sideways view against a green background with the word *Zubrowka* in gold across the top. The vodka was pale green with a grass haulm floating inside. Shane held up the bottle to compare the bison's features with Andrew's.

'Bison vodka!' said Andrew in his liquid bass. '*Na zdorovje!*'

'*Vorsprung durch Alkohol!*' Cait sang out.

It was late when we got to West Berlin. We were drunk. It was dark. A firework rose and embroidered the sky above the dismal high-rises. It happened to be Hitler's birthday. In the tiny club, at the back of the crowd, a clutch of skinheads chanted with expressionless faces and heiling arms. We played on regardless, shooting looks across at one another until Cait swaggered over to the microphone and started to harangue them. I admired her spunk but it just made it worse. The Nazis shoved to the front and gathered before her, a thicket of angled arms and flattened hands.

157

Chevron stepped up to the centre microphone. He was all composure. In measured English he announced that we had come to play for those who had come to see us, and no one else, and that the best thing to do was to ignore the Nazis among them and enjoy our music. Cait backed off and lurked in the shadows.

Backstage we fumed about neo-fascism and regarded our deputy banjo player with wonderment.

⊹

On our journey back to London Andrew regaled us with naval monographs. One of them was his description of what he assured us was known, below decks in the boiler room, as the 'Dance of the Flaming Arseholes'. It involved rolled-up newspapers, bare buttocks and a cigarette lighter. Another was an epigram describing the Royal Navy and attributed to Sir Winston Churchill: Rum, sodomy, and the lash. We all agreed, there and then, that that was the title of the album.

Just the mixing of *Rum Sodomy and the Lash* was left to do. Costello was going to take a break before committing to it. He promised mixes by the time we were finished with our tour of Finland, Sweden and Norway.

We had one show in London supporting Richard Thompson at the Dominion Theatre before going back out on tour. It was a tumultuous and – deemed by the tabloid press – disrespectful opening gig. During our set there was a stage invasion. During Thompson's show the crowd chanted to the tune of 'Cwm Rhondda':

Richard Thompson! Richard Thompson! Who the fucking hell are you?

The following day we met at Elephant to record the B-sides needed for the single release of 'A Pair of Brown Eyes'. Again, we dug into Darryl's trove cassette tape for the traditional songs 'Muirshin Durkin' and 'Whiskey You're the Devil'. Philip Chevron produced. He sat, diminutive and gaunt, bent over at the mixing desk, his head to one side due to a hearing disorder. The recordings were hurried and, after the night before, effortful.

At the end of the week we left Jem at home and departed for Harwich, and the first of our two ferry journeys to Helsinki. After a night of drinking and a ruckus with a handful of etiolated Finns, we arrived in Hamburg. I was tired and hung over. The ship stole through the dawn into harbour, down a foul estuary past the backsides of factories to port and a filthy beach strewn with rotting wooden hulls to starboard. We were not halfway to the first gig of the tour. Helsinki was another nineteen-hour passage across the Baltic Sea.

The tarnished white superstructure of our next ship – the *Finnjet* – appeared in the evening sunlight after an afternoon's drive across Schleswig-Holstein.

Our assigned cabins were cells, pitilessly white, with berths fixed to the plastic walls. Darryl had a scheme. There were first-class cabins for the taking, he said. Almost from under the nose of one of the stewards at what stood for a reception desk, he plucked a couple of keys from a box on the counter. Darryl said to wait at least until the bar closed before squatting whatever cabin the key was for. In the meantime I bought a bottle of apple schnapps and took it down to the Horizon Bridge where angled, salt-rimed windows gave out on a view of the sheen of light cast by the moon on the sea.

I found Philip Chevron sitting with his tiny feet up on the rail, staring out. I took a seat next to him and threw my ankles over the rail. Both of us were already drunk.

Illuminated by the radar images of the coasts of Latvia and Estonia from the sickly screens above the windows, we talked, trading events in our lives, his in Dublin, mine in the north of England. He told me about his days at school, the feebleness of his health – a recurring stomach ulcer – his work with Agnes Bernelle and Costello, his love for musical theatre, his sometimes troubled relationship with his father.

As he spoke he flung his scrawny arms and legs into dramatic angles: an ankle up on one knee, his leg bent wide, spontaneously throwing an arm behind his head, his elbow pointing upward. He moved suddenly and often, as if at pains to show how comfortable he was with himself and me.

I told him about my boarding-school education in Yorkshire, my family holidays in the Lake District, my fondness for solitary twenty-mile hikes in the Yorkshire Dales, my penchant for classical music and my sometimes troubled relationship with my father, too.

I ended up forming the inebriated impression that most of his youth had taken place indoors, in schoolrooms and bedrooms and, now, in studios and the record shop where he worked. By contrast, the synopsis of my childhood turned into a parade of track-bikes and filth, open air and exercise, hiking, hills and lungfuls of fresh air.

When we had finished the bottle of schnapps Philip got up. Before he teetered off he planted a bristly kiss on my mouth.

The sound of the ship's screws going into full astern woke me in the cabin I'd squatted. Huge wooden pilings reflected in the dark water glided by the window as the ship hove into Helsinki harbour. Ice floes nudged one another in the swell. I got up and made my way to the shuddering car deck to find the van.

'What have you done to our replacement banjo player?' Spider demanded. In the night it seemed Philip had had an attack.

Andrew and Spider, who were sharing one of the cabins with him, had roamed the darkened ship looking for a doctor. They found none, only a pilot in the dimness of the bridge who had waved his arms about, shouting, 'You must not be here!'

That morning they had brought Philip up to the car deck and had managed to get him onto the minibus. He was curled in one of the seats, his head nested in a pillow, moaning. His face glowed with a yellow pallor.

'He's been throwing up blood,' Spider said.

'We need to get him to a hospital,' Paul Scully said.

Driving down the incline off the ship, an overalled customs official waved us out of the line and into an aluminium shed. The doors closed behind us and we were all ordered out of the van. We helped Philip to a metal stool where he groaned, eyes closed, arms folded across his stomach. The customs officials let a young golden retriever in through the back doors of the van. We weren't worried. We weren't carrying anything. The puppy padded around the seats, sniffing. Eventually it flopped out through the front door and made straight for Shane, plopped its paws on his thighs and sniffed his crutch.

'Get it off me!' Shane cried out.

We got Philip back onto the minibus. The pain seemed to suck the skin to his cheekbones and temples. He clutched his stomach and moaned at every brake and bump in the road. The prolonged shuddering of one of the cobbled streets on the way to the hotel contorted his face into a grimace of agony. Scully took him to a clinic.

After the sound check Scully, Darryl and I went to visit him. He had ruptured the ulcer he had spoken to me about on the Horizon Bridge. The clinic wanted to keep him for further tests. We expected the worst, but when the lift doors opened onto Philip's ward, we saw him coming down the corridor fully dressed, though gaunt and pallid, and stooping a little. To the bemusement of the staff, minutes before, he had discharged himself.

'I'd prefer to experience my first fist fuck in more conducive surroundings than a clinic in Finland,' he said.

Grim as his determination was to convince us he was better, we forbade him to come down to the gig. Over the next couple of days his resolve to play forced us to relent, and for the next few gigs he taped a folded towel to the back of the banjo to soften the pressure against his stomach.

We arrived in Stockholm with just drumsticks and whistles, gaffer tape and guitar picks. Swedish customs were on strike and had forced Darryl to return on the ferry we'd come on, back across the Gulf of Bothnia. We made it to a club called the Living Room with a minute to try out the instruments Costello and Frank had rented, both men having flown in from London that afternoon. The accordion leaked air through a couple of holes. Costello bent over a mandolin, straining to hear the strings, cursing the clamour beyond the filthy curtain which separated us from the stage. We squeezed through a hole in the wall, to be slammed by the heat in the club.

Afterwards Philip collapsed on the fusty sofa in the dressing room with his eyes closed, his thin mouth drawn into a slit across his shrivelled face. He had laboured with the banjo, not just on account of his burst ulcer, but also due to the scale of the instrument which had been rented for him. It was huge.

We met up with Darryl again in Örebro after his seventeen-hour re-crossing of the Baltic. After Gothenburg Costello returned to London. We continued up the coast. By the time we were approaching Oslo, Shane and Spider were at the roaring stage of an argument. It had started on the subject of whether or not a tomato was a vegetable. It had gone on to the matter of whether dogs could think.

'You fucking stupid fucking ignoramus!'

'Fuck you and the horse you rode in on!'

'Fuck you!'

'No! Fuck you!'

'It's obvious that we've become incapable of conversation,' Andrew said.

A piss stop brought us out of the van into the warmth of a spring afternoon and respite from Shane and Spider's cantankerousness. We lay about in the sunshine on a vale sprinkled with spring blossoms.

I discovered from a couple of the humpers working backstage at the gig in Oslo that Fearnley was a historic Norwegian name, borne by generations of fishers. When I got to my hotel room I found there to be six pages of Fearnleys in the telephone directory. I imagined my forebears, in horned helmets, scudding across the North Sea. It made sense that they would in time turn their skill in the building of longboats to woodworking and joinery and, eventually, to the building of houses. I went about in the spring sunlight as if Oslo were my new hometown. All of Oslo fluttered with flags for Norwegian Independence Day. By evening, the news came from Jem in England that Marcia had given birth to their second daughter. We phoned him from Frank's room, shouting our congratulations in the direction of the handset.

We left the bunting, sunshine and the spring behind and drove up into dense cloud over the Hardangervidda glacier between Oslo and Bergen. Now and again the van pitched into the sulphurous light of a tunnel that bored through the mountain, re-emerging into daylight the colour of galvanised iron. Up on the glacier strange disconnected shapes loomed and drifted noiselessly past. We listened in silence to recordings of John McCormack that Cait had brought with her. It was as if the glacier entered into us.

On the way down, as colour started to return to the landscape, Darryl ploughed the bus to a halt. By the side of the road a water-fall tumbled in full spate from a rock shelf.

We piled out of the van and stood on the side of the road. The air was chill, with the tang of peat. The water was like spun sugar, tinged brown. From a dripping slab between a couple of twis-ted trees above our heads the water lunged and crashed against a pitted boulder jammed in the ravine. The mist which rose from the impact silvered our hair and dripped from the trees. Down an incline, a sapling with a couple of dithering leaves on it grew at the edge.

'Why we stop?' came Shane's slurred voice from the doorway of the van. Everyone looked round. He was clutching a bottle of vodka by the neck.

'Nature,' Frank said.

Shane eased himself down from the doorsill and steadied himself with an elbow. He looked over at the waterfall, rapt.

'Fuck!' he said, with drooping lids. He stepped with flat feet to-wards the roar and the rising mist, stopping halfway across the road to fumble a cigarette out of his packet. After a couple of at-tempts he managed to get one to fall between his fingers.

He succeeded in lighting up and then shuffled down the slope, to come to a swaying stop a couple of feet from the edge. He blinked against the mist and teetered closer, wafting for the sup-port of the sapling. He tilted forward onto the balls of his feet, to look first down into the gorge and then up to the trees at the top. The spray beaded his hair. A dolour came into his eyes, followed by a smile of exaggerated dreaminess.

It occurred to me that communion with anything or anyone would always be impossible for him, shackled as he was to a self-consciousness that rarely rested.

When Shane had clambered back into the van and had

dropped into his seat, Frank drew the sliding door closed behind him.

'Well?' Frank said.

'Well what?' replied Shane.

'Inspired?'

Shane's eyelids drooped. He looked up, bored.

'What you mean?'

'You know,' Frank faltered. 'Inspired? Any ideas? You know, for a song?'

Shane snorted wearily.

'Get fucked Frank,' he said.

Darryl released the brake and we descended from the glacier.

Fjord upon fjord appeared between the trees hundreds of feet beneath the cliffs, each as flat as whetstone with a white scratch of shoreline. The road yawed out of sight round the corners where concrete barriers, barked with tyre marks, kerbed the exposed turns. On the other side, bodywork-paint dashed the rock. Darryl seemed to take delight in swinging the van round the bends, veering at the last minute from a plunge down through the fir trees. Clutching his bottle of vodka by the neck, Shane screamed in the back of the van.

'I'm ready to die! I've been to Norway and I'm ready to die!'

By the time the road levelled out coming into Bergen the vodka had eventually relieved him from the horror of swerving and the sudden vistas. His head had lolled back on the seat and he was asleep.

The last gig of the tour took place in what looked like a school library. Tables abutted the makeshift stage. The room filled with tow-headed students. Here and there an ankle rested on a knee or a hand tapped on the tabletop. Though his face was still the colour of tallow and the expression on it grim against what must have been the pain in his stomach, Philip seemed to have

165

recovered. He dipped and twisted on stage with the banjo, sweeping the headstock up and over his head, to end somehow in a crouch where he stared with a pout out over the audience. With a flick of his head in the direction of a couple of rows of tables going out from the stage into the audience, he instructed me to take one while he took the other. I stepped between people's drinks as best I could, until my cables gave out. I looked across at Philip. He paid no mind to the people gazing up at him from their seats. He crouched with the banjo as if hosing down a wall.

'Ah, lads!' Scully said afterwards. 'It's come to this – throwing shapes!'

In a couple of days, after another seventeen-hour ferry voyage across the North Sea, I was back in my flat on Royal College Street, shaving before the mirror. I had to grip the rim of the basin because the floor pitched beneath me like the deck of a ship. While it alarmed me, there was something strangely comforting about it, as if the tour had become a thing in itself, endearingly reluctant to let me go.

Fifteen

Jem returned to the group. Jem and Marcia's new baby was beautiful. She had a serene face and blue eyes. She was called Kitty. She looked like her dad.

Over the course of the tour of Scandinavia, Shane's guitar-playing had become more and more erratic. During gigs, when he came to an instrumental section, he would lay into the guitar, metronomically and with passion. When he returned to the microphone to sing, his attention seemed to desert his hands, leaving his left hand feeling for the chords and his right hand punching haphazard downstrokes, the pick hardly connecting with the strings at all.

Since Philip was in fact a guitarist and since his ordeal on the *Finnjet* had woven him into the tapestry, we agreed that he should just take over playing guitar. We started rehearsals at a place called NOMIS in Kensington – a place which typified the music industry. Everywhere were walls of exposed brick. An embossed vinyl ramp with a handrail of brushed steel led up to our unit. A blackboard stretched across the wall.

I watched Philip play. He was so fragile that the joints of his left hand seemed to buckle under the pressure of maintaining a chord. He had scant purchase of his guitar pick. His right hand didn't sweep over the strings but snagged on them. On the first day of rehearsals, though, it was obvious that my function along with Jem's as the interpreters of Shane's stop-start, lurching, disjointed creative process was at an end. Philip's ear for harmonic structure was keen. His familiarity with music put mine in the shade. He knew the chords to ABBA, Bowie, Gershwin, Kern, Rodgers, Wagner, Wham! and Weill. He stood with one of his brogues up on the seat of the plastic chair in the rehearsal room and the guitar balanced on his skinny thigh. He motioned Shane to stop just there while he figured out the chord Shane was trying to play. When the sequence of chords became apparent, Philip would rest the guitar against the chair, take up the chalk and write it down – capital letters followed by lines of virgules. By the end of the afternoon I knew that everything had changed. I felt glum and worthless.

One of the songs we started to rehearse was a Christmas song Jem and Shane had been writing. The melody Jem had written for the verses sounded like 'Blow the Wind Southerly.' Shane hadn't finished the lyrics. It was to be a duet, with Cait.

The following weekend, the first weekend of June, we travelled to Ireland to play at an arts and music festival called Cibeal Cincise, in Kenmare, County Kerry. Around the same time that I had returned from Scandinavia, Debsey had arrived back from a week with Sensible after a series of performances in Dubai. She seemed dispirited and tired. Sensible's behaviour had become erratic, veering to volatile. Debsey accompanied us on the ferry over from Fishguard.

It hadn't been a particularly turbulent crossing to Rosslare. The afternoon had been incandescent with sunshine. The sea, though flicked into luminous crests by the wind, had been relatively still. It was a surprise, then, as the minivan bumped off the ferry's steel ramp onto the gravel incline down to the customs post, to hear the sound of retching coming from Spider, sitting next to Shane in the back of the van.

'I'm going to be sick!' Spider shouted. An instant later the van filled with an acrid stench followed by shouts from Shane that he was going to be sick too. He tried to open the sliding windows, but they turned out to be screwed shut – one of the van-hire company's security measures.

'Oh God!' Shane choked. 'Stop the van! Stop the fucking van!'

Darryl pulled out of the line of cars and slammed on the brakes. We wrenched the sliding door open and leapt onto the gravel. Less nimble than the rest of us, Shane blundered against the backs of the seats to get out. He stood in the sunlight, doubled over, gagging. When Spider eventually emerged, the front of his suit and his trousers were covered in a gesso-like substance.

'We have to go through customs,' Darryl said.

'Not in that van,' Shane said. 'I'm not going back in there!'

'We're walking!'

With his head as far out of the window as he could get it, Darryl drove away. The rest of us walked. Debsey's presence embarrassed me. The customs official waved us through and returned to leaning down into the windows of the cars coming off the ferry. With his arms up to keep them clear, Spider edged behind the customs official, leaving a pale brushstroke of vomit on the shiny blue serge of the officer's arse.

Darryl found a hose. We had Spider change clothes in the toilets. We threw the pasted one away. We waited in a bar up on the top of the bluffs while Darryl hosed out the inside of the van. Shane managed to overcome the tang and we carried on.

When we arrived in Kenmare we dumped our luggage in the Irish cottages we were staying in and went into town for a drink. Such was Shane's notoriety that in the first bar we went into a gathering drew up. When we attempted to find somewhere more quiet, the crowd clustered round Shane and shuffled up the street with him, bombarding him with questions. His presence on the high street seemed to verge on the messianic. I wondered for his sanity.

On the Friday afternoon we played elbow to elbow on a stage made of pallets and breeze blocks in the dowdy gymnasium behind a convent. The place was crowded and airless, with people rammed up against the edge of the stage, their faces pink and swollen from the heat. A girl of perhaps ten wormed her way to sit by my feet. Sweat dropped from my nose and cylinders of ash from the ubiquitous cigarette between my lips onto the wood and close to the hem of her dress. On the Saturday night, we played at the more conventional venue of the Riversdale House Hotel.

The festival inundated the gaudily painted market town. The bars spilled out onto the streets. The sun blazed. Everywhere were shining sun-reddened faces and shoulders. Pubs erupted in clapping and clamour. I looked in at the Park Hotel. It was jammed to the point of immobility, the cram extending up the stairs. I got a glimpse of a coterie of fiddle players, a bodhrán player and a guitarist all sitting in wheel-back chairs in the corner of the thronged lounge. A saintly-looking man with flaxen hair and a beard and a tatty scarf round his neck played a beaten-up button accordion. They filled the bar and the stairwell with hurtling lines of music. Except for a hushed hubbub and the odd clink of a glass in the bar and a huzzah here and there as a reel swivelled into a hornpipe, all were silent.

Costello flew from England with mixes of the record. We listened to them in a caravan parked out in the field behind the Irish cottages where we hung out during the day, in the sunshine, playing instruments. I loved the record, from the opening mandolin notes of 'The Sick Bed of Cúchulainn', the low, solitary drone and plaintive round of 'The Old Main Drag', the quivering vibrato of Andrew's harmonica at the beginning of 'Dirty Old Town', the yearning, tremulous wails of the uilleann pipes, to the chiming slashes of the autoharp and the rending of vocal cords on 'The Wild Cats of Kilkenny'. I was exhilarated by how accomplished the record sounded, despite the puerility of the sounds of hammer-priming, gunshots and ricochets which now volleyed through 'Jesse James'. Costello had brought in a cornet player called Dick Cuthell who had lacquered over the accordion solo in 'And the Band Played Waltzing Matilda' with an instrumental break suggestive of a funeral in New Orleans, replete with blue notes and unctuous with *portato*.

In the foreground of the record – guttural, sonorous, nasal and, despite the scarcity of his teeth, precise – stood Shane's almost indomitable voice.

The Bank Holiday not yet over, Monday morning we were up early to catch the ferry back to England. At the beginning of the week we were at BBC Television Centre to record 'Sally MacLennane' for *The Old Grey Whistle Test*. The ramshackle gigs at the festival in Kenmare aside – where the sound had been crashing and chaotic – it was more or less our first proper iteration with Philip as guitar player. Sad as I was to lose the twelve-string, now that Shane had been relieved of it, we sounded better than we had in months.

⸙

'Dirty Old Town' was due for release at the beginning of July, a month in advance of the launch of *Rum Sodomy and the Lash*. The video we made for it was a cheap affair. We stood on a plywood surface in a facility somewhere in London. They closed the doors, set the lights and filled the sound stage with smoke.

There was a gamin brutality about Andrew in his leather jacket, his hand quivering over the harmonica. Cait had had a new haircut – a reddened crest tapering down to her slender neck which disappeared into a starched Windsor collar and tie. Philip had had a duster coat made for himself, similar to the ones we had worn on our tour supporting Costello. He jutted his underlip and frowned out into the imaginary audience. I played the mandolin with a strap over one shoulder. The camera going back and forth made me nervous. I kept my head down. I missed the grandeur and the curiosity-factor of my accordion. I tried to compensate by exaggerating the attack of my plectrum against the strings. Spider stamped his heel. The pulses sent shocks up his body. Shane thrust his hands into the pockets of a new, single-buttoned, dove-grey suit. He closed his eyes, tilted his head back and pulled his top lip into a sneer.

By the end of the afternoon we were done. The only external shot was a cut-away to Henry Benagh and Tommy Keane positioned like buskers, in a backlit brick ginnel in Camden.

⸙

Jem wanted to write songs. He had already collaborated with

Shane on the instrumental 'The Wildcats of Kilkenny', though the extent of their collaboration seemed to be the juxtaposition of tunes they had written independently of one another under a common title. During our tour in Scandinavia, amid the exigencies of new parenthood, Jem had written an instrumental – an homage to Ennio Morricone – for the B-side of 'Dirty Old Town'.

We were not yet teenagers when Sergio Leone's *A Fistful of Dollars, For a Few Dollars More* and *The Good, the Bad and the Ugly* were released. Morricone's soundtracks – the whips, whistles, chanting, trumpets and electric guitar – were embedded in all of us, not least in Jem.

His instrumental conjured up a sedimentary landscape. The melodies in it were ethereal and itinerant. The last tune – played on the electric guitar – seemed at first encumbered by a phrasing which sounded just weird, but was typical of Jem's skewed approach to writing melody lines.

A week or so after our taping of *The Old Grey Whistle Test*, we went to a studio in South London to record it, with Philip producing. We threw everything at it – entitled, by the end of the session, 'A Pistol for Paddy Garcia'. Out came a thing called the vibraslap – a wooden box with a slot in it, against which a sprung wooden ball vibrated. With a bottleneck, I plucked a note of deflation before a repeat of the main melody. I loved to whistle. A job I'd had on one of Fearnley & Sons Ltd's building sites, being the boss's son, was to push a broom pointlessly round the finished empty flats, where my whistling reverberated through the rooms. I had a new accordion, a Paolo Soprani, made in Castelfidardo, the Cremona of accordions I was told. It was large, heavy and black. Its three reeds were lush with musette but there were plenty of switches, one of which selected a single reed, perfect for the dissonance of the countermelody. Lastly, in the studio, there was a set of tubular bells, which we used to underpin the halting electric guitar melody and which brought the instrumental to a close with an ecclesiastical chime.

I was glad to work without Shane in the studio. His absence was a relief from the constant irresolution and second-guessing he provoked in all of us, which culminated more often than not in entrenchment and indignation. His opinions were cruel, unmitigated by courtesy. I didn't miss his bluntness. The fact that the recording was just a B-side and that Shane had nothing to do with it, however, deprived our work of importance, reluctant as I was to concede it.

The writer of the A-sides of the singles we had released so far had been Shane. Because royalties on the sales of singles were based on both A- and B-sides, the criteria for the choice of song for the B-sides were usually in the service of redressing the balance. Our first single with Stiff Records, 'The Boys from the County Hell', had been backed by Spider's 'Repeal of the Licensing Laws'. Spider's writing of 'Repeal of the Licensing Laws', he said, had spontaneously come to him of an afternoon, and we joked that he was unlikely to write anything else.

Because traditional songs were in the public domain, the publishing royalties were shared by all of us. The traditional songs 'Muirshin Durkin' and 'Whiskey You're the Devil' had been chosen for the 7" and 12" releases of 'A Pair of Brown Eyes'. Equally, 'Sally MacLennane' had been backed by the traditional 'The Leaving of Liverpool' and 'The Wild Rover', which we had recorded at the end of a day at Elephant, in the manner of the Jolly Beggarmen, accompanied by an acoustic guitar and clinking bottles.

The attempt at equity in the choice of B-sides was honourable enough but it was a token gesture. The fact was that unless you wrote a song, you weren't likely ever to earn much from the making of records. My talent lay in playing – the accordion, the guitar,

174

mandolin, anything I could lay my hands on – and, with Jem, wresting from Shane the songs he came to rehearsal with.

For the 12" release of 'Dirty Old Town', another B-side needed recording. We went up to a demo studio on Balls Pond Road called the Red House, to record the traditional song 'The Parting Glass'. It was a song Shane was fond of and as close to an apologia as I was likely to hear.

> Of all the money e'er I had,
> I spent it in good company.
> And all the harm I've ever done,
> Alas! it was to none but me.

We had had little opportunity to rehearse the song and just a couple of days to record and mix it. Because Philip had so far produced all the B-sides of the singles since *Red Roses for Me*, we volunteered him to produce this one. I had the feeling that it would be the last time I would play the guitar on anything the Pogues would record. I made the most of the opportunity.

At the summer solstice we drove down to Somerset for the Glastonbury Festival. It was a beautiful afternoon. The summer had come early. From the yawning mouth of the stage, I gazed out at the thousands that crusted the vale. Banners on twisted sticks and drifting smoke measured out the remoteness of the blue and pink sunlit wash of people.

A week later, at a festival at Cheltenham racecourse, we were on the same bill as Captain Sensible and Dolly Mixture. I had been wondering when Debsey and I were going to intersect on the road as musicians. When we met, however, Sensible was bluff with punk seniority, and volatile with it. For Debsey's sake I wanted to find his antics funny. The jockeys' weighing room under the stands had been given over to artists' hospitality. A weighing scale with a chair stood in the middle of the wood floor. When he started to jump up and down on them, Jem lost his temper. In the end, Sensible withdrew, cuffing the air in indignation and spitting oaths behind him. It saddened me that Sensible seemed to exact such loyalty from Debsey.

⛭

We had an album cover ready for *Rum Sodomy and the Lash*. Théodore Géricault's enormous canvas, *Le Radeau de la Méduse*, concerns the catastrophe of the French naval frigate the *Méduse* which ran aground on a sandbank off the coast of West Africa in 1816. After ensuring the safety of dignitaries in lifeboats, the captain cast adrift 150 of his crew on a makeshift raft. All but fifteen of them perished. It was nearly two weeks before they were rescued. By that time the survivors had not only endured hunger, thirst and disease, but cannibalism too.

The picture depicts the survivors' first sighting of a rescue ship on the horizon. Men in the background are attempting to signal, some of them with rags. The raft is strewn with corpses. It is a painting which reveals mankind at the extremity of the human predicament – truly *Eine Reise ans Ende des Verstandes,* as the tag line for *Das Boot* read.

It had been Marcia's idea to use the painting and to replace six of the heads in it with ours. A photographer came to rehearsal to take the headshots to use as models. In the final rendition, Shane's head – wearing shades – replaced that of the crew member in the centre of the canvas. My head replaced that of the painter Eugène Delacroix, who had apparently been the model for the figure in the foreground, my arm draped over Spider's lifeless body. Jem's head replaced that of the man alerting the occupants of the raft to the distant rescue ship.

Stiff Records' publicity department ran rampant with the maritime theme. For the photograph session for the back of the album cover and the paper sleeve, we dressed up in eighteenth- and nineteenth-century naval uniforms. We had cocked hats. We wore twill breeches with knee buttons and tailcoats, full dress and undress coats heavy with metal thread epaulettes and gilt brass buttons, with two-point and three-point pocket flaps weighed down by gold lace. Jem wore an eye-patch. I pulled one arm out of my tailcoat and pinned the empty sleeve to my chest. For further photographs in our naval costumes, we were taken from the photographer's studio and out on a boat into the chill wind blowing up the Thames, across to the Traitors' Gate set into the embankment under the Tower of London.

Between the painting of our heads in *Le Radeau de la Méduse* and the photo session for the rear of the album cover, Philip had officially been inducted into the group.

On the 30th July, the piratical theme reached its apotheosis with the launch party for the record. It took place on HMS *Belfast* – an early venue for Spandau Ballet. We donned our Nelson-era costumes, invited the press and a slew of friends, acquaintances and others, played a short set on the upper deck under a marquee, and then got drunk. At some point in the evening, a journalist fell into the Thames from a landing stage.

For the rest of the summer we went out playing festivals. In the first week of July we performed at an outdoor festival in Battersea Park which went under the title 'Jobs for a Change', staged in protest against Margaret Thatcher's plans for the abolition of the Greater London Council. The previous year there had been fifty thousand on the South Bank. This year, it was so popular that people climbed up into the trees to see. They swelled against the rickety barriers. I watched the yellow-jacketed bouncers brace against the surge. Halfway through our set I happened to catch

sight of a black object turning slowly in the sky, seemingly floating above the trees. I watched it for a moment or two as it twirled
there, bereft of coordinates, until it suddenly dipped from its
zenith and headed straight towards me. There followed a crack of
metal against the front of my accordion and I looked down to see
a can of Guinness spinning on the stage spewing out tan foam
over the plywood.

Backstage in the hum of the generators, amid the barriers and
the Portakabins and in the damp wind blowing off the Thames,
Frank introduced us to Kirsty MacColl and her husband Steve
Lillywhite. We were familiar with Steve Lillywhite's name from
his work with Peter Gabriel, Big Country, XTC, Simple Minds and
U2. He had green eyes, a smile full of teeth and brown hair which
the wind blew over his forehead.

Kirsty, in my mind, was already a kind of national treasure by
virtue of the string of records she'd made in the past few years:
'They Don't Know', 'There's a Guy Works Down the Chip Shop
Swears He's Elvis' and Billy Bragg's 'A New England'. Her autum-
nal tresses of hair, one of them pinned up against her temple,
fell over her shoulders. She had a beautiful face and a brassiness
about her that was infectious. We all loved her.

To end the summer we flew to play at the Vienna Folk Festival,
all of us looking forward to being on the same bill as the Dubliners whom we regarded as patriarchs.

On the bus to Freudenau Racecourse, Jem announced he was
going to smash the mandolin up.

'It's a piece of shit mandolin,' he said. 'If anything, it'll force
me to get a decent one.'

The stage looked out across the park towards long wrought-
iron balconies and the imperial pavilion with its corroded copper dome and spire.

At the end of 'Muirshin Durkin', as promised, and with typical detachment, Jem unslung the mandolin and swung it by the neck in an arc over his head. The body splintered, the side panels came apart and the front burst off. With the strings barely holding the pieces together, Jem dragged it up and sundered what remained on the stage. He finished it off with a couple of footstamps.

The dispassion with which he demolished such an instrument as a mandolin, in front of a couple of thousand at a folk festival of all places, made us laugh.

Afterwards, in the crowded bar of the pavilion we met the Dubliners – older men, hirsute, portly, moist of consonant. There was an air about them simultaneously of the sea and the suburbs. There was an instant acknowledgement of brotherhood between us. We thrust hands into hands and shook our greetings.

Sixteen

Frank's connections had already provided us with a guitarist in Philip Chevron, and, in Paul Scully, a front-of-house engineer. Towards the end of the summer, in the dressing room at De Montfort Hall in Leicester, Frank introduced us to a guy called David Jordan who was going to take over as our monitor-engineer. Jordan had worked on the Specials' first album, coincidentally produced by Costello. He was a youthful-looking guy with a kind of Billy Fury wave of sandy hair. He was broad-chested and wore a leather flight jacket. He had travelled down from Whitehaven where he had been in rehab from heroin addiction. There was a cautious, almost defensive air about him.

At the beginning of September, Frank introduced us to a guy called Paul Verner. Frank had known P.V., as he was known, for a few years, through various Dublin bands. Latterly he had been the lighting engineer for the Boomtown Rats. After Live Aid and Bob Geldof's ascension to world renown, the Boomtown Rats as a band seemed likely to be wound up. P.V. came to work for us. He was a compact, habitually bowed man with watery blue eyes and a mane of tatty hair. There was a heedfulness about him and a sensitivity to slight.

The previous May, on an afternoon off at the Cibeal Cincise in Kenmare, before meeting both D.J. and P.V., Frank had brought a guy across to where we were sitting in the field behind the Irish cottages. The guy was called Terry Woods. We said hello and that was it. We went back to playing our instruments in the sunshine. The encounter had been brief and seemingly inconsequential. It left me with nothing other than an image of curls and the sensation of aplomb.

At the end of August Frank brought Woods to a rehearsal, which took place for some reason at the Boston Arms in Tufnell Park. We had set up on the stage in the club upstairs. A foil fringe curtain provided a bizarre festivity. Woods came in with a curiously shaped instrument case. He had a head of corkscrew hair and sea-blue eyes, the sensitivity of which belied the vague pugnacity of his face. His nose looked to have been broken at least once.

The fact that I had never heard of Terry Woods didn't bother me. With the exception of the bands and players on Darryl's tape from the Elvis Costello tour, and a couple of others besides, I had never been familiar with the identity of Irish musicians, contemporary or traditional, and I had given up trying to remember them.

Shane, however, did know about Woods. The excitement engendered in him by the mention of the guy's name had been enough to stir up our enthusiasm despite token resentment of Frank's imposition.

After having started out his music career in a band called Sweeney's Men, with Andy Irvine and Johnny Moynihan, Terry Woods's musical history impressively included founding the first incarnation of Steeleye Span, though Woods and his wife, Gay, had left soon after the first album. I found myself feeling bad for the man that he should miss out on Steeleye Span's successes – their Christmas single, 'Gaudete', and 'All Around My Hat'. After that, he and his wife had formed the Woods Band. Separating from his wife, Woods had gone on to tour with Dr Strangely Strange, whom Frank had managed. Since 1980 it seemed Woods had gone into retirement from music and, I was to understand, was now working a night shift shelving in a shoe shop. It made me sorry for him, which I couldn't help but suspect might have been Frank's intention by telling us.

I did my best to make him welcome and appointed myself his tutor. I took him through the chords of the songs in one of the tiny rooms backstage. I sat on a chair opposite him, ignorant at that time of his renown.

Woods played with flourish. His fingers swept flamboyantly up the neck of his instrument which he called a cittern. A distant, almost sanctified look came over his face when he played. I was astonished to see how small his hands were, with short, perfectly manicured fingers.

Terry played autoharp and concertina too. When it came to playing 'The Wild Cats of Kilkenny', though he said he had listened to the track, he seemed incapable of playing the instrument the way it had been played on the record. In the studio I had set the autoharp on my knee. I had dug in with my pick. I had slashed across all the strings, ringing in each bar. Terry cradled the autoharp protectively against his shoulder and played it with meaningful caresses of his fingertips and thumb.

His concertina was a Wheatstone English. It was beautiful,

with bright fretworked reed-pans and thumb-loops and bellows of what seemed ancient black leather. Terry played it sitting with his back straight and the instrument resting on one knee. He suggested he should play it on 'The Old Main Drag'. His opinion was that the plaintive single reeds of the concertina would be perfect for the song. I couldn't hear the difference between the single reed of my accordion and that of his concertina. Terry could. We tried it out. His head moved from side to side as he drew or compressed the bellows, adding an occasional twitch as his fingers ornamented the melody.

The refinement with which Terry played, together with the reverence he had for music, seemed destined never to converge with our irreverence and lack of refinement. It made me wonder if he understood what we were doing.

By drafting Scully, D.J. and P.V. into the crew, Frank sought to raise the standard of technical production. Each addition bumped Darryl further and further to the margins. With Philip's admission into the group, expedient as it was, we had regained the synchrony we had been losing to Shane's waywardness on the guitar. Frank's invitation to Terry to join, though, came with Frank's assertion that we lacked a certain finesse. None of us could argue with that. Part of our charm, it seemed to me, derived from our amateurishness and the improbability of our getting to the end of a gig, let alone from the odds of our having become a band at all. In the course of the past couple of years, though, by dint of all the practising we had done, the hundred or so gigs we had played and the two records we had made, our musicianship had improved. We had allowed Frank's power to become so complete that none of us put up any resistance to any of his appointments, though I knew I wasn't alone in my resentment of his opinion of us.

Finesse, as it happened, turned out to be a euphemism for

something weightier, specific to our being taken seriously not by *any* audience – but by an Irish one.

Until Frank came to manage us, as a whole we hadn't much cared whether or not an Irish audience held us in any regard, high or low. We had laughed to hear that when Kevin Conneff from the Chieftains came to our gig at the Riversdale House Hotel in Kenmare, he had listened to the first couple of songs, was heard to exclaim, 'Pah!' and had turned on his heel and walked out.

I wondered if the fact that we were a band that was for the most part English and with just a couple of members who could boast Irish parentage might have been a source of embarrassment to Frank. If I had had the courage to express my opinion, which I dared not in the face of the power he now seemed to exert and in view of the disdain in which I thought he held me, I would have accused Frank of being snobbish.

In the first week of September a disc jockey from Dublin called B. P. Fallon invited us to take part in a radio show at the RTÉ Studios in Donnybrook. In the course of his life's work of tagging himself to what was current, Fallon had been self-styled 'media guru' to Marc Bolan and Led Zeppelin, had mimed playing bass for John Lennon's 'Instant Karma!' on *Top of the Pops* and seemed ubiquitous when it came to Irish rock music. We had met Fallon the previous March after our first show in Dublin at McGonagle's. He was a pixie-ish man and – except for a pair of sable eyebrows and dark collar-length wispy hair – bald. After our gig at McGonagle's he had gone from room to room in the hotel conducting interviews, peppering his language with doo-wop and vocalese. He wore pink-framed glasses to work the recorder. I had ended up standing in the stairwell of the hotel at two or three in the morning, playing my accordion for him.

Fallon's radio show was called *The B. P. Fallon Orchestra.*

There would be a small audience made up of the winners of a competition, which RTÉ had held a couple of days before, together with a handful of Irish journalists and a musician or two. Though the majority of the audience was likely to be fans, we had been primed to expect confrontation. The theme of the evening was to be whether or not the Pogues had the right to play Irish music – in Ireland or anywhere else. Fuelled by the beer in the green room, our dander was up and Frank was on the defensive.

We were ushered into the studio and took our places at a long table covered with a white tablecloth, opposite a couple of ranks of what we assumed would be our inquisitors across the dark floor. Fallon sat at a desk to the side between the audience and us, ready to moderate. There was an indulgent and vaguely parental expression on his face. We set down our bottles between the microphones on stands, the tumblers and pitchers of water and ashtrays. The moment I took my place at the end of one of the long tables, I knew that this studio, with its earth-coloured hessian wall-covering and pine window-frames, was the last place I wanted to be.

Fallon started the proceedings, to our bemusement introducing us as 'probably the most controversial group in the groovy world of pop and roll'. After playing a couple of tracks from *Rum Sodomy and the Lash* he started the interview.

Confronted as we were by a gallery of journalists we assumed had been invited in order to draw a bead on us, we were defensive and impudent. Our responses to Fallon's questions were niggardly. We hoped to present ourselves as people you didn't fuck with, and to offer as slight a target as possible. Fallon faltered a couple of times.

In an attempt to take control of the interview Frank spoke up, cutting off Spider in the middle of a response, paraphrasing him in a voice full of seasoned weariness and thick with drink. When he finished there was an awkward silence.

'If you figured out that you heard an Irish voice there,' Fallon said then, 'you're absolutely correct, a hundred points! Frank, maybe you'd be kind enough to tell us a bit about your rock-and-roll history, up to now?'

'I don't think it has any bearing on what's going on here tonight,' Frank said. Fallon pressed the issue and Frank, with hackneyed flippancy, blundered his way through the list – Skid Row, the Woods Band, Dr Strangely Strange, Thin Lizzy, Kirsty MacColl and, to our mirth, the Commodores. He ended the list with 'big acts, you know, blah blah blah.' I winced in embarrassment for him, and for us.

Throughout the afternoon Frank rode roughshod over the incoherence of our responses and pontificated at length about the band. He referred to the band as 'we.' We came across as witless and incapable of speaking for ourselves.

After the introduction of Frank it was obvious that Fallon was predominantly interested in those of us whose names and associations would be recognisable to an Irish listenership. The rest of us he merely enumerated. Anonymity suited me under the circumstances. After acknowledging Philip Chevron who, it seemed, needed little introduction, he moved on to address the weightier presence of Terry Woods. Fallon enquired as to why Terry found himself at this interview. Terry, it was obvious, had not expected to be called upon to say anything at all.

'Well, frangly, I mean, yeah,' he faltered, surprised by the question and addled by the amount he had had to drink. 'I think the ban's grea. Simmel as tha.' '

'Rumour has had it that you are actually going to join this folkabilly combo,' Fallon went on.

'Rumour'srong,' Terry said.

'You're not?'

'I havn't min asked!'

'Your name's down on the bloody itinerary!' Spider said.

'Oh,' Terry said. 'Then I'm a Pogueen!'

'Well,' Fallon said. 'A round of applause, please. Let's welcome Terry into the Pogues.'

Handclapping concluded our introduction to the radio audience and to the gallery. Fallon moved on to what we had been led to believe was the inevitable confrontation between our inquisitors and ourselves. Fallon introduced an accordionist called Noel Hill, Hill immediately taking pains to point out that he was not an accordionist, but a concertina player, stressing also that he was 'an Irish traditional musician, playing full time.' He was a simple-looking man, bearded and wearing a pair of glasses with large frames.

Assuming our scant knowledge of Irish traditional music and in an attempt at artfulness, Hill wanted to know if we had heard of Séamus Ennis at all. I felt sorry for him that he should think that we hadn't. We rounded on him brutally. Frank led the attack, boxing Hill's ears for his assumption that we in any way sought to emulate Séamus Ennis. He ridiculed Hill for his preciousness about 'Irish traditional music.'

With dogged piety, Hill continued to try to send us up as charlatans and bastardisers of Irish music, distressed as he already was by the likes of Brendan Shine and, to our surprise, by the Clancy Brothers and the Dubliners.

'The music in this country,' he said. 'It's the most bastardised music. But this music that came out of – twenty years ago – the pubs in Dublin – rowdy music, ballad music – that come out of drunken sessions and that, been labelled Irish music, is, is a terrible abortion.'

Jem, Spider, Shane and Frank fell over one another denying that we thought we were playing the Irish music Noel Hill venerated. They came close to denying that we even played the kind of Irish music Hill considered an abortion. Hill sank back into the gallery and into silence. I winced at our duplicity. I hoped that at least one of us would own up and concede that we indeed played Irish music, and, in Noel Hill's opinion, played it badly. The point, to me, was that no one had the least cause to question our sincerity.

Later in the programme, after Fallon had played our version of 'Dingle Regatta', Hill managed to wring some consolation from the drubbing we gave him, interjecting: 'Well, as Beethoven might have said, deafness has got its moments.'

The debate continued on the theme of Irish music – its sanctity and otherwise its versatility – taking in Foster and Allen, Ray Lynam and Philomena Begley, Brendan Shine, the Clancy Brothers, the Dubliners, the Chieftains and De Dannan. Our contribution was either vilified for 'paddywhackery' or applauded for turning Irish music on its ear. Though I told myself that I was ignorant of our supposed significance, I was proud to provoke such polarised reactions.

As the hour and a half of questioning and dissimulation were coming to a close I was relieved not to have been called upon to say anything. When it came to my giving account at all, to anyone, of what we were doing, I had little to say. I told myself that it was a function of my ignorance of the larger issues we stirred up – our subversion of traditional Irish music, our breach of the divide between genres – which disqualified me from opening my mouth. I hoped to be viewed as 'the quiet one', though I ruined the effect by laughing exaggeratedly at anything I found the least bit funny if only to put some sort of oar in.

I had been happy just to play the accordion – and anything else to hand. By the end of the evening, though, I found out that that wasn't enough.

Earlier in the afternoon a fan had had the bad luck to ask Cait whether or not she was going to record further with Pride Of The Cross, the band she had been performing in with Darryl. The question had been so stunning in its irrelevance that she just shut the kid down. At the end of the ordeal, one of the journalists described Cait as a 'pig'. She grunted a succession of oinks.

'Is that behaviour piggish enough for you?' she said in a petulant and sugary voice.

⟩✠⟨

The first show we played with Terry was at the beginning of September at the Haçienda – a former warehouse on the corner of Whitworth Street in Manchester. UV strips mounted in racks above the dance floor threw an unearthly light over the crowd. Riveted iron posts painted red and green, chevronned in black and yellow, interrupted the view from the stage. We played the gig in our customary positions along the front, forcing Terry upstage, subjecting him to a rough apprenticeship.

It wasn't just the fact that he was a new boy that set Terry apart. He was a couple of months shy of his thirty-eighth birthday. The oldest of us at the time, Andrew, was thirty-one. That Terry should have been born in the decade previous to the rest of us conferred on him a remoteness made even more preterite by his musical history. It wasn't long before we started to ridicule his antiquity and make of him an ancient Irish chieftain, embroidering him into a spuriously mythological tapestry of Ireland.

His voice took some getting used to. It was soft with a timbre that was whispery. Its dulcitude made you listen. When he warmed to a subject, which wasn't rare, it was accompanied by a pursing of the lips, a rhetorical device Terry used to accentuate his authority. It didn't take us long to master the piping of his voice and his Irish accent, as well as the declamatory hand gestures he used for emphasis.

Terry and Frank were close to the point of inseparable. They had known one another for years. Latterly, during the period Frank had been Kirsty MacColl's manager, Terry had had the job of tour manager. On our tour bus, they sat down at the front across the aisle from one another where they traded comments, jokes and recollections, back and forth. If there were a couple of hours in the day between sound check and the gig, or on a day off, Frank would seek Terry out. Terry would pull on his coat, don his hat and they would go out. Before gigs, as we assembled in the hotel lobby or when we came back from the venue, the two of them could be found together at a table or propped against the bar. Frank would lean saltily towards Terry, until Terry exploded with laughter, his eyes closed, his head thrown back.

Though we consigned him to the rear of the stage, Terry tolerated his view of our backs for just a few weeks before he took his place in the line next to me. He played loud. A black humbucker pickup, the kind one would expect to see fixed to a Les Paul, disgraced the front of his comely, chestnut-coloured, pear-drop-shaped cittern. His amp stood a couple of feet behind. In the confines of the clubs we played, his speaker cabinet blared such overdriven harmonic distortion that afterwards my right ear whined from the onslaught and the next day felt as if wadded with wool.

'James!' he said. 'I'm playing single notation music! You can't play single notation music if you just can't hear!' I gave up to his seniority and his stubbornness.

When it came to Terry's playing the concertina on stage, an elaborate set-up had to be devised. D.J. together with Darryl and Scully positioned microphones on craning boom-stands on either side of him, well away from the line of monitor wedges along the front of the stage for fear of feedback. The pushing and pulling of the concertina, towards and away from the mikes, rendered the experiment useless. Contact microphones gaffertaped to the reed-pan were dropped too. The concertina went back into its scuffed leather cube and Terry returned to his position at the front of the stage, to flay my right eardrum with the aural equivalent of barbed wire.

As the summer came to an end we went on the road in England, from Glasgow, working our way down through Newcastle and Blackburn to the Hammersmith Palais. Frank engaged a stage manager called Charlie McLennan.

Charlie epitomised rock and roll. He had lustrously blond hair, centre-parted and layered in the fashion of the 1970s. It conjured up such people as Mick Ronson or Rick Wakeman. His jeans were more or less denim sheathing. He had worked with Thin Lizzy, Frankie Miller, Joe Cocker and lately with Joan Armatrading. One of his jobs had been to lift Keith Richards from a couch in Redlands, take him to a nearby airfield and put him on a chartered plane out of the country for tax purposes.

Well tended as his coiffure was, it framed a misshapen face which had a small mouth and a bent nose set in it. His eyes were the palest blue. They moved slowly, without deliberation. He spoke in a slurred Glaswegian accent, low, monotone and soporific.

He was seemingly indestructible. I came across Charlie at the back of the bus outside the Boot on Cromer Street as we gathered to leave for Glasgow. He was telling a story to Shane and Spider at one of the tables near the back. On tour, travelling to the next gig and needing a piss, he had descended the short stairwell from the main deck of the bus and had become confused as to which the toilet door was. The hefty handle he chose had eventually given, but the door swung out over the surface of the motorway. To save himself he grasped the top of it and swung there as the driver swerved all over the road, alerted by the alarm connected to the door. The bus skidded to a stop on the hard shoulder.

'So,' Charlie said. 'I dropped down and walked up to the driver's window and asked the guy, "Where's the fucking toilet on this bus?" '

⊹

Rum Sodomy and the Lash entered the charts at No. 13. A couple of weeks later it had vanished. We consoled ourselves with the explanation that we owed the record's brief but sudden and fairly lofty showing to the vehemence of our fans.

The day before our gig at Barrowland, erstwhile Celtic and Scotland manager Jock Stein died of a heart attack at the end of Scotland's World Cup qualifying game against Wales at Ninian Park. On the afternoon of our show Frank took us all – P.V., D.J., Scully, Darryl and Charlie too – down to Moss Bros on Renfield Street to deck ourselves out in Royal Stewart dress tartan: kilts, black tunics with brass buttons, white socks with red flashings. We went back and forth from the changing rooms appraising one another's outfits, jealous of the fluke of a good fit or politely complimentary if arms extended beyond cuffs or shoulders drooped. Jem filled out his tunic handsomely. His legs were sturdy, his socks drawn neatly up to his kneecaps, the flashings trim. Spider had skinny legs, with pommels for knees. Andrew's were almost Grecian in outline. Shane stood tall, skinny, one sock rumpled mid-calf, both flashings awry, his tunic half-buttoned up and the lace ruff hanging open at his throat.

The unfamiliarity of each of us shedding our usual drabness and becoming a Bonnie Prince Charlie made us hot in the face.

Frank's face shone. His colour was high. His blue eyes flashed and he tittered helplessly.

Barrowland Ballroom was a barn of a place with a latticed ceiling which arched over what looked like acres of wooden dance floor. The capacity was two thousand. It seemed an impossibly large number and the prospect of filling it remote, but half an hour before show time we were sick with anxiety, listening to the mounting chants of the crowd beyond the double doors to the hall.

When the lights went down, in defiance almost of Jock Stein's death, a roar rose up. As it crested, we walked out on stage. When the crowd saw what we were wearing, another roar swelled up. Both seemed to break together and crash across the stage.

The audience was a seething bedlam of wet hair and suet-coloured faces laced together by green and white Celtic scarves.

Hail Hail, the Celts are here,
What the hell do we care?

They continued through the gig. After 'And if you know the history, it's enough to make your heart go whoa-oh-oh-oh!' the clamour of the repeated 'oh' forced us to wait for them to finish before we could start another song.

They chanted 'The Soldiers' Song' and bellowed about how much they hated Rangers, whom the songs referred to as 'Huns' and 'animals'. They scared the shit out of me. I was relieved that these lads – there weren't many girls out there – were on our side. I pitied those who weren't.

After the gig, we strewed ourselves exhausted on the dusty velour seats in the dressing room. Spider raised both hands, in honour of the Glasgow crowd.

'Fucking hell!' he said in awe.

Scully and P.V. came in from the hall in their tunics and kilts, their faces pink from the heat. P.V. smiled with pride. Scully was chortling.

'That was gas,' he said.

I looked around at us all in our tartan finery. We were no longer the six strangers from the tenements opposite King's Cross. We had somehow become a family.

'Meat and two veg,' I heard Frank say. He was nodding across at Shane. Shane was sitting on the wall-seat with his head back, his eyes closed and his mouth hanging open. His legs were apart. His kilt had ridden up and exposed his genitals.

Seventeen

For our tour of Germany in October 1985 – a symbol of our gathering momentum – we journeyed in a forty-five-foot green Van Hool tour bus with a panoramic front window and multiple wing mirrors. Inside, behind a few rows of forward-facing seats, were a couple of tables with domed table lamps and recesses for drinks. Halfway down the bus hung a television monitor upholstered with carpeting and a VCR tucked above it in the luggage rack. Separated by a curtain from the rest of the bus was a back lounge with foam-filled seating upholstered in grey faux suede. Throughout, there was a smell of Glade deodoriser.

With the exception of Frank, we shared rooms. There was a first-come first-served rotation of the coveted single room, if one became free, but this was so seldom as to discourage dwelling on. With Costello accompanying us, he and Cait roomed together. Due to their inseparability, the hours they kept and their predisposition to chronic garrulousness, Shane and Spider often shared a room. What the arrangements were for the rest of the band I didn't know. As a matter of course I shared with Philip.

Outwardly my and Philip's relationship must have appeared felicitous enough. The kindling of our friendship on the *Finnjet*, more or less fused by its near-perilous result, had become lore. Our urging one another to show off on stage, together with our fondness for quality suits, probably supported the assumption that we would room together. When it came to Frank's brusque and impatient distribution of room keys when we checked into hotels a key would come our way with the call: 'Philip and James!'

A few weeks before, after an evening drinking with Philip in South London, I was going to go home. We had happened to be so close by the block of flats in Kennington where Philip was staying with Phil Gaston and his girlfriend Dee O'Mahony that we went up to the flat. We sat together on the spongy leatherette sofa listening to a record. I slouched with my feet up on the coffee table, my arse way down in the seat, smoking a cigarette. I was spent from drink.

Philip reclined next to me with his elbow on the back of the sofa, a hand propping up his head, looking at me. I was drunk but not so drunk that I wasn't aware of Philip's attentions. I had spent the past few months since he joined the group flattered by what had become his obvious crush on me.

Philip suddenly leant over and put his mouth on mine. I was drunk enough to dismiss the shock of the unfamiliar, but even after just a while the kiss seemed to have gone on for ever. In the end, the tedium and my drunkenness overcame me and I passed into unconsciousness.

I woke at the sound of Phil Gaston coming in the front door. By the time Gaston came into the room, Philip and I had done our best to resume our positions and were drinking, lighting up cigarettes and listening to a record.

The episode was never mentioned again. I was happy to assume that Philip considered it to be as much an irregularity as I did. By the time the tour of Germany started, though, it seemed Philip was falling in love with me, if he hadn't already.

After picking up our key from the desk, the business of letting ourselves into the hotel room was straightforward enough. Philip and I deferred to one another as to which bed we wanted. We put our stuff out on the bedside tables and our wash bags by the sink.

We hung the clothes that were still wet from the gig the night before up in the cupboard. We went down to see what could be found to eat or if the hotel bar was open before going down to the venue.

After gigs, back in the room, I went about my business as if he were not there. After a shower, I blithely went about the room clad in just a towel. I was unashamed of sleeping naked. It had been my custom since teenage. Before turning the lights out, we exchanged our good nights.

In a matter of days, once I'd turned over to go to sleep, Philip entered into exaggerated writhing in his bed. I tried to ignore his restlessness but it came to be accompanied by groans and, now and again, the release of a great gust of a sigh. After a while his disquiet would subside and I would fall asleep. I wanted to put it down to poetic agony but knew it wasn't.

At the end of the day I began to dread going back to the room. I would postpone it as long as I could, drinking with everyone else in bars after the gigs. A couple of times I took myself off on a walk through the town. No matter how quietly I might let myself in Philip would still be awake.

One night after his bout of thrashing had died down and I was beginning to drift off, his bedding whistled with sudden movement.

'Say good night to me!' he cried out. 'That's all I want.'

'Oh, fuck,' I said. To pre-empt his getting up and coming to my bed, leaving me less control over what saying good night might mean, I got up and went to his.

My nightly embrace with Philip became the pattern. I got it over with as quickly as I could.

'I'm a gay man,' Philip said to me one night. 'I'm in a group, on the road. You're lucky to be in love. You all have girlfriends, and wives, people at home.'

Strangely, it angered me that he should include Shane in the list, for whom no one seemed to be waiting at home.

'I'm on my own,' he said. 'You don't know how hard it is.'

'We're all on our own, Philip. You just get on with it.'

'That's not what this band's about,' he said. 'We should all care for one another. We all love one another. We're all misfits. It's not just Shane who's a misfit. I'm a misfit. You're a misfit. We're the Town Musicians of Bremen for fuck's sake!'

'I'm going to go to sleep now,' I said. I resented his assumption that he knew anything at all of what the band was about; he had only been in it since May.

'You're all wound up,' he said.

'I'm not,' I said.

'Yes you are!' he said. 'I can see it in your neck.'

I was tired. The marrow in my bones was tired. My ears whined from the gigs.

'Fuck off, Philip,' I said. 'Please.'

In the mornings a couple of times he reached under the covers of my bed to tickle my feet. One morning, I listened to him going through what turned out to be my bag, rattling through the cassettes. His jittery fingers opened one of them up and put it into my Walkman. In a moment or two I felt his shaking hands put the headphones over my head.

'Time to wake up,' he murmured.

'Oh, Christ, Philip!'

On the bus I tried to keep to myself. I sat with my knees up against the seat in front, staring through the window listening to classical music on my headphones. As the tour went on, though, Philip would plop down next to me. I took to piling my coat and bag of cassettes on the empty seat.

⊹

All of us got up earlier than we ever wanted to. Alarm calls bored through our sleep. If we made it down to breakfast at all, it was at the last moment. *Frühstück* was a matter of palate-scouring draughts of grapefruit juice, dry bread-rolls, a tile or two of sweating cheese and some salami. If there was time, we'd wrap a couple of rolls, an apple or an orange in a serviette, check out and then get onto the bus, and wait.

Andrew would lumber onto the bus with his bag over his shoulder. He'd grunt and take a seat in the corner at one of the tables where he would fold his arms, close his eyes, and make a forbidding line of his mouth. Now and again a densely lashed eye would crack open to signal his displeasure at a commotion and then close again.

Spider would come down the aisle, bag bumping on the backs of the seats, in the leather coat he had bought in a second-hand shop in Berlin and had named Wolfgang. He would lean both elbows on the headrests on either side of the aisle and crane his face down towards whoever was sitting at the tables at the back. His eyes were swollen from lack of sleep but tiredness seemed only to goad him on.

'Oh!' he shouted. 'I am seen you of the Pogues! You are hitting yourself over your head with a trampoline! No! I am stupid! I am seen you hitting yourself over your head with a *trombone*!'

Costello and Cait sat together at one of the tables, knees touching, hands dabbling. Terry sat nowhere but at the front, happiest with a view of the road ahead through the panoramic window, with his book on the empty seat by his side – a historic tome or other on the subject often enough of the American Civil War or Irish repression, occasionally a book of poetry. My holdall on the empty seat next to me forced Philip to take a seat down the bus.

The tiredness which set in crowded Darryl's eyes with capillaries. There was a papery wanness about Jem's face. A week into the tour Shane had brought to our attention teardrop-shaped blotches under Jem's eyes.

'Stigmata!' Shane had cried out.

Shane never seemed to look any worse, unless his pallor was more deathly, unless denser stubble encroached upon his mouth and cheeks, unless his lips were rawer from wiping the crust of kaolin and morphine from them with his forearm.

He came out of the hotel wearing shades and in his shirtsleeves, seemingly oblivious to the pinch of winter in the air. His trousers were as shiny with grime as they had been in London. He mounted the step onto the bus, stopped to emphasise to the driver, with stabs of the finger, a requirement about the air-conditioning. He would conclude with an exaggerated nod, push his sunglasses onto the bridge of his nose with a forefinger and make his way, sniffing, up the bus, angry about the way his luggage snagged on the seatbacks. He would briefly take in those of us already sitting waiting to go. He would nod, and then disappear behind the curtain to the back lounge.

As the bus lurched away from the kerbside we'd look across one another and out of the windows and watch the shop fronts, kiosks, banks, the tramlines, trolley-cables and trees go by, until the city gave way to the suburbs and the suburbs to the autobahn. The drives – Berlin to Nürnberg to Zürich to Hamburg – were long and punishing.

The fir forests slid across one another, opening and closing over fields of winter wheat speckled with gulls or, a mile or so later, a clutter of orange roofs and the inky prong of a steeple. Winter was coming and the leaves were turning. Towards the end of the morning, mist still hung in the friezes of woodland which fringed the forests.

'Eagle,' Andrew pointed out, and we strained to pick out the tawny italic soaring against the pines. When dusk drew in, a train of headlights filed past, as the rush hour evacuated the city we were entering.

·✠·

Tom Waits's *Rain Dogs* had been released the previous month. It was never off the bus's cassette player. We loved Waits's cantankerous voice, half lover's whisper, half carney's barking. The clanks of the banjo we loved too, along with the ventilation of the accordion, the bonks and crashes of the percussion, the respiration of the pump organ and harmonium, the wailing of the musical saw, the booms of the parade drum, the clonks of the marimba. The otherworldly grating, creaking and thumping sounded throughout the bus. It was as if we were truly on board a ship with the straining of timbers and the constant motion.

We were already familiar with a couple of Waits's previous records. Jem had played us *Heartattack and Vine* and *Swordfishtrombones* in the past couple of years, but it wasn't until *Rain Dogs* came out that we knew that, if any record pointed the way towards what we wanted to do, this was it.

We waited for our favourite bits to come up, to point them out to one another. We would stare into each other's eyes waiting for a choice phrase or sound. We delighted in spotting 'Chim Chim Cheree' in one of the verses of 'Diamonds and Gold', and Frank Sinatra's 'Witchcraft' in the melody of 'Rain Dogs'. We groaned in wonder at the brutality and spontaneity of the playing: Marc Ribot's angular guitar, Michael Blair's bonkers percussion, the thumb-heavy banjo on 'Gun Street Girl'.

We relished Waits's imagery – as American as Edward Hopper and as fucked up as George Grosz. Along with the brutality of the music came a zoetropic parade of slaughterhouses, roadhouses, shovels, whiskey, pistols, umbrellas, tumours big as eggs, Cincinnati jackets and paladins' hats. The procession of images was as protean, as crystalline and as haggardly illuminated as in Shane's songs.

When we weren't listening to *Rain Dogs*, we were watching Sergio Leone's *Once Upon a Time in America* on the VCR. Along with Tom Waits's music, Morricone's – the minor chord and semitone dissonance of the opening strings, the pan-flute of the title melody, the violins and soprano of 'Deborah's Theme' – became the soundtrack of the tour. Not only did the music weave itself into the fabric of our day, but the dialogue too.

'Noodles!' Spider shouted.

'You coming? We're going. You coming?'

'You dancing? You asking? I'm asking. I'm dancing.'

'Shut the fuck up! Shut the fuck up!'

'You'd be better off you stayed in the Bronx.'

'Woulda been better for *you*, too!'

In the *Raststätten* we pulled into, one or other of us would be sure to stir his coffee for minutes on end, in homage to Noodles's sixty-three seconds of spoon-turning in the film. It wasn't long before the joke wore off.

Contrarily, the long journeys were inspiring. The sequestration, the physical proximity, the boredom, the fatigue, the constant motion seemed to imbue everything with a prodigiousness that drove me to write in my journal whenever I could. Andrew, when he wasn't gazing out over the forests, drew. I could hear Jem at the back of the bus playing a mandolin. He came to find me where I was sitting near the front. At one of the sound checks I had been playing something in what I supposed was an East European mode. It was a scale with four harsh semitone intervals. He took the mandolin back to the back of the bus. I listened to him piecing together a kind of rondo melody.

Shane, too, was writing. If I happened to be sitting in one of the backwards-facing seats at the rear of the bus, I could see him in the back lounge hunched over crumpled pieces of paper holding a felt pen in a clenched fist. Despite it being the end of autumn the roof-hatch would be open. The downdraught snapped the curtain in the doorway and lapped at the sheets of paper pinned between his elbow and knee. It flattened his hair onto his forehead. He'd stop for a minute and look out of the window, working his nostrils absent-mindedly as if something in one of them constantly itched. His foot tapped all the while. Then, after cuffing the paper on his knee, he'd wipe his nose with his forearm and set to again. He filled the flapping sheets of paper with large, angular letters and the margin with violent dots. When he'd finished with one of them he brushed it out of the way. The pages lay scattered. The wind pinned one of them on the floor where it shivered under the gusts from the roof-hatch.

I'd look up again and he'd be unconscious, but never so deeply that he would let go of the pen or the bottle of wine he was drinking. He lay with his arse half on, half off the sliding foam-filled upholstery. His raw hands rested in his lap, an arm clamping one of the half-scrawled sheets to his thigh. The hairs on his forearm stood up. The wind snatched the smoke coming up from his cigarette lying in the ashtray.

·✠·

Ever since he came to join the group we had forced Andrew to stand up to play. I had been the loudest to insist that if everyone else had to stand, so did he. Playing the drums standing up wasn't easy. To play side stick Andrew had both to lean forward onto the snare drum to dampen the skin, and then draw back to wallop it. Within a week on the tour in Germany, he had nicked the knuckle of his forefinger on a burr on one of the lugs. The sticking plaster he wrapped round his finger was no protection. His knuckle continued to knock against the hardware.

Within a couple of days the laceration became septic. He showed me a vein which had begun to trace a pink line up the underside of his arm. Frank took him to a doctor. Andrew came back with his finger in a beak-shaped aluminium cast wrapped around with gauze. He held his hand protectively to his chest. He regretted not being able to play for a few days, but when he said that the injury had advanced to septicaemia and had threatened the loss of his finger, tears welled in his eyes.

In Bremen we talked about who was going to play the drums. Both Darryl and Costello volunteered. We decided to alternate the two of them night by night.

Before he came out on stage to take his place behind the drums, Costello took off his jacket and rolled up the sleeves of his shirt. He bent towards the kit in readiness, head erect, eyebrows aloft, alert to his new responsibility, the expression on his face deferential but convinced of his talent. He counted in the first song. The snare-beats rang out like gunshots. The floor-tom became a battery of explosions. It was a relief the next night to have Darryl take his place at the drums.

Familiar as Darryl was with the songs, and with our ethos, a couple of days later it was a further relief when Andrew resumed playing, but behind the bass drum and hi-hat Charlie McLennan had found on our day off between Berlin and Nürnberg – and sitting on a stool, cradling his bandaged finger against his chest out of harm's way and playing with one hand.

·✠·

'You know guinea pigs can die of fright?' Andrew said, as we drove from Osnabrück to Lübeck, to catch the ferry to Copenhagen. 'Fright, and frost,' he added.

The afternoon in Copenhagen was warm enough to walk around the Tivoli Gardens, but at night the temperature plunged to a stinging cold. None of us were prepared for how bitter it was, least of all Shane who went around everywhere without a coat. I walked across the Rådhuspladsen with him. The night air was opalescent from frozen mist. The neon lettering between the lines of windows and above the buildings seemed to float in the sky. I pulled my coat tight across my stomach and turned the collar up to my ears. Shane seemed unconcerned. Though he might have hunched his shoulders and tucked his elbows in against the chill, he bowled along across the square, hands in pockets, steam issuing from his mouth.

On the way to Malmö the next day he was in his usual spot in the back lounge of the coach – but sitting rigid, his eyes half-open, head back, his arms folded stiffly over his stomach. His lips and face were white. The only motion was his mouth chewing his stomach pills into a chalky glue.

After the sound check Frank helped him up to his room. After Shane had vomited what Frank described as 'bile', he took Shane to the hospital. Frank showed up in the dressing room within an hour of the gig. There was a defeated look on his face.

'Pneumonia,' he said. 'What do you want to do?'

The doors of the club had already opened. We agreed an announcement should be made. We reconfigured the set list, choosing who was going to sing which song. Though Spider put himself forward to sing most of them, Costello took the plum ones.

On stage, as we struggled to salvage what had turned out to be the last gig of the tour, a wretched delirium came over us. I fought with the impulse to let it all go to hell. We passed a bottle of whiskey round the stage. Spider threw himself at the first half of the set, from 'The Sick Bed of Cúchulainn' to 'Billy's Bones'. When Cait sang 'I'm a Man You Don't Meet Every Day', Costello crooned unison in the choruses. Costello's otherwise strident harmony vocals reamed through the monitors. In the second half of the gig, he larded 'The Old Main Drag', 'A Pair of Brown Eyes', 'Dirty Old Town' and 'And the Band Played Waltzing Matilda' with a regret seemingly dedicated to our stricken singer.

Afterwards, in the dressing room we threw dinner plates against the wall until the floor was covered in broken pottery. We bellowed at one another without restraint. Philip got so drunk that he couldn't walk. When it came time to leave, P.V. and I helped him out to the bus. At the hotel we dragged him up to the room we shared and threw him on the bed. I left and closed the door behind me.

In the hotel foyer I came across Cait sitting on the sofa, her elbow on her knee and her chin resting on her knuckles. She and

Costello had fought bitterly in the street outside the hotel and Costello had stormed off. But for a glow of pink under one eye, she was wan with fury.

'It doesn't mean anything,' I said. 'He's drunk. You're drunk. We're all drunk. It'll be all right tomorrow. Forget about it. He's the best thing you have.' I couldn't think of much else to say. I was drunk. I wanted everyone to get on.

'Let's go and find the little man,' she said. We got up and staggered arm in arm to the lift.

The sight of Costello in his black coat and his hat marching up the corridor towards us from their room threw Cait into such a panic that she fled in the opposite direction. I stood, baffled for a moment or two as he chased after her.

I didn't want to go to bed. As I passed, I could hear Andrew's voice talking on the phone behind the door of the room he was sharing with Jem. I explored the hotel, trying handles up and down the corridors as I went. Most of them were locked except for one which opened onto a surprisingly large linen cupboard and another one leading to the service stairs. The staircase took me through the staff changing rooms and the humming, fluorescently lit kitchens until I pushed through a door, surprised to find myself back where I'd started in the foyer.

In the same spot I'd come across Cait earlier in the evening sat Costello, in his coat, his face in his hands. I went to sit down next to him. His eyes behind his glasses were small and slimy with tears.

'It doesn't mean anything,' I said. 'She's drunk. You're drunk. We're all drunk. It'll be all right tomorrow. Forget about it. She's the best thing you have.'

At that moment, Cait came across the foyer. She sat down and put an arm over Costello's shoulders. I was about to leave them to it when another argument erupted. This time Costello was the one to storm off, leaving Cait fuming again on the sofa. I sat with her for a while in silence until Costello reappeared, with his luggage.

'For fuck's sake!' I shouted.

I left and went up to the door I'd heard Andrew's voice coming from. Andrew was still on the phone. Jem was happy to come out.

'That'll be a hundred-quid phone call,' he said.

The lobby was empty of Costello and Cait. The bar was long closed but we persuaded the night man to let us have a couple of bottles of Pripps.

There was nowhere else to go but to the linen cupboard I had come across. We closed the door behind us and hoisted ourselves up to the top shelves where there was room to sit across from one another on bales of linen with our bottles of beer. The light from the bare bulb hanging from the biscuit-coloured ceiling was harsh. We turned it off and talked into the dark, about the band: how worried we were for Shane, his pneumonia, his stomach, his drinking, and how pointless the little we tried to do was. We talked about how things had changed since Frank had come to work for us. Despite such benefits as the acceleration of our career and the living we were now making, we talked about how much we had lost since we had taken him on. We talked about how the dynamic of the band had shifted, since, first, Philip's inclusion, and then Terry's. We talked about Spider's drinking, which at one time had merely been funny but which now wasn't. We talked about Cait's volatility, which, though her relationship with Costello seemed to have dampened it, turned out to be just as prone to combustion. We talked about how much we liked one another.

'I wouldn't want to lose you from the group,' he said.

'Same here,' I said. 'It's not likely. Don't seem to be able to do anything else,' I added.

In the morning, we left for England. Shane had discharged himself from hospital. His bloody-mindedness had vanquished his pneumonia sufficiently to prompt him, to our astonishment, to light up a cigarette as soon as he got on the bus.

We had a three-day journey ahead of us – to Hamburg and then across the North Sea to Harwich. It was decided that Shane should fly home with the Irish contingent – Frank, Terry, Scully and P.V., together with Costello and Cait.

We dropped them all off at the airport in Copenhagen. They collected their luggage from the hold and disappeared into the terminal, leaving Shane standing in the cold outside. He looked up and down the wet pavement, bereft of his bearings. We shouted to him where the rest of them had gone. He lifted a forefinger in acknowledgement and went inside.

Eighteen

We started rehearsals at John Henry's, a converted Victorian factory at the end of a brick alley off Brewery Road in Holloway. But for the sagging black fabric which covered the walls in the rehearsal room, everything in the room was grey, from the cigarette-burnt synthetic carpet to the dinge which managed to filter in through the filthy window.

Andrew's finger had healed, but his first demand at the start of rehearsals was that he should continue to be allowed to sit down to play. He had had Charlie McLennan pick up his kit from home. Around the familiar turquoise cocktail drum and snare snuggled a bass drum, cymbals and a hi-hat.

Shane seemed fully recovered after his pneumonia. He came to rehearsal in a dove-grey suit like the one he had worn for the video of 'Dirty Old Town', freshly dry-cleaned, over a black shirt. He wore latticed leather shoes.

He paced back and forth across the floor with a hand in his pocket, smoking, avoiding our eyes, waiting for us to finish chatting and reading our papers. He tapped on the windowsill as a couple of us drifted in late from the Balmoral on the corner or in from the café next door.

He moved me off the piano to show us a song he had written, called 'A Rainy Night in Soho'. With his index, middle and ring fingers separated in such a way that they moved in a group, he stabbed out the three chords.

There was an introduction to play, repeated at the beginning of the middle eight and at the end. There was a three-note refrain in between each of the verses. He demonstrated it by pecking the keys with a tar-tanned forefinger.

As soon as we started rehearsing it, I understood the reason for his imperiousness and the impeccability of his clothing. The song was gorgeous. The lyrics were generous and grown-up. Despite the mysteriousness of some of the lines, there was a beautiful clarity in the song.

When we had learnt the chords and the structure I took over on the piano. Shane stood tall in his suit, his fingers round the barrel of the microphone, looking with feigned abashment at the carpet as he waited for the introduction to play through. After a while, he took the microphone off its stand and walked up and down, singing. Now and again, he lifted an arm for emphasis. The performance was too artless and too abashed to be pastiche.

His embodiment of Frank Sinatra made me want to look away in embarrassment, but I was simultaneously compelled to watch, the conviction he had of the worth of his song was so conspicuous.

Another song Shane brought in was one he had written for the Clancy Brothers. In endearing hyperbole, it was called 'The Broad Majestic Shannon'. Like 'A Rainy Night in Soho', it was in 6/8 time. The lyrics were vivid with images and locations in Shane's beloved County Tipperary. The melody in the middle eight he had based upon a sixteenth-century harp tune, 'Tabhair Dom Do Lámh' – 'Give Me Your Hand'. Terry closed his eyes and nodded in approval.

The mandolin melody Jem had been playing on the bus in Germany formed the introduction and middle eight of another song Shane brought in to rehearsal. It was a song full of horrific and haunting images. Shane explained to me, with haggard relish, that the figure of the woman with the comb in her hand in the chorus was the banshee of Celtic mythology whose keening presages death. I sat on a speaker cabinet in the rehearsal room with Shane standing over me. He leant close. He mimicked the action of the woman forever combing, her hair falling half over her face, screaming and screaming. It wasn't so much the phantasm of the banshee herself which struck me with horror, but Shane's looming demented phizog, his ruined teeth, crusty lips, mouth blooming with cold sores, the blowholes of his nose and his terrorful eyes.

When we had been in Berlin, in the dressing room, Shane had been surrounded by fans, breathless with excitement to be in his company and desperate to impress, reeling off punk bands and pitching songs to him they regarded as seminal.

'The "Turkey Song" of the Damned!' one of them had shouted.

'What?! Turkish song of the damned!? Fuck!'

212

The title of the new song was 'Turkish Song of the Damned'.

Again we took up rehearsing the Christmas song we had worked on at NOMIS after coming back from Scandinavia the previous May. Marcia contended that a Christmas song without conflict was boring and predictable, and came up with the storyline of a straw-clutching loser bickering with his girlfriend. The song now had a couple of introductory verses. The melody of the first line was an undisguised reiteration of the theme from Sergio Leone's *Once Upon a Time in America*.

Our rehearsals were interrupted by a visit from Dave Robinson, who came to plead with us to stay with the label. Stiff Records, it seemed, was finally going under. Unshaven, the skin around his eyes papery, Robinson sat in front of us on a flight case and implored, his hands defiantly thrust in the pockets of his car coat. The balance of power seemed to have swung diametrically the other way. The record company had now come cap in hand to us. We stood with our instruments hanging from our shoulders and pretended to consider what he had to say.

Almost to spite Dave Robinson, in the couple of weeks we had before going out on a Christmas tour, we went into Elephant Studios to record music for the soundtrack for Alex Cox's film about Sid Vicious and Nancy Spungen, *Sid and Nancy*.

The majority of the music we made for the film was suitably scourging, a synthesis of what we thought were basic elements of the Velvet Underground sound: rigidly down-struck guitar set against a grim Phil Spector beat. Jem had written a melody we submitted to a suite of variations, including one in which, when the location of the film moved to the French capital, the accordion evoked the streets of Paris. Otherwise it was a matter of setting up a groove around two chords with bass, drums and guitar, with Jem laying on banjo and myself a mandolin beaten with teaspoons or a violin meant to conjure up John Cale.

Shane had written a song for Cait to sing. It recalled the Shangri-Las and was called 'Haunted'. In keeping with the music we'd been making for the film, the song relied again on a Phil Spector beat to underpin Shane's favourite chords outside folk music: E, A and B, with the two top strings open, ringing across the chord progression.

By the end of November we had recorded as many as nine pieces of music, before going out on the road for what was becoming our customary Christmas tour of England, taking in the Midlands, the North-West and Scotland.

The tent-pole gig of the tour was the Hammersmith Odeon.

It was deemed a major gig, despite its less-than-grand location under the concrete span of the Hammersmith Flyover and the fact that there was something démodé about the place – the tabernacle for metal and the occasional glam band. Whitesnake, Deep Purple, Lynyrd Skyrnyrd – and Boney M – had played there. On the other hand, so had Frank Zappa, Bob Marley and Ziggy Stardust and the Spiders from Mars. I tried to imagine people saying: 'The Pogues at Hammersmith Odeon? That's cool!' I hoped the ethos I was convinced we embodied would carry us through and transform even the uncoolest situation into triumph.

The Hammersmith Odeon wasn't cool, but then it happened not to be our gig. It turned out to be Frank's. Once the gear was set up, Frank sauntered out onto the stage. He scanned the sweeping balcony with a self-conscious meekness, taking in the plush gloom of the empty seats. He tapped the stage with the metal toe of a snakeskin boot and then knocked a heel against it. But for the cigarette he was smoking, which was unusual for him, he was like a footballer getting the feel for the turf and the terraces.

The gig itself was a matter of the dreadful hurtle of song after song. We played by the seat of our pants and finished by the skin of our teeth. The beginning of each song felt like sheer folly.

Near the beginning, Philip went up to the microphone.

'Hello!' he said, in a voice which instantly invoked Val Doonican's cameo in the Bonzo Dog Doo-Dah Band's 'The Intro and the Outro'. 'We're the Pogues!' The cheering and jeering of a couple of thousand people or more who bore nothing but maniacal goodwill for us carried us to the end of the gig.

Afterwards, drained by the exertion and cowed by the cycle of count-ins and finishing flourishes, we sat with our hands dangling between our knees and our heads hanging between our shoulders.

Frank came into the dressing room. His eyes were opaque with drink. His mouth clacked with dry spit. He laughed breathlessly. He ushered in some other men who more or less looked like him – wearing navy blazers and faded jeans. They gave off a superior air of having rooted for Frank from the beginning. They nodded at us and clapped Frank on the shoulders. As the congratulations proceeded and Frank got drunker, a flap of his shirt came loose and he gave up training back the lock of hair behind his ear that kept coming adrift. His face was flushed with vindication. Recovering from the concussion of noise and heat and light on stage, and because we'd had a drink or two from the fridge – Bloody Marys in pint plastic glasses, bottles of champagne – some of us draped arms over Frank's shoulders. A chant went up.

'Fuck the begrudgers! Fuck the begrudgers! Fuck the begrudgers!'

⚜

I spent Christmas with Debsey's family at her grandmother's house in Cambridge. Granny Butcher had haystack hair from which slid wisps of grey. Her low-ceilinged kitchen was humid with cooking. Upstairs in the room I shared with Debsey's brother, it was so cold that ice formed on the inside of the windows. On Boxing Day, I got up before light to get a train to London to meet up with the rest of the band at Heathrow for another tour of Ireland.

Before we could relish the heady exclusivity and the leatherette seats of the turboprop fifteen-seater Frank had chartered to fly us to Waterford, we had to wait for Cait and Costello to show up – until we couldn't wait any longer. We boarded, leaving to Frank the job of sorting out how to get our bass player to the first show the next day.

Whatever loftiness and rock-and-roll privilege had come with the chartering of an aircraft ended on arrival at Waterford airport. Our plane drew up in the middle of an otherwise vacant plot of tarmac in front of the terminal – an observation tower with canted windows and a squat arrivals hall. The place was deserted. We collected our luggage and walked to where a couple of vans were waiting. Freezing rain drifted across the trees surrounding the scrubby airfield. Lichen grew on the concrete posts which struggled to hold up the chicken-wire perimeter fence.

By the time of the gig the next day, Cait still hadn't shown up. We drafted Darryl into the line-up. He knew all the songs. He had heard them often enough. How could he not know how to play them? Cait didn't show up until our second date of the tour in Tralee.

It was a tour of unrelenting cold. The hotels were interred in the off-season and sparsely patronised, the radiators frigid, the bedding meagre, breakfast dilatory. A few of the gigs took place in drinking and entertainment emporia attached to the hotel we were staying in. They were vast, dowdy places in the middle of nowhere, full of smoke and what we took to be farmers, a lot of whom wore hairpieces of staggering conspicuousness. The gigs provided the only opportunities to warm up. Not even soaking in the bath prior to going downstairs for show time seemed to help much, the water tepid at best.

At the Fairways Hotel in Dundalk we had to be led to the stage down an outside corridor and past the door to the kitchens. My leather-soled shoes slipped on grating slimy with kitchen grease. Keeping my accordion from damage, I went down. The grate tore the skin on my elbow into a hanging lobe. A doctor we found fashioned butterfly stitches out of a couple of sticky plasters a barman came across in a drawer behind one of the bars.

As our opening act, we had travelling with us a singer-song-writer called Ron Kavana. He was a friend of Frank and Terry's – a stocky guy with a flat nose and the beginning of a widow's peak. In Belfast, he and Costello both opened for us, each of them with an acoustic guitar. Before he had even opened his mouth to say or sing anything, Costello was greeted with a gob of saliva spat from somewhere near the front of the crowd.

Kavana stayed in the same hotels as we did and travelled with us – in the bus we had or the car in which Scully sped through the country roads, sometimes within door-handle-striking distance of oncoming traffic, Frank and Terry his usual passengers.

'A Corkman,' Shane sneered. I liked Ron. He was a nice guy, if a little earnest and prosaic.

The drinking and cigarette-smoking and lack of fresh air got to me. In Limerick I became short of breath and my head had started to pulse. I stepped out of the bar we were in, hoping for the refreshment of the cold on my face. The air outside was ac-rid with peat smoke which seemed to have concentrated in the freezing fog hanging in the streets. The sulphurousness of the street lighting made the atmosphere look yet more noxious.

Fresh air, however, we got. On a detour between Limerick and Galway, Darryl took us to Cait's family's hometown of Lehinch, County Clare. The day was Cait's twenty-first birthday. We walked through the town. The roofs of the bungalows shone with orange lichen in the low afternoon sun and their windows gazed out to the ocean. Fresh air we got too, and in great gusts blowing off the Atlantic, when Darryl stopped a couple of miles up the road at the Cliffs of Moher. Ragged piers of black shale marched in from the sea out of the mist and channelled such a gale up the bluff that I could hold my coat out like wings, jump into the blast and float for a second or two.

When we got to Galway we were told the news that Philip Lynott had died in Salisbury Hospital, of renal and coronary failure due to internal abscesses and blood poisoning. I remembered his pallid face and blank eyes at the Clarendon Ballroom the previous March. Backstage at Leisureland, against the seaside-blue paintwork and frosted glass of one of the corridors, Frank, Terry, P.V. and Scully were standing like a bas-relief in the grim fluorescent light. All of them had known Lynott. Each stared into space. The news of his death was a brutal end to an otherwise luminous day of sunshine and cold, sea and wind, sand and cliffs.

No one took Phil Lynott's death more to heart than Cait. Unfortunately, the promoters, having heard that it was her birthday, had stationed beaded buckets of champagne and flutes on both ends of a table to await her in one of the function rooms at the hotel after the gig. A gleaming birthday cake was the centrepiece. It was too much for Cait. Inconsolable over Lynott's death, her voice broken with anger and grief, she scooped up handfuls of yellow sponge and icing and splattered the walls, floor and anyone within range with it. After her fury, her party ended with racking sobs and heaving embraces. Her face was smeared with mascara. When I went back to the function room, corks rolled over the floorboards and broken glass ground underfoot.

Our last gig was in Shane's hometown of Puckane, a few miles outside the market town of Nenagh. It seemed the entire village had come out to fill the sizeable, stone-flagged saloon in Paddy Kennedy's bar, with pride of place by the iron kitchen range bestowed upon the MacGowan family in their navy blazers and print frocks. Towards the end of our set, a man I assumed to be Shane's dad, Maurice, with a little girl in a cotton dress in tow, mounted the stage to speak a few words into the microphone – about his son, about us, about how welcome we were, what a great honour it was and so forth. When the speech was done, Maurice and little girl, bereft of a plan, stayed where they were, staring haplessly at the audience, while we played the last song around them.

⛭

Frank had already given us a sketch of a tour of the United States, to take place at the end of February. New York would be our base for shows up and down the East Coast. The whole thing would take a week and a half. The prospect of going to America filled me with dread.

In order to have some sort of release in advance of the tour, Frank had put forward the idea of recording an EP. Forgetting Shane's animosity or oblivious to it in the first place, Costello had agreed to produce.

When we got back to London we started again at Elephant Studios.

'London Girl' was a pop song, urgently puerile and fun to play. Against a shuffle beat, Shane sang in an American accent.

When it came to overdubbing the accordion part, I played my

219

heart out. Jem tacked a sign up on the hessian wall of my booth in the studio.

'Cajun!' it read.

I'd been listening to Nathan Abshire and Clifton Chenier – and Rockin' Dopsie and the Zydeco Twisters. I played nothing like them, and made it up myself. I chattered chords against Andrew's shuffle in semiquavers, toggling index and middle fingers all the way down the keyboard in a descending scale of couplets. By the time I was done with my overdub, I was exhausted and went to rest on the corduroy sofa in the control room while Terry went into the live room to overdub his parts on one of the other songs: 'The Body of an American'. I lay curled up, going in and out of sleep. Terry's cittern part infiltrated my dreams, the root note he kept striking on the offbeat mutating into a testicle forever dropping out of his Y-fronts.

We knocked out a jig Jem had written called 'Planxty Noel Hill', dedicated to the traditional concertina player who had been so scandalised by the Pogues at B. P. Fallon's radio show at RTÉ the previous September. In Irish traditional music, the prefix of *planxty* denoted tribute. In the case of Jem's instrumental – full of stops and starts and screams and yelps – it was intended ironically.

Before we left Elephant, we tried to record Jem and Shane's Christmas song, which Shane had given the title 'Fairytale of New York', after J. P. Donleavy's novel. In the duet, Cait sang the girl's part. Costello played the piano. The fact that the song was divided into two parts, each with its distinct tempo, gave us no end of trouble. I wondered if the problem was symptomatic of Jem and Shane's writing collaboration. Shane had written both lyrics and melody for the opening verses and the chorus. The main body of the song was Jem's melody with Shane's lyrics. We left 'Fairytale of New York' for a later date.

An orchestra was vital for 'A Rainy Night in Soho'. Elephant Studios were too small. Through Frank's connections with ZTT Records, Trevor Horn's studios in Notting Hill were made available. Studio 1 at Sarm West was a huge place with oak flooring, a Bösendorfer piano in one corner and, in the distance, the window of the control room.

An arranger Frank knew called Fiachra Trench came in with a string orchestra and brass section. Trench had worked with Van Morrison and Phil Lynott. His nobility when he lifted his baton to conduct eclipsed the goofiness of his face. I watched in awe through the window. The presence of an orchestra in the studio beyond the glass and playing one of our songs put me in ferment. Trench's arrangement included here and there a meticulous countermelody or a glissando to hoist the theme to a higher octave. The fourths which underpinned the instrumental verse towards the end of the song classily recalled Ravel's *Bolero*.

In rehearsal we'd been playing 'The Body of an American' with the theme from *The Guns of Navarone* for a middle eight. Averse to sharing royalties with Dimitri Tiomkin, we had Tommy Keane come in and obscure the tune with uilleann pipes. One afternoon, we took pains to teach Tommy to play Hendrix's 'Voodoo Chile', dumbfounded that he'd never heard it. Once he'd got the notes, as we had seen before, his face tilted upward, his eyes staring sightlessly at the ceiling.

We were taken out into the streets of Notting Hill to have our photographs taken for publicity for our American tour and for the cover of the EP. It was the end of January and we wore our coats: Terry, his tweed three-quarter length and his battered hat; Spider, his leather coat Wolfgang. We found a Budweiser hoarding which propitiously depicted Mount Rushmore.

'We should call it *Poguetry*,' Frank said. Thinking it was a pun on 'purgatory', I liked the idea. '*Poguetry in Motion*,' he added.

The EP, Frank was of the opinion, would be our calling card. His excitement to go to the United States was palpable.

'You'll be beating them off,' Frank said. 'You'll all be getting blow-jobs.'

Despite the recent fourth anniversary of my relationship with Debsey, the remark added a twang of cupidity to my eagerness to go to the United States, and to my fear of it.

Nineteen

On the Air India flight from Heathrow we voided the bar of all the miniature champagne bottles. Halfway through what seemed the interminable five-hour flight, we moved on to whatever full-size bottles of Piper Heidsieck the long-suffering steward could come up with. When those had run out I drank vodka and tonic upon vodka and tonic. We took over the back of the plane, standing and smoking. I started to reel a little, gazing down through the fish-eye window in one of the exit doors. Through a layer of haze over Greenland, Newfoundland and New Brunswick I watched the shattered ice fields and the enamel-blue ocean drift by. The sunlight that streamed in through the windows, combined with the drink, provoked a festive optimism in all of us, not least Philip, who clambered all over the seats. None of us slept. We cackled, shouted and passed bottles of champagne from row to row.

The plane descended over forests punctured by sad, slate-coloured ponds, over sere and wintry fields and came in to land over row upon row of clapboard houses and a confusion of factories amid the vaguely purple blush of wintry trees.

We shuffled towards immigration control, tacking back and forth under the rather stiff, hatched quarter-profile of Ronald Reagan up on a banner welcoming us to the United States. Eventually I staggered out of arrivals into the cold February air, taking in great lungfuls in an attempt to alleviate the symptoms of the misspent flight. My head ached. My face burned. My eyes grated.

Dowdy limousines with huge hoods of faded lustre awaited us. The interior of the one Terry, D.J., Philip and I got into was musty with plum-coloured plush.

I sat up front with our driver. He was called Larry. He wore dusty, vaguely maritime livery – a worn jacket and an embroidered cap. He had the pasty and pitted complexion of a heavy smoker. Larry was from a district called Queens. Graciously, he gave me an answer to each question I bombarded him with. If this was the Van Wyck Expressway who was Van Wyck? Those rusted things next to the lake – what were they? Were those things water-towers?

I didn't listen. I heard only his accent. I had never heard anyone talk like that, not in the flesh, not outside television or films, not in the confined space of the front of a cheap limousine bringing me to Manhattan. The limousine coasted down the expressways. The hood drank up the road. Insulated from the imperfections in the pavement by the limousine's suspension, all I was aware of was Larry's granular voice and the slapping of the wheels. Now and again the hood ducked towards the road as Larry braked to pull up to a line of brake-lights and for a paper popcorn cup that was bowling along between the wheels of the cars.

The rusted things next to the lake turned out to be the site of the 1964 New York World's Fair, corroding monsters engraved by the fading light between the trees.

The water-towers were a novelty. That the millions upon millions of people who had come to live here should not get their water from the ground but from tanks built on spidery ironwork above the city was exotic beyond belief. Something about the light, the angle, the intensity, made the paint-peeling timber tubs pulse with maroon, oxblood and zinc under their conical roofs.

The conversation with Larry petered out. I sat in the front of the car, stricken by the scale of the place. There passed a confusion of storage facilities, cemeteries, factories, warehouses, tenements, hoardings, tyre dumps, chain-link fences, razor-wire, yards full of piles of ink-coloured stone, more yards full of glinting mounds of sheared and madly twisted metal, roofs, chimneys, fire escapes, ventilators, cowls. Beyond the chaos, water seemed to be everywhere: razed grey estuaries and sounds bound in by iodine-coloured hursts and threaded together by bridges.

The limousine crossed the Queensboro Bridge. Before me stood a defiant frieze of skyscrapers. As the sun descended in a furnace between the buildings and water-towers, however, it looked as though the whole city was careening towards some sort of crisis and one to which I might as well give in now.

The lobby of the Iroquois Hotel was no more than a corridor with a chequered floor and a staircase. Philip and I let ourselves in to our cramped room. It had walls the colour of soap and a carpet the colour of builders' tea. An ancient push-button television whose plastic had faded stood on a pole next to a cast-iron radiator. There was a blocked-up fireplace and a mantel. The drink and the jet lag caused me to sit so heavily on the loose-jointed chair next to the television that my weight snapped the webbing underneath. I sat with my arse on the floor and listened to the sound of traffic through the window.

We walked through the streets around Times Square, staggering a little down the sidewalks, our hands thrust in the pockets of our overcoats against the chill. It was dark. The air was thick with the smell of honey-roasted peanuts and burnt chestnuts. Plastic orange flues vented steam into the wintry air.

The avenues were floods of lights, red on one side, white on the other.

We marvelled how everyone in New York City seemed to wear overcoats such as ours. The men wore suits, the women pencil skirts and heels. It was our kind of town. We stood before the statue of George M. Cohan on 47th Street and Broadway.

I had never come across such commotion. Black delivery men still working this late in the evening leant against a wall with a hand truck, conducting a conversation at bellowing level with a couple of other guys in the back of a lorry. Cars banged going over ill-set steel plates in the road covering a construction hole. Horns sounded constantly and at the least provocation. Hubcaps rattled. Detached fenders clanked. Doormen blew into pea whistles or emptied lungs into pipes that sounded like trains. Constantly in the background motors were running – diesel, petrol, air-conditioning vents, fans. The sounds blended into a tireless tinnitus. Above the commotion, the winter clouds obscured the tops of the skyscrapers in a sulphurous veil.

Bill Rahmy was our driver. He was a big, burly guy with dense hair. He had a huge face, with eyes close together beneath lush, dark eyebrows. He drove us down to our first show – at half past eleven in the morning – in what was billed as a ballroom but which turned out to be the concourse of a community college on Long Island, for the benefit of students filing through between classes. None of us questioned the hour of the gig. Those of us who hadn't been up since four in the morning from jet lag had been up all night in any case. Through the windows we had a view of dry couch grass, and in the middle of the expanse the wheeled yellow reader-board with our name on it. The students gawped up at us in bemusement as they passed by. A couple of them stopped to listen but then moved on.

The next show was in Manhattan, at a club called the World

and at a more civilised time at night. We climbed out of the van into the cold and across an intersection to the back door of the club. Steam swirled in the slipstream of a yellow cab, spookily revealing Cait in her new suit, with a guy called Bill Flanagan.

Costello had stayed back in London. His record *King of America* had just been released and he was doing promotion. Bill Flanagan, a journalist friend of Costello's, seemed to have been engaged as Cait's chaperone. Flanagan had a lofty hairline, a long nose and a small mouth. At all times, a shoulder bag hung from him.

During our gig at the World, through the heat of the lights burning down from the ceiling, my attention was drawn again and again to Rick Trevan's American girlfriend, Heather, who stood in the middle of the crowd.

I had met Heather at Rick's flat on one of her visits to London. She was something called a performance artist, and a writer. I had come across her huddled against the radiator in Rick's living room, wrapped in a long tweed coat. She was talking with way-worn authority about New York to Spider, who was sitting on the sofa listening, his fingers in the shape of a church roof.

She was beautiful, with her blonde hair and slender shoulders. Beneath the old coat, she wore a short dress of kingfisher blue and white knee socks. I watched her rake her bony fingers across her forehead up into her fine hair. As if in confirmation that she was a writer, I saw her fingers were blue with ink. She fascinated me. It had been wondrous to come across someone so exotic in the Victorian tenements round King's Cross.

At the World she was standing by herself leaning up against one of the columns away from the moil of heads and shoulders in the middle of the crowd, wearing a sleeveless dress. Though it was difficult to tell from that distance it seemed that every time I looked up, she was staring right at me and so intently that I had to look away. Throughout the rest of the gig I tried not to look in her direction again though I was constantly aware of where she was standing.

In the backstage bar afterwards, Heather's blonde hair, incandescent under a recessed spot in a corner, led me to her like a beacon. She was staring into the rout, cupping an elbow, a cigarette propped in the V of her fingers, her forearms sheathed in satin opera-gloves. I sat down and flopped my arms on the tilting Formica table.

'Hey,' she said.

'How are you?'

'I'm doing good,' she said. She was lovely with her aquiline nose and the thin dark lines of her eyebrows. Her mouth was lustrous with lip-gloss. Now and again her hair would fall across her face from where she had hoisted it. She would take it up again and push it back.

All I knew was that I was in New York for the first time with one of the most attractive women I had ever come across. To my shame and annoyance, Frank's remark about us all getting blowjobs when we came to America had put me in a fever of anticipation. I could think of little else than what was going to happen next, what we were going to do, where we were going to go, how we were going to get there. I deferred all the concerns I might have had regarding Debsey back in London to an indistinct point in the future. I put off thinking, too, about the friendship Jem and Marcia shared, it occurred to me, with both women.

There was a move to go to a bar on the Lower East Side. Out in the street a couple of taxis veered into the kerb to pick up the people shifting around on the sidewalk. Heather linked me from behind.

'Yo!' she said. 'Let's get this one.' She pulled me across the sidewalk, stepped out between parked cars and hailed a cab on the far side of the street.

Our thighs touched as she put her face up to the window in the hazed Plexiglas screen.

'We're going to Attorney and Houston,' she said to the driver.

We sat and smoked cigarettes with the window down. Though the storefronts were shuttered and it was one o'clock in the morning, the city showed no sign of abatement. Streams of cars and taxis jockeyed up and down the avenues. The fast-food joints and the corner delis lit the sidewalks. It felt as though the city, like me, was hurtling towards some turning point.

'It's a fucking mad place,' I said.

'I won't live anywhere else,' she said. 'It won't let me. If I try to leave it stops me somehow. If I leave, it brings me back. I can't imagine living anywhere else. I'd wonder why I wasn't living here. I'll never leave.' She fell silent for a second or two.

'I have beer at my place,' she said then. 'No I don't, but do you want to come back to my apartment anyway? We just passed it.'

Against the free-standing wall that bisected her apartment, Heather had a four-poster which seemed to rise in valanced tiers. The summit was misted with mousseline and chiffon hanging from the metal rails. She climbed up and sat on her heels with her palms on her thighs.

'Shoes,' she said.

The following morning, I managed to get up without disturbing her. West 14th Street was clamorous with traffic and the honks of taxi cabs. The air shuddered from the engines of passing buses. Loudspeakers on the sidewalk in front of stores brayed Latin music. The speaker-cones had all gone but the vendors didn't care or didn't notice. I jumped at every noise. I seemed forever to be in people's way. A man cursed me for sending him against a scaffolding pole because I hadn't known which side to pass him on.

New York couldn't care less about what I had done. It was loud, preoccupied, and indifferent to my infidelity. In desperation I went from store to store picking up things to take home for Debsey, things she would like, things that would distract her from asking questions.

Combined with the drinking we were doing and the hours we were keeping, our unfamiliarity with jet lag only went to magnify the five-hour time difference between New York and London. Cait, though, seemed to have a slenderer hold on sleep than the rest of us and was having problems. There was a nagging restiveness about her. Her complexion was wan. Her disposition was mettlesome. Her regression seemed due to more than just her being stricken with Costello's absence. There was an ominousness about Bill Flanagan's ubiquity.

On the morning we were to leave New York City for Washington DC we gathered, bedraggled, in the lobby with our luggage. To add to the mêlée, a journalist and a photographer working for the *NME*, Mat Snow and Bleddyn Butcher, had turned up with their belongings for the journey down to Washington. Amid the confusion of checking out, no one else heard one of the receptionists tap on the glass of his cubicle.

'Phone call for the Pogues?' he said.

I went across. Cait's voice sounded distant. She said she had left for the airport and that she was getting a plane back to England.

'I'm splitting,' she said.

'What do you mean?'

'What do you think I mean?' she said and hung up.

'Who was that?' Frank wanted to know.

'Cait,' I said. 'She's splitting.'

'What do you mean?' he said.

Frank exploded into supposition and after that into action. It was Costello who had orchestrated Cait's escape. It was Bill Flanagan, upon instructions from Costello, who had picked her up from the hotel and taken her in a taxi to the airport and had bought her ticket back home.

Frank took the second Econoline we had and assigned to it as many as would fit in, to travel down to Washington DC. The remainder – himself, Terry, Spider and Shane, along with Snow and Butcher – would go in Bill Rahmy's van to try to intercept Cait at the airport.

In our Econoline on the way down the New Jersey Turnpike, Jem and I taught Darryl what bass-lines he didn't already know. It had only been a couple of months since Cait and Costello had missed the charter plane out to Waterford.

Later, I leant my forehead to the window looking out onto the wintry landscape, the grey woods rimmed with spruce. I watched the cars passing us. Many were rusted, tail pipes clanking underneath, panels loose. Inside a couple, the upholstery was burst. Dingy fabric hung down from the ceiling and snapped in the wind coming in through the windows. The cars floated over the slabs, but the wheels shivered over the uneven concrete ledges of the pavement which slammed underneath our bus. The sill of one particularly ill-set slab bounced the entire back axle and wheels of a dump truck off the road surface. It banged down, released a cloud of rust and skittered back to equilibrium. Everywhere I looked it seemed the place was driving itself into the ground.

I became distracted by the replacement driver we had whose large-frame glasses I could see in the rear-view mirror. He wore a baseball cap with an exaggeratedly curved peak.

'You guys had any Mercan pussy?' We pretended not to hear. 'No?' he added.

'No,' Jem said. 'I'm happily married.'

'You don't wanna go home and not had some Mercan pussy,' the guy said. 'It's the best in the world.'

In a couple of weeks, I would be going home to Debsey.

Frank's Econoline arrived at the airport too late and Cait was gone. We played the next couple of shows without her. We played well enough, though tentatively, at least in Washington DC. Andrew was relieved. He had been complaining about Cait's bass-playing for a few months, frustrated at either her inability or her unwillingness to synchronise her playing with his bass drum, irked but thankful for her lack of eye contact on stage. In Darryl, Andrew was relieved not just to play with someone who actually had a talent for bass-playing and for music in general, but with someone who evinced enthusiasm for it too.

After Andrew's septicaemia it all seemed to have changed. Once he had returned to what was considered a drummer's rightful place sitting down with his battery of instruments around him, Andrew became a musician again. Cait, though, hadn't been playing along. If anything, she was going in the opposite direction.

Cait returned to the tour with little fanfare at Maxwell's in Hoboken. How Frank had managed to get her to come back didn't interest me. Some of us teased her about having jumped ship, but from a safe distance.

Once the tour resumed and we headed north to Massachusetts she kept herself to herself. I interpreted her insularity to signify contrition, until she happened to show Spider the diamond and emerald engagement ring she had returned from England with.

For the rest of the tour Andrew committed to suffering her bass-playing. He ignored her on stage and off. We played three more gigs – in Massachusetts and Rhode Island – before returning to Manhattan where we played at Danceteria, an after-hours dance club where we were told Madonna had once worked as a hat-check girl.

Perhaps in unconscious resentment of having had to suffer Cait's indifference to the synchrony of bass drum and bass guitar,

Andrew dropped Ecstasy and ended up pitying his drums so much for the walloping he was supposed to give them that his playing became a matter of delicate and apologetic taps.

·✠·

A week after our return from New York we had a three-day run of St Patrick's Day shows at the Hammersmith Palais. On the first of them, Mat Snow's article appeared in the *NME*. His report of the conversation in the van on the way to intercept Cait at John F. Kennedy airport sent her into a smouldering fury. The atmosphere backstage was thunderous with animosity.

In the article, Spider and Shane's allusions to the size of Cait's breasts were harmless compared to what must have been the damage to Cait's spirits when she read that our revenge against her for deserting, according to Shane, should be to 'post her Elvis's head with his cock in his mouth' and that in reference to Costello's girth we should all 'dress up as Michelin Men and gang-bang her.'

We cared less and less for Cait. She had made it too difficult for us to retain even the most rudimentary sympathy for her. Jem was civil enough, but privately showed the scantest compunction when it came to revealing his true feelings about her. Off stage, Andrew barely tolerated her. On stage, he struggled to make sense of playing in the same band. Ironically, the two people who it seemed had done her the most damage were the ones who defended her.

'She's a bloody good bass player!' Shane had been quoted in the *NME* article.

The fact was, though, she had never been much of a bass player. As her relationship with Costello developed, it seemed to me that she was more than ready to sacrifice her interest in bass-playing to what was now her new life. After spending most of his time in the studio and on the road with us, the release of *King of America* – and within a couple of weeks the commencement of recording his next album – meant the resumption of Costello's career. Costello, it was obvious, was ready to return to the lofty stratum he'd come from. Cait, it seemed, was eager to go with him.

Twenty

I let myself into my flat the morning of our return to London from New York and had to hold my breath against the smell. I opened a few windows. There were dead flies on the sills. There were crusts of penicillin mould in the tea mugs. Once I had tidied up and aired the place out, I rang Debsey.

Banishing the words 'Mercan pussy' from my mind, I traded my guilt for Debsey's delight in the gaudy string of plastic beads, the striped tights and the parrot-blue wig which had been hanging under one of the awnings on the sidewalk of West 14th Street the morning after our show at the World.

'Your face is all blotchy,' Debsey said then, looking at me. 'What's the matter with you? You're drinking too much.'

My hair was falling out too. That week she remarked on the hairs I left in the sink after I washed. Over the past couple of months an open sore had appeared on my left foot. My arm hurt from forever dragging open and hooking closed the bellows of my accordion. After gigs I couldn't hold anything in my left hand without my arm going into spasm.

'You should go and see a doctor,' Debsey said.

After our three nights at the Hammersmith Palais, we had a week off before starting a month-long tour of France and Germany. Mindful of his appeal to give him two years of our lives, I surrendered to Frank's urgency to break us, territory upon territory. I wasn't unhappy to be going away again, and so soon. I was glad to pack my belongings in the canvas holdall from my dad's days in amateur dramatics and lock up my flat for weeks on end. I promised Debsey I'd see a doctor before we were to go to Europe.

The last thing we had to do before going away was to finish recording our contribution to the soundtrack for Alex Cox's film *Sid and Nancy*. Cox wanted another couple of songs. We met at post-production studios in Soho.

'Hot Dogs with Everything' was a song I had played with Shane in the Nips. After going through all manner of versions of the song – in the style of Costello and the Attractions, as a reggae song – Frank burst into the studio.

'Just play the fucking thing how you used to play it!'

Shane took up a guitar. We ended up lashing through the song even more unflinchingly than the Nips had ever played it. Spider bleated the lyrics. Shane abraded the middle eight with a guitar solo. He fisted the guitar, head down, and with such recklessness that I was embarrassed how quickly at my audition for the Nips I had admitted that I could do disconnected shards of industrial noise. I ducked out of playing guitar on the next song – a minute-and-a-half Millwall Chainsaws' song called 'Glued up and Speeding'. Abandoning the tyranny of tuning and refinement, Spider, Shane, Cait and Andrew hurtled through it.

The recording done, Alex Cox took Shane and Spider out to dinner in Notting Hill. Afterwards, as Shane was getting into a car, a black cab coming up Westbourne Grove knocked him down. He broke his arm and tore ligaments in his leg.

⚜

Portugal at the end of March was beautiful. Debsey and I stayed a week at a farmhouse in the Serra de Monchique which a German friend of mine shared with the other bus drivers in his hippie coach company.

What marred the otherwise paradisiacal interlude was the sleepless nights I had, while I nursed the conviction that I was falling out of love with Debsey. After the farm-dogs had finished their barking, my predicament regarding our four-year relationship seemed inextricably linked to the baleful rectangle of moonlight which slipped from the bedcovers to mount the wall and fill the room.

When I got back to England I went to visit Shane. His leg and arm were in plaster and he was going about with a walking stick.

'How was your holiday?' he sneered.

'How are you?' I asked. In pubs, he told me, people moved to let him put his leg up and got him drinks.

'Not much changed there, then,' I said.

It was the first time in a couple of years I found I had nothing to do. There was a rerun of the eleven-episode *Heimat* on the television. I took up driving lessons.

I went to see the doctor about the suppurating lesion on my foot and the pain in the crook of my left arm. For my arm the doctor prescribed an ointment, made, he said, from the pituitary gland of a pig. He suggested weight training and swimming.

D.J. was a keen weight trainer. He took me to enrol at a fitness centre he went to in Camden. Though we laughed that D.J.'s enthusiasm for weight training was due to the similarity of the endorphin rush to that of heroin, we respected his commitment.

Guilty about the ebb of my feelings for her, I spent a lot of time with Debsey. We went swimming at Kentish Town Baths. We went up again to my parents' country cottage in the Yorkshire Dales. In the course of an afternoon spent holding her hand while she sat crying on the bed in one of the upstairs rooms I finally admitted to myself that the end of the relationship was near.

Two days after the explosion at the nuclear power plant at Chernobyl, we went into the studio to re-record, as a single, Shane's song for *Sid and Nancy*: 'Haunted'. Frank had attached a producer by the name of Craig Leon. Leon had produced the Ramones' first record and had been producer's assistant on Blondie's début album.

Leon exuded the air of an American living in London. A smile played on his lips as if he was aware of being ahead of some sort of curve. He had grey hair and a dark beard. He had the flattering knack of making you feel that what you had to say he hadn't heard before.

We recorded the backing track at Olympic Studios in Barnes. It was another huge room with a venerable hardwood floor and walls of wooden panelling. The control-room windows frowned from beneath a tiled overhang. The Rolling Stones had recorded *Their Satanic Majesties Request, Beggars Banquet, Let It Bleed* and *Sticky Fingers* at Olympic. Led Zeppelin had used it for all their studio albums. So had the Small Faces, the Jimi Hendrix Experience, and Blind Faith too. 'A Whiter Shade of Pale' had been recorded there. The place was imbued with the sanctity of a cathedral.

The Phil Spector beat which had so far characterised the music we had made for *Sid and Nancy* found its apotheosis in Leon's production of 'Haunted'. He ladled guitars, electric and acoustic, over the pounding drum part. I sat in a huddle in a booth with Ron Kavana, Terry Woods and a guy I didn't know, each of us with an acoustic guitar on his knee. Terry played the guitar as if he were sweeping lint off his lapel. Ron Kavana dragged his pick backwards across the strings with elaborate flourishes. While we waited for the next pass, Kavana let me into the secret of strumming the mirror image of the take we had just done – starting the strumming on the upstroke.

'Makes it sound bigger,' he said.

After Cait had left Darryl's band Pride Of The Cross, Debsey had taken up singing with Darryl and Dave Scott in what was now known as the Troubleshooters. Debsey came into the studio one afternoon to sing backing vocals on 'Haunted.' Underpinning the staginess of Cait's voice, the line of backing vocal Debsey sang was limpid and unadorned.

Once construction was properly under way of his wall of sound, Leon brought up the matter of what was going to happen in the middle eight. I brought up an idea I'd had for ages, something I'd been doing at home, which was to set a mandolin flat on my lap and beat the strings with teaspoons, in the manner of a hammered dulcimer.

'Let's give it a try!' Leon said.

I knew Philip to have been waiting to play what would obviously be the guitar break. Philip happened to be out at the dentist. I was glad not to have to enter into a contest with him that I would probably have lost. By the time Philip came in at the end of the day, the middle eight was done. He looked crestfallen. The idea, though, was so direct a descendant of the rolling semiquavers of John Cale's piano on 'All Tomorrow's Parties', and so self-abnegatingly monotone, that I regarded it to have been inevitable.

Though not able to reinstate the entire European tour cancelled by Shane's broken leg, Frank and our agent Derek Kemp managed at least to put together a tour of France, with a sketch of another tour of the United States in June. The French tour began at the end of May, after an appearance at a charity festival in Dublin.

Using Live Aid as its template – and featuring Bob Geldof – the purpose of Self Aid, held at the Royal Dublin Society Main Arena in Dublin, was to highlight the quarter of a million unemployed in Ireland.

We met to go out to the site in the bar at Jurys hotel. The remaining members of Thin Lizzy, who were going to close the festival, sat nearby: Scott Gorham in a denim jacket, the chafed pinchedness of his face belying the silkiness of his locks; Gary Moore with a face that looked as though it had been wrapped in barbed wire.

We didn't see Cait or Costello until Cait turned up, in beatnik costume – leather jacket, leather hat, black slacks – at the RDS itself, where she announced her marriage to Costello that morning at a registry office in the city. The stage looked as if it had been decorated for their nuptials. It was all white, with white-painted monitor wedges, a white floor and a white backdrop – with the outlines of white Fender Stratocasters on it.

After playing the short set, I spent the rest of the day in a greenhouse of a bar backstage, paying scant attention to the concert, getting drunk with Eamonn Campbell of the Dubliners, missing Rory Gallagher, Costello and the Attractions and what was billed as the last performance of the Boomtown Rats. Towards the end of the evening I sensed the day reaching its climax and worked my way into the huddle of people by the side of the stage, where I craned to watch U2: Bono in a fringed suede jacket, his fingers continually sweeping his hair back; the Edge in a cut-off jean jacket and a brown derby with a playing card stuck in the hatband.

After the tribute to Phil Lynott by what was left of Thin Lizzy came the finale – as had become usual at events such as this one. The occasion and the pints of Smithwick's with Campbell up in the bar had gone to my head. I was among the first to heed the call for all the performers to come out onto the stage. I strode in. My drunkenness made nonsense out of the shards of coloured shadow from the lights. Everything besides was painted white. I didn't see the monitor wedge in front of me. One minute I was headed for the centre mike and Gary Moore and Bob Geldof and Bono and Chris de Burgh. The next it was as if my legs had been swiped from under me. I lay on my face for a second or two before I picked myself up and strode to the apron of the stage and threw my arm around Bob Geldof's neck.

In Paris on the first morning of the reinstated tour I woke up on the bed in the hotel, still dressed, with my legs hanging off the edge. My pockets were empty of all the money I had changed at the kiosk at Charles de Gaulle airport the day before. I lay there hopelessly trying to reconstruct the events of the previous evening.

If the amount I was imbibing had not affected my understanding, I would have known that, along with the amount I was already putting away, the nightly binges on the road over the next couple of weeks constituted heavy drinking. Debsey had not been so distracted by the trinkets I had brought back from America as not to have remarked on the blotchiness of my face from alcohol.

The day after we arrived in Paris was the first day of the World Cup, hosted by Mexico. Football was an enthusiasm shared by most of the group. Darryl was a keen Nottingham Forest supporter. Jem's allegiances were to Manchester United – as were mine, though nominally. Spider was an avid Arsenal fan. Costello and Terry, who I was given to understand had been something of a player in his youth, supported Liverpool. Charlie's loyalty to

Glasgow Rangers was so obdurate as to disable mockery. Shane was only capable of seeing football in terms of the sublimation of humanity's drive to annihilation. P.V. avoided taking sides. Philip seemed not to be interested.

'You're mistaking me for someone who gives a fuck,' D.J. said, when it came to the sport.

The first game of any significance for us was the match between Algeria and Northern Ireland. Our Irish connections sided us with the latter. Though the majority of its citizens were loyal to the English crown, the province was occupied by a colonial power. The Algerians, once occupied themselves but twenty or so years independent from France and still seemingly universally despised by the French, demanded our sympathy and respect.

We travelled along the Mediterranean coast from Marseille past the dream-like turrets and battlements of Carcassonne to watch the match in the time we had before the show, in the barely tolerable humidity of a bar in the centre of Toulouse.

The match was a 1–1 draw. Scully paid homage to the Algerians.

'Ah, the Al-jaysus-gerians!'

It was hot in Toulouse, so hot that one of the lads in the opening band we had – a Scottish band we had come to know called Nyah Fearties – fainted. After the gig the heat was no less intense, even when we had come off stage and were away from the lights.

One of us found a swimming pool in the grounds behind the club. Most of us stripped to our underwear and dived in. Despite the sweltering heat, Shane seemed happy enough to sit on the rim of a planter with his drink, watching.

I was treading water in the deep end, relieved to cool down, when a dark shadow blotted out the night sky for a moment. The black shape exploded in the middle of the pool, sending the water lapping over the sides. In a moment or two Costello broke the heaving surface, blowing spray, and swam to the edge. He had left his hat on a window ledge, but otherwise he had been fully clothed, wearing his black caftan and his shoes.

Provinssirock festival took place on the first weekend in June, two hundred miles north of Helsinki and towards what looked to be the north-westerly curling path of the radioactive plume issuing from the explosion at Chernobyl. On the four-hour van journey through the forests and lakes and the late summer sunlight, I shouted for a piss stop. The driver pulled over. Shane and I got out and made our way over a trench to the trees and out of sight of the road, Shane carrying a bottle of rum and smoking a cigarette.

I'd seen Shane piss before but not with such a clear view. We stood feet apart on the far side of a large fir tree. When it came to the matter of pulling down his flies, encumbered by the bottle of rum, he hooked down the band of his Y-fronts with his thumb and stood with his foreskin lolling in the gap. He looked round the forest without interest, squinting through the smoke from the cigarette in his mouth. He adopted no stance. He didn't even pull his foreskin back to piss, but allowed the rush, artesian rather than ejaculatory, to gout from the tan rosette, unconcerned about the drips going on his shoes or down the leg of his trousers. I looked down at the nose of darkened bark on the tree I had been pissing against. I carefully shook the last drops, stowed and zipped up. Shane's flux petered out. He lodged his cigarette between his lips, blinking against the smoke, tucked the bottle of rum under his arm and rummaged his penis away. We walked back to the bus.

At the festival, our evening set felt like the middle of the afternoon. The sun gave little sign of descending and slanted brutally down on the stage. It was hot too. Shane came so adrift with the words to the songs that we were forced to scramble, falling in behind him as he lurched unpredictably from choruses which should have been verses, into verses which should have been instrumental sections. In the sweltering Portakabin afterwards, P.V. came in from his redundant lighting desk, shaking his head.

'And he wrote the fucking songs!' he said.

I changed out of my sodden suit. Our driver that afternoon had indicated the lakes all around on our drive up to the festival and had warned us of mosquitoes. I counted forty-seven bites on my ankles.

At two o'clock in the morning I found myself wandering round the festival site. Diffused daylight, soft and ethereal, bathed the trees and grass and the multitudes of the sleepless, staggering about the site like me. In the hotel car parks I passed a barefoot group rummaging in the boot of their car full to the rim with tins of beer.

When I got back to the hotel and tried to sleep, the room was bothersomely bright. I lay in bed worrying about the path of the radioactive smoke trailing north-westward from Chernobyl. The Finns were restless too. From the car park below the window a prolonged and guttural bray of exhaustion broke the quiet.

Back in Paris, we finished the last three dates of the tour. In a week and a half, we would be returning to the United States – and to New York where I knew I would be seeing Heather, my blonde performance artist. Sooner than that I would be going back to London and to Debsey's possible admonishments about my drinking. I decided to put a buffer of sobriety between the tour so far and my return to London.

In Paris, we spent a day going from television studio to television studio performing 'Dirty Old Town' to a backing track. There was just one more gig to do on the tour and the impending sense of relief was palpable. Everyone else got drunk. As the morning went on, the more drunk everyone got, the later we became for everything. We swaggered into each studio, passing cheap wine between us. We were obnoxious. We slighted the director and laughed out loud at the voices that came through the speakers. At the end of the last taping before lunch Andrew kicked his drums all over the studio. His eyes were swimming in his head. No one but me seemed to notice.

We were taken to a restaurant on the banks of the Seine. I looked around at the other people in the restaurant. None of them seemed all that bothered by the rowdiness at our table. I tried to catch the eye of the girl attached to us by our publicist but she passed me over without eye contact. Not only did she seem not to notice Shane and Andrew and Spider's drunkenness, but she seemed not to care whether or not they would be capable of playing or mouthing in time to the backing track at the next taping after lunch.

I knew it was my sobriety which made their behaviour offensive. I knew it was my apprehension about returning to London which necessitated my sobriety. I knew it was my guilt about both falling out of love with Debsey and looking forward to going back to America which were the causes of my apprehension. I yearned for the day to be over.

Northern Ireland were on their way home from the World Cup in Mexico. England were through to the Round of Sixteen – to meet Argentina in the quarter-finals, two days before we were due to fly to the United States, in the first bloodless conflict between the two countries since the Falklands War. We would be in New York for the final. On this tour, we would strike out from the Eastern

Seaboard to Canada, the Midwest and California. I had never been to these places. The exoticism the upcoming tour held for me was both dreadful and exhilarating.

Twenty-One

Though Frank had been accompanying us on all our tours, when we returned from France he engaged a tour manager for a handful of dates. Joe Cashman was a guy in his mid-thirties of medium height, and thin. He had a sour-looking mouth with a derisory twist to it. He came from Dublin – 'from the Northside', he said, pridefully – and had been in a handful of Dublin bands: the Fast Skirts, DC9 and Tokyo Olympics. He was nimble of wit and mordantly sarcastic.

He worked with us for a week of gigs in England. Saying he would meet up with us in the United States, he was leaving to join the crew of a schooner sailing up the Eastern Seaboard to Providence, Rhode Island. That, together with the information that Cashman seemed to have been a professional potter in Norway, led me to build a romantic image of him.

The penultimate show of our sequence of dates in England was an early evening set on the opening day of Glastonbury Festival. The bill for the balmy Friday afternoon had been put together with an Irish flavour and included That Petrol Emotion and the Waterboys. We greeted the O'Neill brothers – two-thirds of the Undertones and now two-thirds of That Petrol Emotion – awkwardly. A couple of the Waterboys we knew. Anthony Thistlethwaite and Mike Scott had come over to play mandolin with us at Cibeal Cincíse in Kenmare.

The clouds started to come in and the temperature dropped.

As the rain began to come down on the Psychedelic Furs' set, to Cait's disappointment, we left to drive overnight up to Sheffield, our last gig before flying again over the Atlantic.

We had a meeting the following day. We hadn't agreed on a clear agenda other than Frank's hiring of Joey Cashman and the tour of America coming up. We took our places at the wooden table in one of the dowdy, panelled conference rooms at the Royal Victoria Hotel. Shane finished the bottle of wine he had been drinking and, if only to break the silence, released a belch. Spider groaned and rested his head on his arms on the tabletop. We were all tired after driving all night.

'Who wants to start?' Jem said.

'Spin the bottle,' Cait said. We didn't contest. She pushed Shane's empty bottle onto its side and sent it into a whirl on the top of the table. When it finally came to a standstill, it pointed straight to her. She slid her elbow into the middle of the tabletop and rested her face on her open palm.

'You know what I want to talk about?' she said. 'You,' she said to Shane. She twisted to look at Spider.

'And you,' she said. 'You both drink too much.'

Shane snorted, but when he saw Cait's earnestness he hoisted his eyebrows and dropped his chin in an expression of cartoonish culpability.

'I put it to the meeting,' she said, 'that Shane and Spider stop drinking.'

'Oh dear,' Andrew said.

'If you don't stop drinking,' she said, 'it's simple. You're going to die. You first,' she said, looking at Spider. 'Probably.'

Jem spoke up.

'I understand what you're saying,' he said, 'but I think this isn't the forum for this kind of discussion. I think it's something you would have to bring up with them, personally.'

'This isn't the *forum*?' she sneered. 'This is a fucking meeting, isn't it? I am so bringing it up with them, personally, I think, actually. I love him and I love him. I love all of you. To my detriment. I don't want to see anyone fucking die. He drinks too much. So does he. So do all of you, really, but these two are the ones who are the worst for it.'

Indicating Shane and Spider respectively, she continued, 'He can't remember his fucking words half the fucking time, and he can't handle drink.'

'Let's consider it having been put in the fucking minutes,' Spider said, bitterly. 'Shall we?'

'I don't want you to die,' she said.

'I'm not going to fucking die!'

'You will if you go on drinking the way you do.'

'Oh, shut the fuck up,' Shane moaned.

She was right. Off stage, Spider drank with reckless annihilation. In Norway, first thing in the morning as we were setting off to the next gig I had watched as he had tilted a bottle of vodka to his mouth so that it choked him, exploded from his face and gouted from his nostrils. After a show in Germany the previous autumn after upsetting his drink over the tabletop in a restaurant, he had picked up the straw and sucked the spillage up from the plastic tablecloth. In Nuremberg he had staggered round the stage holding a bottle of vodka and a knife, wearing his leather coat Wolfgang and shouting lines from *Once Upon a Time in America* at the audience. In the end, he had fallen over behind the drums.

I'd look across at Spider on the far side of the stage sometimes. When he wasn't playing, he held the whistle down by his side and waited with his eyes closed for the moment to play. He used to beat his thigh with his whistle in a fist. He used to snap his knee back and forth, jerking his skinny body, making his head flick. Now, he hardly moved. He became lost and would turn from the microphone in puzzlement at how the song we were playing had got away from him. In the studio too, some songs seemed to be a phantasmagoria into which he would step, full of purpose, only to realise in a couple of minutes that he was lost. He would stop where he was, take the whistle out of his mouth, and would shout out petulantly:

'Hey!'

Shane's alcoholism was a more intricate concern. Shane's condition was somehow innate, intrinsic to the subject matter and imagery in his songs, and consequently more worthy of attention. Shane's drinking was a more venerable enterprise, a swath cut by the likes of such writers as Brendan Behan and Dylan Thomas, not to mention Faulkner, Chandler, Fitzgerald and O'Neill. Shane's drinking came with the job. More and more the question on people's lips was whether Shane wrote so beautifully because of the amount he drank, or despite it.

In comparison to Shane's alcoholism, Spider's drinking seemed uncomplicated, and somehow temporary. It seemed to be performed with such irony that it drew us into a conspiracy of denial with him. It was so self-conscious that it distracted him and us from the addiction to which he was already committed. Because he made such a fuss about drinking, I had to assume that he knew what he was doing.

Spider's need for attention made matters worse. The more he sought it, the more we ignored him. The more we ignored him, the more he seemed to seek our attention. In the end some fucked-up covenant seemed to have been reached. His prating became background noise which we ended up tuning out. We dismissed Spider's musical contribution to the group. He aided and abetted us by sloping off to the pub when the process of extracting the songs from Shane became too boring for him.

The meeting closed with nothing decided. In a case of the medium obscuring the message, Cait's blundering artlessness prevented us from hearing what she had to say.

The first gig of our revisit to the United States was in Washington DC. At the hotel, after handing out A4-size itineraries, bound in black with a window in the cover, Frank distributed per diems. Both were such a novelty that I thanked him for the money, forgetting that it was actually ours. The following morning Jem, Andrew, Darryl and I had to go to the bank to get change for the hundred-dollar bills Frank had given us, indignant that the teller should charge for the service, and then to the post office where we sent money and our itineraries home to our families and the girlfriends we had left behind.

Once we were outside, Jem raised his face to the sunlight.

'It's beautiful,' Jem said. The sky was pellucid. The trees seemed to have been scored into the blue of the sky. The new growth on the branches was incandescent. The white-painted eaves in the neighbourhood were blinding.

Otherwise, after that, once the tour started, things were different. On the road, intersection after filthy intersection went by, the paving broken and the grass blackened. In the used car lots, the windscreens were blind with dust, the prices daubed with tennis shoe whitener. Everywhere were boarded-up windows and stores gone out of business.

Outside the window of my and Philip's room in Philadelphia, day and night, a queue trailed round the corner under an overhang. Men and women in filthy parkas or wrapped in blankets stood against the wall shuffling forward every now and then. One of the runners who plied between the venue and the hotel took a couple of us on a diversion through the African-American area of one of the towns. Couch grass covered mangy front yards and grew from the tops of street signs and in the gutters. Siding hung away from the houses. Stretches of rent chicken-wire clung to rusty poles. Fires made of railway sleepers burned, while men and dogs stood around and people sat on porch steps with their forearms on their knees.

⚜

During the furlough enforced by Shane's injury, I had welcomed the respite from Philip's ritual nightly, and bristly, embrace. During the tour of France I had occasionally managed to avoid it by staying out late or not coming back to the hotel at all or through the fluke of getting the single room. In Washington the ritual had looked like resuming. I held out. In Philadelphia a few minutes after we'd turned the lights out his bed erupted in a turmoil of rustling and thrashing.

'FUCK!' he shouted.

'What the fuck's the matter with you?' I said.

'I can't sleep!' he cried.

253

'You want to know how to get to sleep?' I said. 'You put your fucking head on the pillow and close your fucking eyes.'

'Oh!' he said. He fell silent. There followed a few moments of quiet before I thought I could hear laboured breathing. I lay in my bed and listened. The panting became more and more urgent until it sounded as if someone were going at a cinder with a set of fireplace bellows. I lay in the dark as he fought for breath, my mind veering back and forth from the possibility that it was a ruse.

'I can't breathe!' he cried out into the dark. 'I'm hyperventilating!'

All I knew about hyperventilation was that it was a symptom of panic attacks and that breathing into a paper bag somehow helped. I found a bag for the disposal of sanitary napkins in the bathroom. Soon, after a few cycles of inflating and emptying it with my hand to his face and my arm round his shoulder, he calmed down. When I finally got to bed, I was exhausted and miserable.

After our gig at the City Gardens in Trenton on the Friday, we drove up to New York. The city was festive. The Puerto Rican Day Parade was in a week. Already, fleets of cars snapping with Puerto Rican flags sped through the streets of SoHo sowing firecrackers behind them as they went. I sought out Heather. She was just as ethereal and lovely as I remembered. I was chuffed to see taped to the wall of her apartment a promotional poster for Jim Beam whiskey, which read: 'James is back!'

With a grim sheepishness though, she told me that she now had a boyfriend. They had been going out for a few weeks. I went out for a drink with them in the East Village. I went back to my hotel room on my own. For Debsey's sake I was relieved. For my own I was heartsick.

The day of our gig at the Ritz in New York City, it was over the mundane matter of whether or not we were going to be late for our sound check that my relationship with Philip came to a head. My patience had worn so thin with him that his peremptory injunction to wait before leaving to go down to the gig resulted in a final explosion. I picked up my stuff and slammed the door behind me. I managed to hail a cab before he came out of the hotel.

The only person to talk to about the state I was in with Philip was Frank.

'Why didn't you come to me sooner?' he said. 'We'll change the rooming list.'

I laughed at how simple the solution was. Without fuss, Frank put Philip in a room with Andrew. I went to share with P.V.

We left for New Haven in the evening after Argentina beat West Germany in the final of the World Cup. We hung out in a bar waiting for the minibuses to come. Heather came to see me off. She had left her boyfriend somewhere. Bill Rahmy came into the bar to usher us out to the Econoline which was parked out on the street. As Heather and I sat together on a wooden bench at the back of the bar we entered into prolonged kissing, her hand on my arm, my palm against her face. Caving in to Bill Rahmy's entreaties, I left Heather in the bar and walked across with Spider to where Bill had parked the van.

'Well,' Spider said archly, 'I wonder what Debsey's going to say when I tell her you've been mashing face with a blonde Yank.'

'What you don't know can't hurt you,' I said. Before I knew it Jem had lunged across and had pinned me up against the side of the van.

'You make me sick,' he said. 'Debsey is your girlfriend. She's my friend. And Marcia's too. The what you don't know stuff makes me sick. Fucking sick. I hope you have the courage to actually tell her what you've been doing in New York, though I suppose you won't.'

Jem stood for a second with his arms stiff at his sides like a bulldog's and then got into the van. Of all people, Jem's esteem was the one I valued the most. Bill Rahmy's huge arm round my shoulder could not assuage the doom I felt.

'That was beautiful,' Rahmy said. 'That was one of the most beautiful things I ever saw.'

For the next few days I found myself listening to the Stones' 'Gimme Shelter' over and over again on my headphones, loud. Such was the state I'd got myself into that the amp tremolo of the guitar tracing the song's opening chords did nothing but herald ruin, and on an almost mythical scale. The second guitar, the high backing vocals, Charlie Watts's syncopated drumming together with the rasp of the jawbone seemed hell-bent on turning the sunset into an apocalyptic cremation of my life. In the misery I was in over Heather and Debsey and Jem, when the low doomful piano chord sounded and when Watts smote the two snare drum beats and the cymbal on the downbeat of the next bar, and when the bass-line started up, and when Keith Richards's cruel blues bent-note swooped down on a menacingly constrained vibrato, it was the sound of the end of the world coming.

I drank heavily. After gigs, I drank pint glasses of the cocktail one of us had invented from tequila and grapefruit juice, topped off with champagne, and which Jem had called the Time Wharf. Striking away the remaining pillars that held up my relationship with Debsey, instead of going back to the hotel, I went home with whoever would take me. After our show in New Haven, predictably enamoured of American cars and the highway, girls and booze, but full of Time Wharfs, I made the girl who picked me up give me the wheel and drive her back to her place in the woods. Her car – not the Oldsmobile Delta 88 or Buick Skylark I wanted it to be, but a Toyota Corona – veered across the lanes. My companion reached over to steer it between the lane markings.

In Montreal, I found myself with a Canadienne française who took me down to her place near the St Lawrence River. She kept horses and fed me strawberries on the bed in the spare room until we ended up eating them out of one another's mouths.

Canada's sallow landscape – mile on mile of sere grass and bleached fence-posts – drifted by as we followed the St Lawrence Seaway to Toronto and back into the United States.

On our way to Cleveland, we stopped at a liquor store. I bought some grapefruit juice and miniatures of Gusano Rojo mezcal. A curled bug the colour of old paper floated in each bottle. Before long we all had pockets and bags full. We continued on our way, skirting Lake Erie and through Buffalo.

Shane appeared from the back of the bus.

'You supposed to eat the worm?' he said.

'Yes,' Jem said.

In a while Shane returned. He stood in the doorway. His eyes swam in an attempt to focus. His head tilted this way and that, as if the lashings tying something down in it had come loose.

'Got any more?' he said.

'You've had enough,' I said.

'Cunt,' he replied.

There was a nautical theme to the bar we set up in that afternoon. A galleon with rigging and mast pitched in the middle of the room. In place of the deck was the front-of-house mixing desk. The gig we played was atrocious, interrupted by vomiting and mezcal-induced vertigo and memory loss. Philip was incapable of standing. A chair had to be found for him. Spider became entangled in a stook of microphone stands by the side of the stage. Shane filled a bucket with puke.

'Jem's fault!' Shane said afterwards. 'He told me to eat the worm!'

'If Jem told you to eat your own shit, would you?' Spider said. Shane looked at Spider, surprised.

'Yes!' he said.

⛭

Outside the window of the hotel room in Los Angeles stood an immense, cut-out hoarding of Arnold Schwarzenegger as the T-800 Series cyborg in *Terminator*. His frowning visage was clawed open on the right side to reveal his hyperalloy endoskeleton. A penetrating red eye stared into the room. Beyond him a lattice of streetlights receded, twinkling in horrific perspective. Whatever preconceptions I had about Los Angeles – as a palm-fronded playground for lovely-looking people – were swept away. The scale of the city behind the Austrian bodybuilder did me in.

On our way to Hollywood from the airport, P.V. had pointed out a place called Barney's Beanery. Moments later we pulled up outside the Hyatt on Sunset. As was the custom, we had agreed to meet in the lobby in half an hour, to eat. As was the custom too, when I walked out of the lift, the soap-coloured lobby was empty – except for Shane, who was wandering about, seemingly lost.

'You eating?' I said.

'Yeah,' he said.

We waited a while for the others. In the end, exasperated and hungry, I suggested we just go to Barney's Beanery ahead of everyone else.

'You know where it is?' he said. I didn't but I reckoned it wouldn't be too difficult to find.

'Let's get a taxi,' he said.

'Let's walk,' I said.

'Walk?' he said. He clawed his face at the idea. 'This is fucking Los Angeles! No one fucking walks!'

258

My northern upbringing wouldn't permit the wastefulness of getting a taxi to a place I knew was walkable.

'I'm not getting a taxi,' I said. 'It's just round the corner.'

'Where round the corner?'

'I don't fucking know,' I said. 'Round the fucking corner. I saw it from the bus. We'll ask someone.'

I was shocked that he consented to come out onto Sunset Boulevard.

For a city of fifteen million there were surprisingly few people about. The boulevard was awash with orange light. Cars went up and down the street, their tyres slapping on the joins in the concrete road surface. We walked a couple of hundred yards along the pavement. A black guy appeared on the street.

'I'll ask him,' I said to Shane.

'You don't ask anyone in Los Angeles anything!' he cried. 'It's Los Angeles! No one's from here!'

I asked the guy where Barney's Beanery was. He shrugged and walked on. On both sides of the street the pavement was empty.

'See?' Shane said triumphantly. 'I'm going back to the fucking hotel.'

He turned round and started to walk back.

'Fuck,' I said.

Back in the lobby there was a guy in a cheap suit with a plastic name tag on the lapel.

'Ask him,' he said.

'Why don't you ask him?' I said.

'You're the one who wants to know where this fucking place is,' he said. 'I want to get a taxi. I don't need to know where it is.' I walked up to the fake marble desk.

'Do you know where Barney's Beanery is?' I asked him. He blew air through his lips, shrugged and lifted up his arms.

'Get a taxi,' he said.

I sat in the taxi fuming at Shane's victory. The cab plunged down a street opposite the hotel. At the bottom of the hill the brakes whined. The driver turned the corner and pulled up under a green-striped awning.

I sat in silence with Shane at an excessively varnished table in the back of Barney's Beanery, unsure if either of us was the winner.

⊹

During the day before our gig at the Palace, we traipsed miles in the stultifying heat hoping to come across a neighbourhood, high street or a centre of activity. The scale of the city under the beating sunlight seemed to defy the covering of distance by foot at all. Spooked, we ended up lounging around the pool up on the roof and, between cooling swims, puzzled about how the city worked.

The Palace on Vine Street was a Mission-style playhouse. The entryway dripped with ornamental stucco. Inside, everything was painted black, the gloom punctuated only by brass railings and strips of white tape on the edges of the stair treads. The bouncers wore black too. They were immense men, pyknic and broad-chested. They had hams for arms which were unable to rest flat against their sides because of the accretion of musculature. Each had a white-wall haircut and a black 4-Cell Maglite in a holster. Once I had become familiar enough with the guy on the door between the dressing rooms and the stage, I had a go at slapping him on the back as I passed through the door, as if earthing voltage. His shoulder was hard as concrete.

What need there was for a phalanx of such gorillas in the theatre, I couldn't see. The audience in Los Angeles, though appreciative, was subdued.

'Pot-smoking surfers,' Spider said.

At the beginning of August 1985, Alex Cox had organised a concert with Costello, Joe Strummer and us, at the Fridge in Brixton in support of the Sandinista National Liberation Front in Nicaragua.

On the strength of the success of the gig, Eric Fellner, the producer of *Sid and Nancy*, came up with the idea of organising a tour of Nicaragua, with the same line-up, in support of the beleaguered Sandinistas. Fellner's plan was to subsidise it by means of a video deal. All parties had apparently agreed to what would have been a month-long commitment. In the end, Fellner hadn't been able to find a company to fund the tour and the project fell through.

Instead, Cox's next project was to make an homage to Sergio Leone, with the same principals as the Brixton gig and the failed tour, along with a good proportion of the cast of *Sid and Nancy*. It was to be filmed in Andalucía, where Leone had made *A Fistful of Dollars*, *For a Few Dollars More* and *The Good, the Bad and the Ugly*. A script had been written. Eric Fellner was the producer. Finances had been settled. A start date had been set. It was to be called *Straight to Hell*, after the Clash's song.

After our show at the Palace and before we went home, Cox convened a meeting of the cast and crew in one of the conference rooms at the Hyatt hotel. The only actors I had come across had been those in my father's amateur dramatic circle – men dressed in tweeds with dewlaps under their eyes, women in polyester twinsets and a handbag hanging on a forearm. The table opposite us in the conference room filled with the most exotic creatures: a beautiful flame-haired woman with slender shoulders and a figure that was simultaneously girlish and voluptuous; a black guy with a face as mournful as a bloodhound's and an eyebrow cocked in perpetual quizzicality; a short man with a vaguely clerical face but with a beard which belonged to a mountaineer; an exquisite young girl, tawny, with hair of jet, whose shining half-bite alluringly prevented her mouth from closing. They were Hollywood actors. The fact that I did not recognise any of them did not dim their lustre.

Cox ranged from one end of the table to the other, talking the film up in his mid-Atlantic South Wirral accent. Now his gangly arms gesticulated. Now he thrust them in his pockets. We sat the length of one of the trestle tables, alternately tittering with the novelty of it all and gawping at the actors opposite.

On the plane next day, sitting across the aisle from me, Frank slapped a couple of blocks of A4 held together with brass fasteners on his knee.

'When he comes to visit Hollywood,' he said, 'the successful manager always leaves with at least two film scripts.'

The scripts made their way round the plane. One of them was a script for a Jonathan Demme film called *Something Wild*. The other was the script for *Straight to Hell*. If the plot was indiscernible, the characters indistinguishable and the dialogue gobbledygook, it was because all I could think about was that I was flying home to end my five-year relationship with Debsey.

I spent a day by myself in my flat. I threw the windows open. I swept the dead flies into a dustpan and flung their bodies into the courtyard. I broke the discs of penicillin in the coffee mugs with a spoon and scooped them into the sink. The next day I rang Debsey.

'I need to talk to you,' I said.

'Oh, it's chuck time,' she said.

'Yes it is,' I said.

Twenty-Two

It was September and it was hot in the south of Spain. As the sun passed over the open sea of the Mediterranean, the angled frontage of the Hotel Gran Almería focused the sun's rays onto a pool the shape of a dart-flight surrounded by crap loungers upholstered with slack plastic tape. First thing in the morning they would be empty but by eleven were full and would stay that way until evening. Regulars at the pool were a woman in a bathing costume slashed into slits at the waist and whose skin hung in bronzed silken folds from her arse down, and her partner, a guy with steel-grey hair, skin similarly russet, who I saw one morning standing in the poolside shower, his arm extended from the twinkling stream, holding a lit cigarette out of harm's way.

Some of us had rooms overlooking the breakwater of the Club de Mar and the palms of the Parque de Nicolás Salmerón, the grid of olive trees, the train tracks of the Cable Inglés elevated on rusted iron trestles which ended at the wharf and, beyond, the glittering Mediterranean. I had a room at the back with a view of a car park, the clock tower of the Palacio de Justicia and the palm trees lining the Avenida de Federico García Lorca. I would have been envious but I was too relieved to have a room to myself. We'd just finished a short tour of France and had flown from Colmar to Andalucía by way of Madrid.

As the cast of *Straight to Hell* arrived, the cool rotunda of the lobby with its pillars and its gleaming composite floor echoed with Americans trying to make themselves understood to the Spanish staff. The joke was that, sooner than repeat themselves more slowly, the Yanks merely raised their voices as if the concierge or the receptionist or the barman was deaf. The Americans whose voices reverberated in the rotunda and whose laughter exploded in the bar were Hollywood actors. The loudest of them all, when she arrived to play the part of the bank-robbers' moll in the film, was Courtney Love, between myself and whom I made sure to put at least twenty-five yards whenever I could.

To the Hollywood actors were added a slew more from London, just as striking to look at but less divisible into stereotypes. Whether they were from London or Los Angeles, most of the actors knew one another, having either worked on at least one of Cox's previous films, *Sid and Nancy* and *Repo Man*, or having otherwise crossed paths in their careers. The fact that I did not recognise any of them didn't matter. I was in awe of them and glum that my incorporation in the 'composite character' of the Pogues made me unremarkable.

I was Jimmy McMahon, one of the twelve siblings of the McMahon clan. Our dad was the American actor Biff Yeager. Our mother was Sue Kiel, the voluptuous flame-haired actress from Hollywood. Our grandfather was Jem, who since the filming of the video for 'A Pair of Brown Eyes' had been typecast in Cox's eyes as an old man.

The shooting location was twenty miles north of Almería in the Tabernas Desert. A dusty road from what was called Tent City, where the car park and catering were, led down past a couple of shabby brick buildings – a saloon with a covered walkway and opposite it a hardware store – to the plaza. Round a circular stucco fountain stood a Mexican-style pueblo of blindingly white, crumbling, mostly adobe buildings, including a church with a tiny bell in a tower above the front door. Beyond the plaza lay the otherwise biscuit-coloured expanse of the desert. The clarity of the light rendered the weathered wood of the window-frames and the water-tower luminous.

We didn't start off on the right foot with Cox. We had been given instructions not to shave for at least five days before arriving on location. Towards the end of our ten-day tour of France before flying to the south of Spain, a consensus had developed that we couldn't allow ourselves to be dictated to over the matter of our facial hair.

On the first day of work on the film we went to the costume department in one of the dilapidated outhouses up the dust road from the plaza. As we were tugging our gaucho outfits on, Cox strode in. He chided us about the unprofessionalism of arriving on set unprepared.

'Not acceptable,' he said, 'to have to change the shooting schedule until the band's ready.' He swept out of the building. I believed him and went hot with guilt that our collective vanity should affect the circumstances of a multinational cast and crew.

After that, I tried to demonstrate to the people I took to be seasoned practitioners of the craft of filmmaking that strangers to their profession as we were could at least be relied upon not to fuck up. As it turned out, make-up compensated for our lack of swarthiness until our stubble grew in. Cox's bluffness had been just bluff.

Nonetheless, as soon as shooting started I made sure I was quick to learn what the assistant director's honking instructions 'first positions' and 'checking the gate' over the walkie-talkies meant and to show that I could be relied on to pay attention to the orders 'hold the traffic' and 'quiet on set'. I showed the crew that I knew where to stand, how to get out of the way, how not to wander into shot. I remembered what I'd been doing in what I found out was called the master shot. I could be relied upon to replicate it in the medium and close shots. Above all, I wanted to distance myself from the disorder I expected Shane to wreak on a daily basis.

He never knew which one his costume was in the corridor of bare brick and exposed beams that was our dressing room, but we all figured it out by process of elimination. He looked puzzled on set, but it turned out to be the severity of the sunlight which I realised must have hurt his blue eyes. To my surprise, he paid attention and stood in the right place, if sometimes unsure of where his mark was supposed to be. He spoke his lines at the right time, though the ferocity and precipitation of his delivery seemed to startle him.

The heat was punishing. The crew went about in canvas shorts and T-shirts. They tied bandanas over their heads, squeezed fluorescent strips of zinc oxide down their noses against the sun. Our costumes were heavy black suits of ill-fitting trousers and jacket, decorated with gold thread and buttons, a grey flannel shirt and a bandana tied round the neck. They were suffocating. The black sombrero I had to wear trapped my head in a vice of hard felt. At the end of each day I was filthy with the dust. I reeked from the heat.

In the hotel, the actors in *Straight to Hell* for the most part came across as a professional, homogeneous and oddly suburban bunch. The odd voice might have been raised in an attempt to clear the language barrier, but by and large, proprieties and civility were observed. The men went about in loafers, chinos and polo shirts, the women in halter-necks, blouses, shorts, the occasional muu-muu.

When they turned up on location, though, the passage through wardrobe and make-up wrought such a transformation that when they arrived on set, they had been possessed by the most grotesque of psyches, the fellowship replaced by a hydra-headed monster of suspicion, supremacy and sexual tension. Why many of them needed to inhabit their characters so intensely and for such long stretches of time mystified me. The men lowered at one another with a mixture of hatred and suspicion. The women sneered with a combination of hatred, suspicion and lust. I tried not to let it go to my head. I told myself that they were actors, that they were acting. I tried to give as good as I got, but, being merely an element, and a fairly lowly one at that, of the composite character of the coffee-addicted McMahon family, and feeling increasingly out of my depth with these graduates of the Anna Scher Theatre School and the Lee Strasberg Theater Institute, I knew I would be the one to blink first.

Their behaviour on set resulted in my being leery of them when we got back to the hotel. I befriended Kathy Burke, one of the few actors who managed to maintain some sort of immunity. She was a doyenne of *Sid and Nancy* and had appeared in *Scrubbers* and a BBC production of *Bleak House*. We met in the bar most nights. Hers was Holsten Pils. Mine was a *Cuarenta y Tres con leche caliente*.

One of the worst was Joe Strummer, who seemed never to be out of costume, never out of character. He hunched about the set, squinting here and there, or sitting on his haunches in the dust idly drawing something in the sand with a stick, glamorously lost in his thoughts, or combing his hair into bituminous striations above his ears with a steel comb and machine oil, flicking the excess into the sand. He had comely eyes, shaded by brows set at a more or less dolorous angle. If he looked at you, it was from a level lower than your own, clerically askance, as if he expected to be pained by a secret from the confessional. It seemed he rarely slept in the hotel. The rumour was he walked about Almería instead or slept up in Blanco Town. An undeniable charisma clung to Strummer, not just from his history, though it helped.

Strummer played the part of Simms, one of the bank-robbers who arrive in town with a suitcase full of money which needs hiding. In the script, members of the McMahon family go up to where the bank-robbers are holing up in the saloon, to point guns in through the windows, block the swinging louvred door and otherwise scrutinise the bank-robbers' intentions. We'd done a couple of takes when Strummer came up to me.

'You've got to pick one of us, man,' he said. 'And that's the one you're going to kill if it all goes to shit. Pick me! Don't take your eyes off me! Not for a second. Do you know what I'm going to do next? No, you don't! A lapse in concentration and you're dead, man!'

In the script, as much as the arrival of the bank-robbers in Blanco Town threatens the town's equilibrium, and as much as the hidden suitcase full of money sets the townsfolk against each another, it's the bank-robbers' sexuality – particularly that of Simms and Willy – which deranges the entire community. The womenfolk vie for Simms's and Willy's favours, and not merely in the hope of discovering the whereabouts of the suitcase.

Dick Rude, another doyen of *Repo Man* and *Sid and Nancy* and the co-writer with Cox of the screenplay of *Straight to Hell*, played Willy. Rude was a diminutive guy with sloping shoulders. There was a steely dispassion in his eyes that gave me an attack of self-disesteem whenever he looked at me. I was baffled what women saw in him, both when he played Willy and when he played himself.

In the third week into filming, 'sexual tension' became the repeated phrase on set. Before the shooting of any scene which included Simms and Willy and the town's womenfolk, it was muttered as an incantation. Afterwards, it was huzzahed in celebration of its achievement.

It had been six weeks since I had ended my relationship with Debsey. I had a room to myself. It was the summer. We were surrounded by women. My susceptibility to sexual tension had been whetted by Olivia, a schoolgirl from the South of France whom I had encountered during our recent tour. A gaggle of teenagers outside the Roman amphitheatre in Nîmes, where we had just played, parted to reveal Olivia's severe profile as she pulled her blonde hair back and snapped it into a hair-tie. We ended up in the hotel pool where we played like dolphins until our eyes were raw from chlorine.

On the set of *Straight to Hell*, sexual tension clogged the air when it came time for the shower scene featuring the hardware-store owner's wife, Fabienne. Fabienne was played by Jennifer Balgobin, the tawny girl we'd seen at the meeting of cast and crew in Los Angeles. We studied her contours under the shower-head as she rinsed herself off – daftly, in an outside stall, and even more daftly in her clothes, skimpy as they were. Cox notched up the sexual tension even further when we were treated to the sight of Fabienne, again scantily clad, washing the chrome muffler of her husband's motorbike with a foaming sponge.

Jennifer had long, tan legs and slim shoulders. She was gorgeous, with dramatic eyebrows and abundant black hair. During shooting I would take in her form. At lunch I made any excuse to gravitate towards her.

She welcomed my flirting. She laughed at my jokes with the guttural abandon of a teenager. It turned out, though, that there was something going on between her and Strummer. I put it down to the script and the predatory and violent relationship between Fabienne and Simms the Englishman. Off set I saw little evidence of any relationship at all. Yet, when I squeezed myself in next to her on the bench in Tent City, I became aware of sidelong glances. In the end it seemed best policy to separate myself from her when it came time to return to the set where Strummer invariably hung out during lunch.

In the last week in August, the Parque de Nicolás Salmerón erupted with the Feria de Almería. Strings of lights looped from lamp-post to lamp-post. In the middle of the palm-fronded promenade a huge Ferris wheel turned, bright with bulbs. Huge caged barrels of iron and wood with seats bolted inside spun and tilted, flinging out over the park the screams of the people inside. There were teacups, twisters, waltzers, dodgems and orbiters. The seafront resounded with the cracks from the shooting galleries, the clangs of bells, the interminable squawking of the bingo callers. There was shrieking and rumbling, the hiss of hydraulics, the blasts of air horns, and reiterated again and again the blowzy trumpet theme of the 'Liechtensteiner Polka' which brayed throughout the dusty park as soon as the sun went down. Kathy Burke had one of the coveted rooms at the front of the hotel overlooking the park. She took to sleeping in the bath to escape the noise.

On the dodgems at the Feria one night, as I slewed my car around the edge of the rink, I saw Spider pass me. He was wearing his suit. He drove with a foot up on the dashboard. His left elbow lolled on the back of the seat as if framing an invisible passenger. He steered the car with just his fingertips. I came in on an angle and rammed him from the side. When I saw him again he was driving with both hands on the wheel, sitting forward with his knees together. Blood was trickling down his face from above his left eye. I couldn't bring myself to tell him who had rammed him.

One afternoon on a day off from shooting I wandered out of the hotel across the road to the amusement park. The Feria was quiet, though the Ferris wheel still turned above the strings of light bulbs pointlessly lit in the brightness of the afternoon. The sound of guitars at the far end of the park drew me to a warren of stalls with a small plaza in the middle and a makeshift bar. It was busy with stall-keepers and ride-operators before the Feria opened. In the bar a man and a woman were dancing flamenco to the accompaniment of a couple of guitarists sitting on boxes. The man's white shirt stuck to his back with the heat. The woman's face was haggard and red. Amid the abrasive *rasgueados* of the guitars, the cracks of fingernails on scratch-plates, the smacking of their audience's *palmas*, and shouts of '¡*Vamo' ya!*', the couple circled each other, their arms raised as if keeping an invisible veil aloft. They showed each other nothing but their profiles. The woman wheeled around as if to keep the man in her sight. She stamped, as if simultaneously to warn him off and bring him into line. Though their arms snaked, though her buttocks passed maddeningly close to her partner's groin, though her shoulders swept inches beneath his chin, they never touched once. Their deferred appetite for each other made me sulky with longing for Jennifer Balgobin.

Day after day, Cox strode about the set in shorts, dusty boots, a T-shirt and a bandana. Such was his will and his domination of the set that his eyes became all pupil, organs of total concentration, permitting not the slightest deviation from the matters at hand, one at a time: the length of focus, an actor's mark, the blocking of a particular scene, the motivation of one of the characters. If his focus and commitment were not reciprocated, he would become angry.

Cox looked benevolently, though, on our attempts to comply with his procedure. We had a rehearsal of the death of Spider's character, Angel Eyes, by a shotgun blast to the chest. The McMahons came running to the scene. We knew that Cox was going to ask us all what we had been doing off-camera.

'Burning an insect with a magnifying glass!'

'Squeezing Lance's nipples with a pair of pliers!'

'Good! Good!' Cox said.

The only sympathetic character in the film was a hot-dog vendor called Karl, played by Zander Schloss. Karl becomes the scapegoat for both the inhabitants of Blanco Town and the outsiders. In the script, at the culmination of an orgiastic party, Karl is marched to the plaza fountain to have his head dunked in the water.

The fountain was a stagnant sump. For weeks, it had been used as a general refuse bin. Everyone threw their cigarette butts in it. The grips extinguished brands in it. As the scene of Schloss's and his character's submersion in the filthy water approached, we were sitting around in the sand between the arches of the McMahon house, watching the grips set up the camera and the lights, rekindling the flaming torches around the fountain. Schloss appealed to us as to the legitimacy of having his head shoved into the water. He looked at us each in turn, his face mournful with foreboding, orange from the lights in the plaza.

We all agreed that the water was noisome and in all likelihood toxic with the fuel they put on the flaming torches.

'People probably piss in it too,' someone said.

'It's a film for Christ's sake,' Schloss said. 'It's supposed to be pretend.'

We all agreed that just because films looked real, they didn't have to be.

Emboldened, Schloss got up and walked across to where Cox was leaning with a foot up on the camera dolly and his long arms dangling crosswise over his knee. The conversation between them was inaudible. Suddenly, Cox stood upright.

'My God!' he shouted over Schloss's head. He tore his bandana off and threw it into the sand. 'You want to know how easy it is?' he shouted, as he strode past Schloss in the direction of the fountain. 'It's this easy!' He stopped at the low wall. 'This is all you have to do!'

In one movement, Cox plunged his head down over the edge of the fountain wall into the rank water until all we could see were the treads of his boots and his arse. After a few seconds, his head burst back into view with an explosion of breath and a cascade of water. He strode back to where Schloss had timidly returned to sit with us, stooping to retrieve his bandana on the way.

'Got that?' he said, his face dripping. 'Just keep your eyes closed and your mouth shut!'

·✠·

Soon we all started to be killed off. First, Jem's head was stove in by a Mayan sculpture and his body pushed off a roof. Spider, his chest full of buckshot, died in his mother's arms. In the dénouement, the McMahon family fanned out, to be dropped one by one: Shane by Strummer; Philip by Rude with a bullet in the middle of the forehead; me by our mother, the blaze-haired Sue Kiel.

As the tyranny of the heat, the boredom, the dehydration and the director set in, not to mention the sexual tension and the line that separated what was real from what wasn't, Shane seemed to have started to lose it. A couple of days later I came across him in our baking changing room, sitting on the lath bench.

'Can't you see what he's doing?' he said, his eyes staring out of his head. 'He's brought us out to the desert and he's going to kill us all out here! That's the plan! It's been his plan from the beginning, to bring us all out here and kill us all!'

I tried to reassure him. We were on a respite from the slog of touring, with plenty of time between scenes to doze in one of the hammocks that were slung in the shade in one of the crumbling buildings. It was pleasant to stretch out on the sand beyond the plaza and listen to the wind blow across the mouths of the empty bottles of San Miguel that were stuck in the sand.

Four weeks of desert heat, dust, sweat, filth, ill-fitting clothes, fireballs, gunfire, manic cackling, mock menace and sexual tension seemed to have turned his head.

At the end of the last day of shooting I dumped all my filthy clothes in the hamper in the wardrobe and got into the van back to the hotel. There was going to be a wrap party at a restaurant in town. Jennifer had consented to be my date. Strummer's wife and kids had arrived in Almería. The film finished, the tyranny of the script would be forgotten. In the course of the next few days, we would all be going home – myself to London, Jennifer to Los Angeles. I showered and, finally, after five weeks, shaved.

I found Jennifer in the darkened back room of the restaurant.

The place was as yet fairly empty. Chairs had been backed up to the wall for dancing. Fairy lights hung over the doorways. A mirror-ball hung from an extension cord in the middle of the ceiling. I was happy to be back in my suit and shirt. Jennifer was wearing a black satin dress, mascara and lipstick. I put my arm round her waist. She pulled away.

'He might walk in!' she said. I was stunned. I saw how Shane had come adrift of where the line was between real and pretend. I had thought that all the on-set relationships would end simultaneously with the wrapping of the film and the reversion to real life. Neither the end of shooting nor the arrival of Strummer's family changed anything, in effect. Strummer and his wife came in. The transformation from Simms into Strummer was hardly dramatic. He looked clean and wore a new pair of black jeans. His wife was blonde with long hair, parted in the centre. She looked round the room with neutrality. Jennifer stepped a couple of inches away from me.

It was hard to leave Jennifer. She was standing beautifully in an archway in the room, her eyes darting across to where the Strummers were standing. I ended up getting drunk and walking back to the hotel alongside the park, which crepitated with the sounds of the Feria.

Twenty-Three

At the beginning of October we went up to rehearsal rooms in Islington. In a month we would be going away to France, again, and Germany. We had been invited, with Irish musicians such as Paddy Reilly, Finbar Furey and Stockton's Wing, to record with the Dubliners to mark their twenty-fifth anniversary. There were a couple of songs they wanted us to learn: 'The Irish Rover' and 'The Rare Old Mountain Dew'. In addition, Shane had written a couple of songs for *Something Wild*, one of the scripts Frank had slapped on his thigh on the flight back from Los Angeles two months before. The songs were a departure from the kind of music that we had made our own. One of them drummed home, on end, the title of the film. I hoped the departure was temporary.

After rehearsal, the day before my thirty-second birthday, we packed up to leave. Cait laid her bass in its flight case, fastened it up, said cheerio and went home. We had never seen her take her bass home. Rehearsals were booked until the end of the week.

'What she take her bass for?' Spider said.

'She's going to practise, obviously,' Shane said.

'She never practises.'

The following day we remarked upon Cait's absence, but still thought little of it. I had brought champagne to celebrate my birthday. After an hour or two of rehearsal, I got drunk for the rest of the day.

By the end of the afternoon on the Friday, Cait still had not shown up. When I got back to my flat, I set about finding out where she was. I listened to half of Costello's outgoing message on the machine, in which his voice apologised for being unable to come to the phone due to a Bulgarian Secret Service poison-tipped umbrella, and then rang up his management.

Costello was in the United States on tour. The day Cait left rehearsal, Costello had been due to start three dates at the Warfield Theater in San Francisco.

Without much of a plan, equipped with the phone number of the hotel where Costello was staying under his current *nom de guerre*, Napoleon Dynamite, and careless of the time difference between London and California, I rang Costello up. He put Cait on the line.

'I've left the band, James,' Cait said in a tone so derisory that I found myself stumped as to what to say next. As in February, when I had taken the phone from the receptionist at the Iroquois Hotel in New York, I chastised myself for my lack of strategy. I had been naïve to expect her to give some sort of explanation. I put the phone down and sat for a minute staring at the carpet between my shoes.

We continued the rehearsals with Darryl once more standing in for Cait. He played the bass with sure upstrokes of his pick. Andrew was thrilled to play with someone who instinctively understood the importance of synchronising the bass guitar with the bass drum. Andrew's relief at not having to play with someone he had ended up loathing was palpable.

At the end of October the Dubliners arrived at Elephant Studios. Ronnie Drew was moist of lip and had doleful eyes which seemed eternally teary. John Sheahan wore a cheap jacket unbuttoned over a portly tummy and carried his violin case under his arm. An endearing derangement, as if he were continually getting his bearings, accompanied Barney McKenna as he went around greeting everyone, getting our names wrong. Eamonn Campbell, the Dubliners' producer and guitar player, had a head swathed in a Christmassy mist of nicotine-tinged white hair. With their hoary ostrich-feather-shaped beards they filled the control room with an air of the nineteenth century. A guy called Sean Cannon seemed to be the fifth Dubliner. Compared to the others, he seemed a boy with bum-fluff.

Terry quickly became the liaison between the Irish and the London-Irish, between the old guard and the vanguard, between the folk and the punk. Taking the Dubliners under his wing, he conducted a quick rehearsal, came up with a connecting figure between the umpteen verses of 'The Irish Rover' and otherwise guided us through the simple arrangement.

It was a hoot to play with the Dubliners, particularly with John Sheahan whose smile, exaggerated by his grey beard, never left his face as he gleamed in avuncular approval of me over the top of his fiddle.

After a couple of days in the studio, we applauded ourselves on our collaboration, sanguine with the consensus that it had been long overdue. Frank's suggestion that we should release 'The Irish Rover' as a single provoked Eamonn Campbell to give double-handed handshakes all round. We all parted company amid robust, manly body-hugs and fare-you-wells.

Our tour of Europe started off in Brittany. Such a bank of dry ice swathed the stage at L'Escalier in Saint-Malo that we were able to crawl undetected under it while our intro tape played. When the music had finished, we stood up into view.

The following morning at four we left the hotel to catch the train for Berlin. We were only one show into the tour and already we were done for. We were strewn around the waiting room at Saint-Malo Station in various postures of exhaustion. Shane was lying on his back on one of the wooden benches, his hands joined over his stomach, and his head tilted forward so that his chin was on his chest. Spider's hands dangled from his knees as he squatted on the floor with his back to the wall, his head sagging. Andrew sat cradling his head on top of his luggage. Frank came in to tell us that our travel agent had mistaken the weekday train timetable for the weekend's. It was a Sunday. I collapsed into hysterics.

In Paris, on our unexpected day off, Philip and I were crossing the Pont de la Concorde when we came across Costello and Cait coming in the opposite direction. Costello and the Attractions happened to be playing the first of two shows at the Olympia near the Boulevard des Italiens. Costello, dressed all in black, held his hat onto his head against the wind blowing up the Seine. Cait was tall in a long coat and felt hat. She'd dyed her hair red again. Costello hung back as she greeted us with a merriment that was brittle with *froideur*. Breezily, and I guessed to shorten the interaction, she invited us both to the Olympia that evening.

'Fuck me,' Philip said. 'What were the chances of that?'

I ended up going to the Olympia by myself. Neither Philip's name nor mine was on the door. I was about to turn away and go back to the hotel when I happened to see the Attractions' drummer Pete Thomas's face peering through the door which the security guy was about to close on me.

'I know you,' Thomas said. 'Don't I?'

After the show, I talked my way backstage. I paid my respects in the general dressing room where someone gave me directions to Costello's. I found myself in a plush chamber with damask wallpaper and red velvet upholstery where Costello and Cait were sitting on a sofa in a regal tableau. I said nothing about the absence of my name on the guest list. I hardly said anything at all. I could see that Cait's contentment to see me was that of a monarch for a public appearance at the crowd-control barrier. Cait's transformation from a kind of Olivia to Shane's Orsino, to a kind of Cleopatra to Costello's Mark Antony was complete. I didn't overstay my welcome.

We left the next morning for Hamburg and then to the Ruhr Valley. Throughout the tour so far, to let Darryl carry on playing bass had been the most straightforward solution to Cait's quitting. Yet we were persistent in our quandary about who should permanently replace her. We would find ourselves in huddles on the tour bus, muttering the names of various prospective candidates.

One of the names mentioned was that of Ron Kavana. I liked Kavana. I knew him to be a talented guitar player, he was good company and he was Terry's friend. The prospect of replacing the slender and proud, and above all female, form of Cait with such a boulder of a man – with the complexion of a rustic and the physiognomy of a pugilist – seemed wrong. We continued on our way down to Bavaria and into Switzerland.

In Geneva, Scully, Jem and I sat at the window table in the elaborately furnished upstairs room of a café, talking about Cait's replacement.

'I can't see what your problem is,' Scully said. 'You've got your bass player right there in the band already!'

Disinclined as I was to have Kavana play bass in the group, I baulked at admitting Darryl as a permanent member.

'He's just not cool,' I said. I sickened with shame as soon as I said it. It didn't help that Jem seemed to agree. I blenched at the idea that Scully might think we had such an elevated idea of ourselves. In an instant, the idea that we thought ourselves too cool for Darryl detached us, and without recourse, from any 'coolness' at all.

Scully laughed in our faces.

'What's not cool about him?' he said. We stared at him like a couple of schoolchildren caught in a lie. I willed Jem to take up the explanation, hoping to be able to hide my wretchedness behind Jem's authority while pretending that in fact we were shoulder to shoulder on the matter.

'I don't know,' Jem said.

The assumptions I had made about Darryl – that he was in some indefinable way not a 'Pogue' – were difficult to dislodge. Darryl was as indefatigable and as uncomplaining a musician as he had been our roadie, our driver, our sound and lighting engineer and our tour manager. Whenever one or other of us fell ill on the road, he was 'Dr Daz'. In the past couple of months we had given him the title 'factotum'. Yet his transition to band member remained unthinkable. It was as if the various manifestations of his uncomplaining devotion to us were accretions, like the unprepossessing shell of a geode, which prevented us from seeing the crystal core of Darryl as a member of the band.

When it came to our resolution of the problem of Cait's permanent replacement, Scully, Andrew and Philip shamed us out of our reluctance to take Darryl on board. As the rhythm section, Andrew and Philip were relieved to play with someone so dependable and so benevolent.

⊹

To share rooms with someone so carefully respectful as Paul Verner had been a relief. Though P.V. was predisposed to fretting and grumbling, he had been courteous in the extreme. When he had been in the room for some time, though, I noticed a strange smell of solvents. Not being able to pinpoint it, wanting to reciprocate his courtesy, I never remarked on it.

It didn't surprise me to learn that, rooming with Andrew since Frank had separated us in New York, Philip had formed an attachment to his new roommate.

The days of outvying each other with our acrobatics seemed to be over. Philip tended to range behind Shane no further than a couple of yards to either side of the centre microphone. His capers – pointing his guitar at the audience, twirling it round in mimicry of the tango, or spontaneously springing into the air with his feet tucked under his arse – he executed with a po-face. The byplay that I got up to became equally insular. For a time it was restricted to wagging my head a lot, stamping my feet or dropping to my knees at the end of a song.

In a beer hall in Germany though, I watched an accordion player in full regalia – lederhosen, Tyrolean hat and white knee socks – turn around in tiny shuffling steps, holding his accordion over his head. It looked stupid, but the image of someone holding an accordion over his head – even someone looking as though he'd just stepped out of a Grimm Brothers' illustration – was so improbable that I wanted to try it. My accordion was twenty-five pounds in weight, not to mention the three microphones that were gaffer-taped to it. I was hampered, too, by an udder of XLR connectors and their cables. Aided by something I'd read in a teach-yourself-judo book when I was a child – which stressed using your assailant's weight to your advantage – in the middle of one of the gigs, I managed to hoist the accordion in an arc over my head and to sweep it down as if it were a flag. I was so chuffed with myself that I made sure not to betray the slightest sense of pride in what I'd done by doing something so crass as to look to see if anyone had noticed.

As the tour continued I persuaded myself to become inured to the volume Terry played at. If I could, I got out of the way and into whatever safety zone I could find. I decided to regard his amp as if it were a turbofan I could be sucked into at any moment if I stepped too near.

Shane spent most of the time in the back lounge of the bus, writing and drawing cartoons crowded with hideous, densely drawn characters called Bim and Bom, a Russian clown duo from the 1920s whom Samuel Beckett featured in his writing. Occasionally he came aft to sit at one of the tables where he would sit and talk, tap the tabletop or the side of his bottle of wine, sniff, clear his throat. He never set his drink down in one of the holes in the Formica table for the purpose. He preferred to let it dangle between his knees. He never reached over to the ash-tray to flick ash off his cigarette. He preferred to let it smoke away between his onionskin-coloured fingers. After a while, he would fall asleep.

It was seldom that I sat near him. On a recent flight I had had the misfortune to be seated next to him. I was relieved that he had fallen asleep, his tray full of various drinks, one of his hands, again, unwilling to let go of the glass of wine on his tray. My relief was short-lived. He woke with a spasm that caused him not only to shout out loud, but also to jerk his knees upward and send everything on his tray everywhere.

One afternoon he happened to come to join Jem and Andrew and me at one of the tables near the door to the back lounge. We let him in to the seat by the window, where he sat, sniffing, bash-ful of the attention he thought he had caused by coming out of his den. He tried to downplay it by staring with fake concentra-tion at the passing trees.

We all talked for a while. Andrew got up to go and lie down somewhere. Jem retreated into his book. I watched the frieze of forest slide by the window, punctuated by the occasional ham-let or the forest dropping away beneath us as the bus went over a bridge. I could see Shane falling asleep, his feet stretched

283

beneath the table. Soon his tatty head had lolled back. His eyes closed, but not quite. His jaw hung open, revealing the adhesive barm which collected in the corners of his mouth. A twisting blue sleeve of smoke undulated from the soggy cigarette between his swollen knuckles. In his other hand his bottle of Piesporter nestled precariously between the Zantac-encrusted legs of his trousers.

Sleep came upon him this way. He never planned it. He was heedless of the fact that the passage of time was divided into dark or light. Whatever sleep-cycle he might once have had, he had bent into more or less a straight line, punctuated with random periods of unconsciousness. These periods didn't synchronise at all with the diurnal round, nor much with the routine of being on the road. I pitied him for it and for what seemed not so much his fear of unconsciousness but the transition into it. The workings of his intellect were tireless and gave him no release. A malevolent energy possessed him. It goaded him to talk, draw cartoons, scrawl lyrics across crumpled pieces of paper, clink the rings on his fingers incessantly against the side of his bottle of wine or on a tabletop, tap his foot on the floor.

With him sitting dozing off opposite me, I found myself in a constant state of watchfulness. I knew the butt was going to fall out from between his fingers onto his filthy trousers. I knew that it would burn down to his skin. I knew he would wake in a fury of batting and shrieks and resentment. His bottle of Piesporter made me anxious too, suspended from his fingers.

I tortured myself as to whether I should remove the dangling bottle to safety. I fretted about whether I should nip the smouldering cigarette out from between his smoke-tanned fingers and put it out in the ashtray. The trouble was that I couldn't entirely convince myself that Shane had actually gone to sleep, since, as when he sang, the pale blue of his irises was visible through the lashes. If I didn't act now, though, the outcome looked likely to be not only that the bottle would fall and spill and the cigarette end burn him, but also that he would blame me for wetting his trousers and shedding his Piesporter all over the floor of the bus. As much as I told myself it would be a simple act of kindness I couldn't put out of my mind the time I had aided him down the street from Dingwalls, after the two Black Zombies had rendered him spittingly abusive, resulting in his calling me a sanctimonious cunt.

At the end of it all, I leant forward to pluck the bottle out from between his fingers and nip away the burning cigarette. He woke up instantly and lunged for the Piesporter.

'Aagh!' he screamed. 'What the fuck!'

He flashed a look of fury at me. I regretted my compulsion to help him, and to try to do so without detection. I burned with shame at my presumption to think that I could help him at all, with anything.

We ended the tour – a cold, drear and dismal three weeks – in Utrecht. It was a freezing night. The sky was wintrily mauve. A fog had descended which formed a nimbus round each of the street-lights outside the Muziekcentrum.

After the gig we flopped on the wheezing leatherette banquettes round the walls of the dressing room, a huge chamber with white walls of breeze block, harsh with fluorescent strip lighting. A grand piano stood in the middle of the fibrous, rust-coloured carpet. I felt vaguely disappointed to have completed three weeks of a tour with a gig that was indistinguishable from all of the others we'd done. We would be going home in the morning, but a couple of days later were due to play the National Ballroom in Kilburn, followed by another two weeks of what seemed to have become the expected Christmas tour, ending the Saturday before Christmas in Dublin.

The separation of tours had become illusory. The transition from landmass to landmass had become more or less meaningless. The printed itineraries which Frank handed out to us at the beginning of each tour looked identical to one another. The exchange of one bus driver for another had become irrelevant. By the last gig of the year in Dublin, we would have been on tour for thirty weeks.

Twenty-Four

At the beginning of February 1987, we went again to Elephant Studios to record music for the soundtrack of *Straight to Hell*. Shane had written a couple of songs. I had once criticised Shane's songwriting as a matter of stringing a load of swear words together and making them rhyme. He never let me forget it. 'Rake at the Gates of Hell' was a stream of invective submitted to meter and a rhyming pattern. He was so unsure about its biliousness that he went to seek Jem's absolution for having written it. The second song was called 'If I Should Fall from Grace with God'.

The opening melody of 'If I Should Fall from Grace with God' was gorgeous. I loved the unaffectedness of the pentatonic scale and its passing embodiment of 'The Bonny Banks o' Loch Lomond'. The song was as elemental as the best of all Shane's songs. It had mud and land and rivers and oceans and corpses in it, in a landscape as expansive and ancient and threatening as the melody, bringing to mind the high road and the low road, one of which – after the Jacobite Rising of 1745 – led to death.

The remaining pieces for the soundtrack were instrumental, inspired by our five weeks in the south of Spain: boleros and tangos, with *zapateado* and *palmas*.

After recording 'Rake at the Gates of Hell' and 'If I Should Fall from Grace with God', Shane did not return to the studio much. The week at Elephant was my first experience of composing: a bolero based on a melody from Anton Brückner, played on a pan-flute; a piece of incidental music using the drone made by blowing into the mouth of a bottle of San Miguel – the sound I'd listened to, lying out on the sand beyond Blanco Town. Cox also wanted a treatment of Mussorgsky's *Night on Bald Mountain.* I sketched out an arrangement on a couple of pieces of foolscap and played it on a honky-tonk thumb-tack piano.

Spider showed up a couple of times during the recording. Snow had descended on County Cavan and had isolated Terry in what I imagined to be his lodge – a squat, rain-lashed pile in the wilds of the Irish countryside with a clapped-out BMW of rare vintage immobilised in the driveway.

Cox had finished editing the film and came to us wanting a version of Ennio Morricone's 'The Good, the Bad and the Ugly'.

'To save the film!' he said.

In an attempt at hip-hop, we built a beat on the drum-machine they had at Elephant Studios – instead of a real drum kit and against the advice of D.J., who knew about hip-hop. We layered samples taken from Morricone's original music – bells, gunshots and Eli Wallach's shouts of 'Blondie!' – over the top, along with the banjo, accordion, tin whistle. I borrowed Darryl's Gibson SG guitar with the late-night idea of emulating Steve Vai's guitar-playing on Public Image Ltd's *Album/Cassette/Compact Disc* which had come out the previous year and for a time had taken a place in the constellation which included *Rain Dogs.* I didn't possess a shadow of Steve Vai's talent, but I thought at least I could pull off a handful of stock heavy-metal licks. I had never yet been able to rid myself of the sometimes elegiac compulsion to impress Shane. The Eden of his estimation of me, it seemed, had been when I had been a guitarist.

We pridefully brought a cassette of our finished version of the song into the Devonshire Arms to play over the pub's sound system. As soon as the drum-machine beat started, I knew it was wrong. I wanted it to sound powerful and authoritative, but instead my shirt stuck to my back to hear how lame it was and how my playing sounded like guitar-shop guitar licks. The drum pattern turned out to be several thousand miles distant from Run-DMC and more in the province of Ultravox.

·✠·

Soon after we'd finished recording, Philip admitted himself to hospital. Other than his looking more haggard than normal at Elephant, I hadn't noticed anything particularly the matter with him. The explanation was that he had been drinking too much and had cutaneous oedema.

I went to visit him. He was sitting up in bed in a hospital gown, reading. There was a stack of books on the bedside table. There was a hollowness to his cheeks which made him look mournful. Though his complexion was only ruddy at the edges, he looked hale enough. His hair had a lift to it as if the hospital barber had been to visit.

'I'm an alcoholic!' he said. 'I had to admit that to myself. It's the first step to my recovery.'

I was surprised. During the months he and I had shared a room, his drinking had been nothing to remark on. I hadn't noticed that he had been drinking any more than the rest of us. Our drinking of an entire bottle of schnapps on the Baltic Sea, resulting in the perforation of his ulcer and near-death, was a distant memory. He swung his downy leg out from under the bed covers.

'Look what happens when I do this,' he said. He leant down with the full weight of his mop-handle forearm onto the top of his bare thigh. We both watched as the impression it left filled in.

'Water retention,' he said.

In the third week of February, seeming to have neither improved nor deteriorated, he was out of hospital in time to begin promotion of the single release of 'The Irish Rover'. Frank's suggestion after recording with the Dubliners had become a reality.

First we flew to Dublin to appear in *The Late Late Show*'s tribute to the Dubliners, where we performed with Christy Moore and U2. The latter and their entourage drifted through the corridors with ecclesiastical gravity.

His appetite for acting whetted by our four weeks in Andalucía, Spider left for Nicaragua to take a part in Alex Cox's next film, *Walker*, with Ed Harris and much of the cast of *Straight to Hell*. We flew without him to Northern Ireland for our next promotional appearance at the *Tom O'Connor Roadshow* in Derry's Guildhall.

The damp countryside of the Six Counties was still bleak from the winter, though the ochre turf, where it was exposed in banks and in the hillsides, was almost lambent in the late-afternoon sunshine. In the middle of the fields stood small A-frame pens, we guessed for the sheep to find shelter, though in each there would only have been room for one.

'You know what they're doing in there,' Terry said, in a low voice.

'What?'

'They're plotting,' he said.

We were staying in a hotel just outside Derry. Ronnie Drew, we were told, was staying at a hotel across the border between the Six Counties and the Republic. The very idea of staying in the part of Ireland that was still under British rule was anathema to him.

Most of our promotional appearances were a matter of miming to a backing track. With the exception for the most part of the Dubliners – particularly Drew, who I was told had been off the drink for a few months – and Philip, recently out of hospital, it relieved us of the necessity to stay sober. At the minimum, for the cameras, it should look as though we could be playing our instruments.

At the *Tom O'Connor Roadshow* we performed in a large hall to an elderly audience in frocks and blazers. Shane and Drew sang live. Shane stood tall, jug-eared by virtue of a recent haircut, one hand in a pocket. During the alternate verses he turned to watch Drew singing, then, closing his eyes, sang his own verse, awkward and suffering with abashment.

Afterwards, we found ourselves in the mayor's office. It was a severe, wood-panelled room with a couple of huge oak desks, one of which spanned the bay window. Part of the room was lined with bookcases, the other ranged with portraits. Pediments capped the hefty doors. We sat around one of the desks with the mayor Noel McKenna and John Hume, the leader of the Social Democratic and Labour Party. Hume was a red-faced teddy bear of a man. He had a chin set halfway up his face and wiry sprouting eyebrows. His eyes flashed with the thrill of being in the same room as the Dubliners.

A bottle of Tullamore Dew appeared and went from man to man. It wasn't long before we were all singing 'The Auld Triangle' – the mayor, the leader of the SDLP, together with the journalist and Northern Ireland Civil Rights Association organiser, Eamonn McCann, and James Ellis, the actor who played Bert Lynch from *Z-Cars*, the Dubliners and ourselves. Hume's face glistened red with drink. Terry's head twitched with emotion. Shane sang to the floor, his face solemn with meaning. I regretted Spider's absence. He would have exulted in the occasion.

'Well,' I overheard John Sheahan murmur to Eamonn Campbell. 'Ronnie's well and truly off the wagon.' I looked round at Drew. His eyes were swimming in their sockets, red and straining to focus. He was resting on Barney McKenna's shoulder, leaning into his face, cackling piratically into his ear.

When it came time to leave, the bottle of Tullamore Dew was gone and most of us were drunk. Drew stated his intention to drive back to Dublin that night. The other Dubliners implored him to stay.

'I'm not staying one fucking night in this fucking province,' Drew said. Red-faced and gesticulatory, they argued about how they were going to get him home.

'For fuck's sake let Barney drive your fucking car!' they beseeched. In the end, Drew consented. We hugged the Dubliners goodbye, clapped them all on the back and said safe home, see you in London. We were all booked to appear that weekend on a programme called *Saturday Live* for Channel 4. We got into the van to go back to Belfast.

When we met again for camera rehearsals in London, as he came into the studio in mackintosh and wine-coloured dark glasses, there was a contrite air surrounding Drew. As it turned out, his car had been an automatic. McKenna had become confused by the scarcity of pedals and had set the car off lurching down Queen's Quay to the Foyle Embankment where the alternating screeches and bursts of speed attracted the attention of a patrol of the Royal Ulster Constabulary Traffic Branch, who pulled the car over.

Realising who they had in the car, charges of drunken driving or even driving without due care and attention were not brought. Instead they were each given a cell at a nearby police station to sleep it off.

When Drew woke the following morning, he woke the others with his shouting.

'Barney! What kind of fucking hotel is this you booked us into?'

I could only imagine his chagrin on coming round: the ruination of his principle of never staying a night in the Six Counties, and in an RUC cell.

At *Saturday Live* the Dubliners were introduced to the floor of predominantly teenage dancers as the Dub Liners.

When 'The Irish Rover' reached No. 12 in the charts, we reconvened at BBC Television Centre in White City for *Top of the Pops*.

During the rehearsal, before we ran through the song for the cameras, I saw Frank take Sean Cannon to one side, to inform him that since Spider was away in Nicaragua he would be playing the whistle. Cannon demurred.

'Sure everyone where I live knows I don't play the whistle,' he said.

'You do now, right?' Frank said, his falciform nose a foot away from Cannon's schoolboy face.

Again, I had no real work to do, other than pretend to play the accordion and do my best not to indulge Campbell's excitement too much. During performances of 'The Irish Rover' his yellow-toothed smile and his crazed face, surrounded by a haze of nicotine-coloured hair, would appear bobbing in front of me.

Towards the end of April, our last television appearance with the Dubliners was for RTÉ's *Sunday Night at the Gaiety* in Dublin. By the end of the week 'The Irish Rover' vanished from the charts.

⸎

At the end of March, between our performances on *Saturday Live* and *Top of the Pops*, we started our next album, in the Penthouse of Abbey Road Studios. In order to circumvent our contract with Stiff Records – from legal necessity or not, I didn't care – Frank enjoined us to let no one know, going so far as to pretend we were assisting Terry in a solo project. The sessions became known as the *Terry Woods Solo Album*.

We had already been rehearsing what we thought might be described as a Tex-Mex song, called 'Fiesta'. Jem had not only written the melodies of both the verse and the chorus, but had composed an instrumental section too, folding into it a couple of lines from the 'Liechtensteiner Polka', which we had all heard blaring out over the Parque de Nicolás Salmerón during the Feria de Almería. We walloped the song out over a norteño beat, with a bass-line restricted to fifths, the guitar on the offbeat, and as much as I could replicate on the accordion from a couple of tracks on Los Lobos' *How Will the Wolf Survive?*.

We played the song back in the control room in the Penthouse. The gaps after the choruses and throughout the instrumental melodies begged to be filled up with the cracks from the shooting galleries and the clangs of bells, the whistles and shouts we'd heard throughout the Feria de Almería. To demonstrate, I detached the top of one of the steel ashtrays in the studio and at the right moment dropped it into the metal waste-bin in the control room. Otherwise I made finger-pops, stuck my fingers in my mouth to let loose a Swanee whistle, or, as I had as a kid, mimicked gunshots with a plosive clearing of the tonsils.

Though still apparently embroiled in an endgame with Stiff Records, we came out of our bolthole in the Penthouse of Abbey Road in order to start work recording our next album in plain sight. As a precaution, Frank suggested we finance the recording ourselves. We set up our own label, Pogue Mahone Records, owned by Warner Music Ltd. Through his previous management and tour management of Kirsty MacColl, Frank was able to secure Kirsty's husband, Steve Lillywhite, to produce the record.

We were excited to start, and with such a producer as Lillywhite. Frank was also in high feather, though he tried to hide it behind managerial aplomb, having persuaded Lillywhite to accept a reduced royalty and to decline an advance. Spider was back from Nicaragua with a goatee and moustache and a face swarthy from the sun.

RAK Recording Studios was a converted Victorian schoolhouse in St John's Wood, with stern pillars framing the front door. The studio itself – the control room and the live rooms – was bright with light from the windows which ran the length and width of the building.

Steve Lillywhite was resolutely but ashamedly English, well spoken, meticulous in his manners and genial. His breezy affableness, though, tended to bring on a discomfiture which he would cut short by moving on and getting on with matters in hand.

Lillywhite was quick to admit that he had never recorded instruments such as the cittern, banjo, accordion and whistle, but

he doughtily clapped his hands, rubbed them together and said:
'Right! Let's get started shall we?'

Lillywhite's engineers, Nick Lacey and Chris Dickey, divided the large window-lined live room in half with a screen. It wasn't long before those in the front half – Philip, Andrew and Darryl – were calling themselves the Engine Room, and the rest of us – Jem, Spider, Terry and myself – the Bridge. Shane had a booth to himself by the side.

We had already rehearsed many of the songs. 'The Broad Majestic Shannon' and 'If I Should Fall from Grace with God' we had been playing for six months. 'Turkish Song of the Damned' we had been playing since the previous August.

Philip had been writing his song 'Thousands Are Sailing' for months. He managed to finish it after the end of our session for the soundtrack of *Straight to Hell* and a few days before he went into hospital. It dealt with the ocean passage of Irish emigrants to New York. I adored the song and let myself be persuaded that at least part of the lyric was about me. There were lines about a couple of guys in New York City visiting, as Philip and I had, the statue of George M. Cohan, and a line about whistling.

Shane had written a song about the Birmingham Six. It was as powerful as any song he had ever written, and sharpened to goading point. Terry happened to have written a song from the point of view of someone leaving Northern Ireland during the Troubles, vowing never to return. Because of the congruence of theme, we spliced the two songs together. Terry sang the first part, and plaintively. Shane sang the heavy end of the song, which concerned the continuing incarceration, after twelve and a half years, of the Birmingham Six, sentenced to life imprisonment for the Birmingham pub bombings in November 1974.

Halfway through recording at RAK, Lillywhite took a break to work on a Talking Heads record. We used the hiatus to play more or less weekly festivals in Europe, and support slots for U2 on their Joshua Tree tour.

We arrived at Wembley Stadium for the first of our opening gigs for U2 early enough in the afternoon that the turf hadn't yet been covered and before even the goalposts had been taken down. Jem and I broke out from the mouth of the goal furthest from the stage. We deftly passed an invisible football between us, leaving behind us a trail of wrong-footed, imaginary opponents. When we got within eyeshot of the goal, I went wide, sent my non-existent marker the wrong way and lifted the ball over the baffled defenders. The ball met the lateral arc of Jem's left foot and he volleyed it into the back of the net. We both went down on our knees and raised our fists to the sky.

A couple of weeks later we opened for U2 at Croke Park in Dublin. Before our set, Frank went to stand on Hill 16. After our set, I went out into the audience and jammed my way as far towards the front into the crowd as I could. The pounding of Adam Clayton and Larry Mullen Jr, in andante tempo, supported a glittering superstructure of the Edge having as much fun as can be had with a WEM Copicat and an electric guitar. Bono's singing was the grand incantation of phrases resembling advertising copy. I jumped up and down in synchrony with the crowd, pulling my arm out of the squeeze to stab the air like everyone else. I hoisted a girl onto my shoulders to give her a better view. Her bare thighs muffled the pounding of U2's music.

In Paris we opened for U2 again at the Hippodrome de Vincennes in front of a crowd of two hundred thousand. We wandered out onto the stage like lambs, gawping at the immensity of the horde. It stretched so far back that the details of the sweaty heads, the waving banners, the girls on shoulders, the bare chests, merged into the colour of Plasticine before seeming to curve out of sight beyond the horizon. Somewhere in the middle of the throng, as if to illustrate the magnitude of the crowd, I watched a distant refuse truck slowly part the multitude, going from one side of the field to the other, like a bug.

Intimidating as the size of the stage and audience was, it came along with a requirement to produce something resembling a grand gesture, a vindication of swinging my accordion over my head, buckling up over the keyboard, foot-stamping, dropping to my knees.

·✠·

Back at RAK in the second week in July, the heat was oppressive. We came upon Lillywhite standing with his back to a fan wobbling in the open fridge he had had brought into the control room. It blew damp air into the room to a distance of maybe three feet.

The irony of tackling Jem and Shane's Christmas song, 'Fairytale of New York', in the sweltering heat was lost on us. By now, our problems with it had become so chronic, threatening to inure us to the idea that the song was probably just impossible to record, that we became even more determined to find a way of recording it. Lillywhite's solution was so straightforward as to provoke you to slap your palm to your forehead: to record the introduction – the piano and Shane's voice – first, and treat the duet with the full band as a separate song. We postponed the problem of who was going to be Shane's partner in the duet. A couple of names had been put forward. Shane had been keen to have Chrissie Hynde sing. She had been at RAK in any case. She had come across us in the canteen and berated us for our carnivorism.

Lacking someone to sing the female part, we recorded the section in 6/8 time with Shane supplying both. It still made as much sense as it had in rehearsal. We moved on.

In preparation for the piano and voice introduction, I took whatever opportunity I could – while the others had lunch, or after dinner – to go down into the darkness of the live room to figure out and practise, again and again, my piano arrangement. I wanted my accompaniment to sound sophisticated and adult. Because the song was set in New York, I wanted to include identifiably American harmonies in the chords – chords with second and seventh intervals that I'd heard in Aaron Copland and Leonard Bernstein, in Tom Waits's songs too. Shane had a maddening talent for metabolising artlessness into beauty. Everyone else had to work at it.

When it came to recording it, I didn't want merely to play the chords and follow Shane's vocal melody. I wanted to make what I had come up with inextricable from Shane's voice. I made the appoggiaturas I played synonymous with the ones Shane sang. I made myself Shane's equal, at least for the time it took to play the introduction to 'Fairytale of New York.' I made myself not fuck up too, despite the fact that the more coloration I had put into it, the harder it became to concentrate on what Shane was singing.

The whole agonising precarious minute and a bit, as I hung on every moment in which neither Shane nor I fucked up, was an ordeal. I attended to every syllable of Shane's voice in my headphones. I was morbidly aware of the rest of the band listening in the control room. I strove to remember where my fingers were going next. I was ecstatic to get through it.

Of all the takes, the keeper was the one in which, after Shane had finished singing and I was on my own, in the very last measure, I hit a top E instead of a D. The mistake for ever imprinted on my mind the phrase's similarity to Charles Parry's arrangement of William Blake's 'Jerusalem.' I wanted to do it again, but the rapture which met Shane and me when we came back into the control room was such that Lillywhite and everyone else declined to re-record it.

Lillywhite had a studio at his house in Ealing. One Friday, he took the tapes home. Over the weekend he set up his studio for his wife Kirsty to have a go at the female part of the duet with a view to seeing if the song was going to work as a duet at all.

He came into the studio on Monday. We sat around the control room to listen, perched on the back of the couch, on a cabinet, down the stairs to the door. Kirsty's vernacular, familiar to all of us from the records she had put out, so suited the lyrics that it was as if they had been written for her. Her voice, with her slightly nasal South London accent, now breathy, now brassy, embodied the alternating buoyancy and bitterness of the girl in Shane's song, agog with New York City, then betrayed. The harmonies in the choruses were one thing, but the layered vocals when she sang 'Well, so could anyone!' opened up the reprise of the opening melody as if it were a gift.

We sat in awed silence while the melody cycled out.

The summer ended with two last shows opening for U2, the first at Sullivan Stadium in Foxboro, Massachusetts, and the second at Madison Square Gardens in New York City. Our set at Madison Square Gardens was a matter, as Jem said, of providing music for people to find their seats, but to play at such a place, on such a stage, struck terror. The stage had been rid of all equipment. Inclines made of metal grille hid from view the backline and the technicians. Mindful of the scale of the auditorium, the grandeur of the event and the empty expanse of the stage, I yearned to swing my accordion around and rove the metal platforms and ramps. My shoes had leather soles. Remembering my accident at the Fairways Hotel in Dundalk a couple of years before, I spent a lot of my time rooted to the spot, summoning up courage every now and then to shuffle tentatively up and down one of the inclines.

The première of Cox's film *Walker* took place while we were in New York. I went with my New York girlfriend Heather. We happened to sit behind Paul Newman and Joanne Woodward. Newman and I were both wearing the identical Prince of Wales check suit. Neither of us remarked on the fact, and I suspected I was the only one of us to notice.

Heather had recently rented a performance space on the Lower East Side. She let us in through the sliding lattice metalwork. It was a black-painted corridor with a pressed tin ceiling. We kissed for a long time in the dark, on the plywood stage.

By the end of the summer, the record had been mastered. Frank had come up with an idea for the cover of the album. It was another spin on the theme of the head-replacement which Frank had co-opted for the cover of *Rum Sodomy and the Lash*: an undulating line of replicas of a photograph of James Joyce's face, but with our faces flanking the original, each of us wearing Joyce's fedora. We rejected the idea, and opted for a photo session in a studio in East London, a group tableau with our instruments and a steamer trunk.

Our failure to come up with a title for the record exasperated Frank so much that he burst into one of our rehearsals and demanded it.

'All right!' Shane shouted out. '*If I Should Fall from Grace with God!*'

Twenty-Five

'Mr Fearnley! Covered in sweat, man! The hardest-working musician in rock'n'roll!' Strummer was fond of saying, adding, more often than not: 'After Mr Ranken!'

His exhortations after the gig we played with him at the Electric Ballroom in Camden in November reminded me of my games teacher at school, who said that if you came off the pitch without being covered in dirt, you hadn't played football. I was drenched. My shirt stuck to my back. The sweat plastered my hair to my head. Sweat fell from me into the keyboard of my accordion, to the point that the wood swelled and pinched the metal rod the keys pivoted on. After a while, each key stayed down when I lifted my finger off it, until the accordion played by itself. There was no point in carrying on. I pulled the cords out of the mikes and mimed.

The previous June, on one of the weekend breaks during the recording of *If I Should Fall from Grace with God*, we had performed at RTÉ in Dublin, for a programme called *The Session* which featured ourselves, the Dubliners, John Prine and Strummer. With the Dubliners we played the two songs we both knew, 'The Irish Rover' and 'The Rare Old Mountain Dew'. With Strummer we played 'London Calling' and 'I Fought the Law'. He was no longer the insular and bituminous Simms from *Straight to Hell*. He was boyishly curly of hair, munificent and magisterial. In 'London Calling' we relished the vertical slamming of the chords. Spider rejoiced to join Strummer in howling out during the break.

Within a week of leaving England for America to film the video for 'Fairytale of New York', due for release at Christmas, and to continue on tour across the United States, Philip forlornly let it be known that he had been to see a Harley Street doctor. The ulcer which had hospitalised him in Helsinki a couple of years before had flared up. The doctor had debarred him from touring.

'It's all your fault,' Spider said to me. 'You tried to kill Philip.'

The obvious and august choice for his replacement was Joe Strummer. Amending the slogan of the Protestant campaign against the Anglo-Irish Agreement in 1985, Spider shouted out:

'Ulcer Says No!'

Quoting the slogan from a recent television advert for citrus fruit, Shane shouted out:

'But the man from Del Monte, he says "Yes!" '

'And he's an Orangeman!' Spider yelled.

In the third week of November we left for New York without Philip, but with Kirsty MacColl and Strummer.

We set up for a rehearsal in New York City. Strummer had written out the chords for the entire set list on a strip of card which he stuck to the side of his acoustic guitar. It followed the curve of the body from the neck to the tail block. By the end of a run-through of the set, Strummer had to hold his guitar out to the side, away from his body, bending down to see what the chords were for the last songs of the set list. A lock of hair dangled over his forehead. His eyes squinted.

The week of Thanksgiving, New York City was magical. Cars and taxicabs whipped the steam venting from manholes into rags. Everywhere we went, strings of lights spiralled the dark trunks of the trees, uncoiled into their limbs and twinkled among the branches. Jem and I went to the Village and the apartment

of a friend of Heather's for a Thanksgiving dinner. The candlelit table spanned two tiny rooms on the second floor. Heather dampened us with the story of how the Puritan settlers stole Thanksgiving from the Native Americans.

Before our gigs at the Ritz, the first couple of days were taken up with the making of the video for 'Fairytale of New York'. I hung about in the freezing cold in my suit, waiting, as Matt Dillon in the role of policeman dragged Shane by the scruff of the neck into the police station, and as the NYPD's Irish pipe band performed in Washington Square Park – not 'Galway Bay' as Shane's lyrics went, but the 'Mickey Mouse Club March'.

We loved Kirsty MacColl. I felt irrationally privileged that her birthday was the day after mine. There was a staunch impishness about her, unflaggingly full of brass, except when I happened to catch sight of her while the grips set up, staring tiredly blank at the ground, waiting.

For the cutaway shots from the story of the fighting couple to the band performing the song, it had been Jem's idea to stylise the video after footage he'd seen of Billie Holiday singing at a late-night session in the back room of a bar. On our set, smoke similarly curled up from cigarettes left in ashtrays. Jem wore a pork-pie hat. Darryl was given a string bass to play. Andrew, curiously, sat behind a bass drum large enough for a marching band.

I took my place at the piano. As I was playing the introduction over to myself, Peter Dougherty, the director, came over.

'We'd like Shane to sit at the piano for these shots,' he said.

'Shane doesn't play the piano,' I said. I'd seen Shane play the piano. He made chords with three stabbing fingers, rarely moved them any further than the neighbouring three keys and avoided black notes. Frank happened to be nearby.

'Shane's going to play the piano,' Frank said. 'It's just going to look better if he does.' I remembered Frank's nose inches away from the face of Sean Cannon when we'd appeared on *Top of the Pops* with the Dubliners the previous April.

'But I play the piano on the record,' I said.

'And so you do,' Frank said. 'Only, it'd be better if Shane played it in the video.'

'No,' I said.

'It's just a video,' Jem said. 'We all know you play the piano. You play it very nicely.'

'You're a very good piano player,' Andrew said. I pushed the chair back and went across to join the others who were in their places.

Later, Dougherty came up to me again. Because Shane was no piano player, close-ups would be needed – of my hands playing the introduction.

'You'll need to wear his rings,' Dougherty said. I waited for

Shane to work the rings over his swollen knuckles. One was a heavy, scuffed signet ring. The other was set with a yin and yang symbol inside an alloy flower. He cursed and twisted until they finally came off. He pushed them into the palm of my hand with a sort of peck as if I were the cause of the botheration. I played the introduction a couple of times, bridling for the song to be over. The weight of the signet ring kept turning it on my little finger. When the take was finished, I handed them to an assistant to return them to their owner.

We left MacColl in New York. Our first gig of the rest of the tour was the Metro in Boston. Strummer's presence on stage with us seemed to be a weapon so secret that the least acknowledgement of it would amount to hubris. Strummer kept his place where Philip would have stood, but a couple of feet back from the line, tilting his guitar further and further as we got through the set in order to read the notes he'd written on his cheat-sheet.

When it came time to bring him to the front to sing 'London Calling' and 'I Fought the Law', he stood with one leg bent, stamping a heel, his arms hanging out by his sides as if reluctant to take control of his beat-up Telecaster. He'd turn this way and that as if calling us to muster and then dig into his guitar, head bent down and his leg going.

During Strummer's songs, Shane found himself with little to do. He would stand staring at the floor while Strummer sang the verses, occasionally lift what he was drinking to his mouth and look across at Strummer with a combination of leniency larded with irony, but full of awe.

Wherever we went, before and after shows, groups of various sizes gathered round Strummer. Between sound check and the gig I would come across him in huddles – in catering or seated along the wall of an empty hall, in a sagging sofa, round a table – leaning forward on his knees, talking to anyone who wanted to talk

to him. His pow-wows were not so much platforms for pontific-
ation but symposiums for his cherished themes of brotherhood,
solidarity, outsiders and underdogs. Scattering his discourse with
watchwords and apothegms, he let his circles know that he would
take up the cudgels for them, that he had their backs.

In Toronto, Strummer came into the dressing room in a lather
about the Toronto Blue Jays' near-success against the Detroit Ti-
gers. Both teams had been in contention for top of the division in
American League East baseball.

'The only Canadian baseball team in the American League,
man!' he said.

On stage too, he took up cudgels with us, stirring us up with
foot-stamping, chin-thrusting, and guitar-stabbing.

'ANDREW RANKEN! ONE, TWO, THREE, FOUR!' he would
shout out at the beginning of 'London Calling.'

'JAMES FEARNLEY!' he would cry, to signal an accordion
solo.

'TERENCE WOODS!' he would yell when the break for 'I
Fought the Law' came up, and then wheel away from the microphone.

I swelled with self-worth when, with barely discernible sly-
ness, Strummer broke the fourth wall and glimpsed up from his
guitar at me to wink in comradeship.

At the end of 'London Calling' and 'I Fought the Law', finished
with his Telecaster, in one motion Strummer ducked under the
strap of his guitar and, his hand under the tailstock, launched it
spinning over Darryl's head in the direction of the wings in the
trust that someone would catch it.

In Montreal and Toronto, the kerbsides were lined with com-
pacted snow, blown hard by the wind. By the second week in
December we were on the West Coast, where it seemed the
winter did not exist.

The frontage of the Arlington Theater in Santa Barbara was white as a wedding cake with a scalloped awning and a vaguely astronautical spire rising above the pantile roof. The ceilings in the lobby were heavy with weathered beams, but the interior of the auditorium gave you the impression, in spite of the plush theatre seating, that you were sitting outside in the plaza of a colonial pueblo. An earthenware roof spanned the stage between what looked like a pair of bell-towers. Stucco town-houses with balconies, staircases and arched windows were built out from the theatre walls. The ceiling was painted night-blue.

We opened for Los Lobos, though we all agreed that the gig was really a double bill.

On our tour of Scandinavia in 1985, Costello had been eager to have us listen to their first album, *How Will the Wolf Survive?*, in the van. It was a selection-box of music. There were country songs, something rockabilly and a drinking song. The two tracks on the record played on traditional instruments threw the rest of the material into shadow and confirmed that Los Lobos and the Pogues were kindred.

During Los Lobos' performance, I longed for them to play tra-ditional norteño music, and when David Hidalgo drew on his accordion, and when the guitarrón, bajo sexto and saxophone came out and they plunged headlong into it, I laughed out loud with joy. I loved their polkas, the guilelessness of the marching 2/4 beat. The vocal melody passed from man to man. An instru-mental passage flipped the metre on its head. I was glad to hear how much of 'Fiesta' we had got right, from the polka beat to the blowzy saxophone melody.

We met them backstage in the green room after their set. There was a conspicuous aura of success surrounding Los Lobos. For a week at the end of August, their version of Ritchie Valens's hit 'La Bamba' had been No. 1 in the *Billboard* charts. Los Lobos had provided much of the music for the soundtrack to the film, which had been released that July. In a matter of months they had been promoted from pets to paradigms.

César Rosas was a stocky guy with a goatee and impenetrable behind shades. Louie Pérez looked like a boy. David Hidalgo was a giant, with sloping shoulders and a florid face. When it came to meeting Hidalgo, once the introductions were over, we stood in front of each other in awkward silence. I wondered if, like me, he beseeched the hubbub in the green room to beckon each of us to something less uncomfortable.

I went into our dressing room to get myself something to drink. A couple of girls were doing the same. It wasn't unusual to come across people I didn't know helping themselves to drinks in our dressing room. One of them was tall as a model, with shoulder-length ginger hair and angular shoulders, wearing a white T-shirt and a short skirt. The other was a blonde in a green vintage zip-up jacket, short black skirt and dark tights. I waited while they fished inside the plastic drinks cooler. The ginger-haired model re-assumed her full height. She was half a head taller than me. She smiled wanly at me. The blonde girl wiped water from a bottle and stepped out of the way.

'Sorry!' she said. Her face was astonishingly symmetrical, framed by long, straight hair. She was limpidly beautiful with blue eyes. 'Thanks!' she sang.

'Not a problem,' I said. The girls went past me into the green room with their beers. Spider appeared at my shoulder.

'She's gorgeous, isn't she?' Spider said.

'She's lovely,' I said.

'She's Ritchie Valens's girlfriend in *La Bamba*,' Spider said. 'And Joe Strummer's in real life. Bastard,' he added.

The following night we turned up at the Palladium on Hollywood Boulevard in Los Angeles, again opening for Los Lobos. I came across the girl from the Arlington Theater backstage. She was carrying a shirt on a hanger.

'This is Joe's,' she said. 'I'm going to put it in the dressing room.' I was going the same way.

Her name was Danielle. She couldn't have been more than twenty or twenty-one. I asked about *La Bamba* and if I would have seen her in anything else. She had started acting, she said, when she was still at school. For a year she'd had a part on a soap opera until her character got killed off in 1984. She had done a couple of things for television since, and an independent film. She described herself as bi-coastal. Her apartment in New York was draped in wisteria. The one in Los Angeles was next to a shopping mall. I struggled to pay attention. She had remarkably level, perfect teeth. Her complexion was pellucid. A slight cast to her eye prevented her pupils from completely aligning their focus.

We talked about England. It turned out that her parents owned a sixteenth-century cottage in the Cotswolds. Her dad was a television film producer and her mother a product of something called the Philadelphia Main Line. Her voice was as beautiful as she was, her diction precise and her voice young. The following night in San Juan Capistrano would be the last gig of the tour. I would be going home to England.

'I'd like to write to you,' I found myself saying.

'I'd like that,' she said.

'Okay then,' I said.

'Okay,' she said. We wrote out our addresses on scraps of paper and swapped them.

The next day, we drove in a couple of Econolines down to the Coach House, an hour or so from Hollywood down the freeway under sweeping concrete overpasses, past huge car dealerships and the bleached flanks of the Laguna Hills.

The Coach House was a single-storey roadside restaurant just off the freeway with a hardwood floor and a wrought-iron balcony. Dining tables and bentwood chairs were set together in lines extending from the small stage. The dressing rooms were a pitilessly white-painted suite of rooms with walls of hardboard. I kept coming across Danielle in the narrow corridors backstage. We smiled awkwardly.

During the sound check she sat at one of the dining tables, watching. Though I was careful to begin with, to check to see whether or not Strummer was aware, I could not prevent myself looking over at where she was sitting. The more we met each other's glances, the less I cared if Strummer knew of our flirtation. The strength of my yen for Danielle overrode my compunctions about going behind Strummer's back. They had been eroded by my crush on Jennifer Balgobin in Almería, not to mention his infidelity to his wife. After the sound check I went over to sit with Danielle, caring nothing for what Strummer might think.

We played in front of people having their dinner. Strummer shuffled over to me on stage. With a flick of his head he beckoned me to follow him stepping out over the monitor wedges and onto the tables. I did my best not to lose my balance. My feet flipped plates, spilled glasses of water and overturned a couple of red glass candle holders. We went the length of the dining tables. A table tilted under me. A woman shrieked and held her hands up. I turned around and made my way back through the spillage to the stage. When Strummer got back, head bent over his guitar, he winked at me.

Danielle offered Jem and me a lift in her car back up to Hollywood. She drove a Honda. It was more cramped than I expected. Jem and I sat in the back with our knees against the seatbacks. Strummer got in the passenger seat.

As we set out he put on a tape the two of them had been listening to. It was a collection of Roy Orbison's songs called *In Dreams: The Greatest Hits*. We were listening to 'Oh, Pretty Woman'. It sounded more fake than I remembered. It was difficult to tell. All the parts were there. There was the thumping downbeat on the snare, the tinkling piano. There was the tremolo guitar. There was the wooden part-meow, part-purr, part-snarl after the words: 'Are you lonely, just like me?' The more I listened though, the more I became convinced that these songs were not the originals.

'These aren't the original recordings,' I said. 'Listen.'

We all listened.

'It's Orbison,' I said. 'But it's someone else playing the instruments.'

'You sure?' Strummer said. I felt sorry for him that he didn't know.

'Pretty much,' I said.

Danielle brought the tape cover out of the glove compartment. Strummer turned on the ceiling light. It was hard to read the lavender printing on the fold-out against the blue background.

'*A collector's fantasy,*' he read. '*A treasury of nineteen Roy Orbison classics totally re-recorded for the best state of the art sound possible.* Can you believe it? Man! For fuck's sake!'

I felt awful. Strummer clapped the cassette case closed and put it back in the glove compartment. Before he could shut it, Danielle ejected the cassette and tossed it in.

Danielle pulled into the subterranean car park of the hotel on Franklin Avenue. We all got out and stood in the unforgiving light and the sour air.

'Thanks, Danielle,' Jem said. He stretched his shoulders and yawned. 'I'm going to go to bed.' Jem's brevity did not surprise me. Though I knew he liked Strummer and appeared to like Danielle too, I was familiar with his view of illicit affairs.

'I'm going up too,' I said, not knowing what else to do.

I hugged Strummer goodbye, suddenly guilty to realise that this was his last night on tour with us, and Jem and I were just going to bed. I took Danielle into my arms and kissed her cheek.

On my way up to the room I stared at the scuffed steel shell of the lift in a mopish rapture.

··✠··

While we had been away in the States, 'Fairytale of New York' had been released in England. The day after landing at Heathrow from Los Angeles, we performed on *Top of the Pops* with MacColl. Two days later, our last gigs before Christmas, we played three nights at Glasgow Barrowland. I took a late train down to Manchester to spend Christmas with my family. At Preston I had an hour or so to wait between trains. I hadn't let anyone know when I would be arriving in Manchester. I rang up my brother.

'It's at No. 2,' he said.

'Fuck me,' I said.

To kill time until my connection to Manchester, I crossed the rusted bridge over the railway lines to a pub I'd seen from the station. Halfway across, I burst into tears.

Twenty-Six

'It's the other side of the world!' Spider said. 'It's Christmas in the middle of the summer! The water in the plughole goes round the other way! We're two years ahead in *Neighbours* and two years behind with *Eastenders*!'

Even the moon was upside down. Andrew and I spent a day on Bondi Beach. It was a beach like any other but patrolled by people in kepis and mirrored shades with fluorescent frames. Their noses were luminous with zinc oxide. Andrew and I alternated between the sea and the sand until the sun went down. We bought a bottle of champagne at a bottle shop on the Parade and clambered in the dark along the rocks under the headland out to Mackenzies Point. We found an uncomfortable shelf in the sandstone, opened the champagne and with our backs to the rock gazed out over the ocean. Time slowed down in Andrew's company. There was little cause for words. We passed the bottle between us.

'The Southern Cross,' Andrew said, pointing up at the constellation in the sky. 'I've never seen that before.' There was a pause. 'Look at the moon,' he said. We stood up, bent over and looked at it between our legs to see it the way we were used to.

As soon as we had set foot in Australia, three weeks into 1988, we were agog with the country. Everywhere we looked there was some new wonderment: a church covered in its entirety in livid green ivy; the seagulls endlessly circling the red-and-white spoke of a communications pylon; a giant 'Mr Moon' face flanked by the vaguely Moorish towers at the entry gates to Luna Park in Melbourne. There were gum trees and galah birds, bottle-brush trees and bull-roarers, clap sticks and cane-toads.

Our arrival in Australia coincided with the bicentennial celebrations of the landing of the First Fleet in Sydney Harbour in 1788, bringing the first European settlers to New South Wales and marking the beginning of convict transportation to the Antipodes. Required reading was Robert Hughes's *The Fatal Shore*, which described the degradations of the convict ships and the devastation of the Aboriginal culture upon the arrival of the settlers.

We drew poetic comparisons between the barbarities of penal transportation and our own seemingly relentless voyaging in conditions we weren't ashamed of thinking were cramped, and for weeks at a time, if not the three months it would have taken an actual convict ship to make the journey from Portsmouth to Fremantle in the 1700s. We never forgot our visit to U-boat 96 at the studios of Bayerischer Rundfunk in 1985. We drew romantic parallels between our particular narrative and that of every last damn mariner there ever was – convict, fortune-seeker and explorer alike. We had all read *Moby-Dick*. Every aspect of seafaring fascinated us.

Ever since our playing 'Greenland Whale Fisheries' in the earliest days of the Pogues, we had been haunted and inspired by the ocean, the ships that sailed on it, the creatures that lived under it, the hopes it built up, the misery it inflicted. In nineteen hundred and eighty-two, in October the fifth day, we had hoisted our colours to the top of the mast, as in 'Greenland Whale Fisheries'. As in 'Muirshin Durkin', we had been bound away across the foam to seek our fortunes, and not just in America. We were the brave boys, again of 'Greenland Whale Fisheries'. As in 'Sea Shanty', there never were wilder bastards than us on the sea.

We were outraged by the scant regard in which the Aborigines were held. Spider, as sympathetic as Strummer to the downtrodden and the disenfranchised, went about in a T-shirt that read: 'Rock for Land Rights.' It hadn't been long since Australian Aborigines had been able to claim rights to their own land. One of the Australian roadies spotted Spider's T-shirt.

'Land rights?' I heard the roadie say. 'Two bob a flagon.'

Spider brought backstage a large Aboriginal flag – a yellow disc on a horizontally divided field of black and red – to hang as a backdrop. The yellow, Spider said, represented the sun, the red the earth, and the black the Aboriginal people of Australia. Halfway through our set, word came that the flag was the wrong way up. Spider was stricken at the possibility that hanging the flag upside down meant we were taking the piss and that we intended the opposite of what the symbol signified. His inadvertent betrayal of the Aborigines horrified Spider.

I had family in Australia. My aunt and uncle had emigrated in 1956 to settle in Adelaide, where they grew a sizeable family and a building construction empire that made them comfortably rich. The Evinses came out in no small number to welcome us from the aeroplane at Adelaide airport. I spent an evening round the barbie, where we bogged in on tucker and stubbies. I was open-mouthed at the privileges enjoyed by the European culture and the extent to which it seemed to be a stranger both to racial and sexual equality.

Our tour promoter was a guy called Vivian Lees. Lees was a mild-mannered man and softly spoken. He came everywhere with us and even drove one of the minibuses. It was rare for a tour promoter to be so ubiquitous. His delight to have us on tour in Australia was palpable.

On a day off in Melbourne, Lees took us up to Hanging Rock, where we picked our way through eucalyptus trees and the eruptions of what we were told was volcanic solvsbergite. The mounds were riddled with holes large enough to put your head through. Philip had recovered from his ulcer but was fragile. He strained almost geriatrically, pushing down on his knees to get himself up onto one of the rocks. A terrain more complicated than a pavement or pub floor tended to baffle Shane nowadays, but he clambered up the rocks with the rest of us.

On a large pitted slab away from the trees, away from the others, I came upon a view over the Bush. It was the largest uninterrupted plain I had ever seen. Scrub and dry grass stretched for miles all around to a horizon which faded into the rim of the vast dome of blue sky. With such a view in front of me, on the other side of the world, in the middle of nowhere, it was as though we had all been set adrift and there was just the subtlest, sketchiest of networks holding us all together.

After Sydney and Byron Bay, on the way up the Gold Coast, new developments were beginning to spring up with such names as Koala Town, Dream World and Industrial Paradise. At the far end of the sweep of coast, between the almost acrobatic branches of the Norfolk pines ranged along the edge of the cliff, stood the hazy pilings of the high-rises of Surfers Paradise.

P.V. couldn't tolerate the heat. The further north we went on our way to Brisbane, the more tropical the weather became. Miserable from the humidity, he sat in the minibus, his hair lank, his upper lip beaded with perspiration. Now and again he let out a great sigh and elaborately rubbed his face.

Frank joked about his drinking. On the Pacific Motorway, we stopped at a roadside fruit stand. P.V. stumped back to the van with a plastic bag full of papayas.

'You have to have it,' Frank said, mimicking a phrase we heard a lot from P.V. 'Papaya daiquiris in P.V.'s room when we get to Brisbane.'

From Brisbane, we went to New Zealand, an Eden with livid green hills and beaches of black sand. Spider greeted us at every opportunity with '*Kia ora, bro!*' From the fans he met after the gigs, he learnt whole phrases in Maori. Walking around Auckland, alert to such a mellifluous language preponderant with vowels, I was elated to come across a Maori word I could bring to Spider. It was printed on a wall behind a block of flats. I started mouthing the word TOWAWAYAREA in order to be able to repeat it accurately, when I realised my mistake.

On the drive down to Wellington we pulled over at Pukerua Beach and gawped at the barrelling of a seal among the orange tendrils of bladderwrack heaving in an inlet, as it swam up to us, curious, its wet-whiskered snout breaking the water and its mournful, liquid eyes staring up. From Christchurch, we took the train to Dunedin. Rhododendrons grew so close to the railway line that now and again a branch would thwack the windows.

⊹

When we got back to England in the second week in February our tour of the Antipodes seemed a keel-upwards, anomalous interlude full of wonderments. When our ship righted itself, it brought us up in the middle of an English winter and time to go back to work.

Though while we were away 'Fairytale of New York' had slipped to No. 10 in the charts and had vanished from the top twenty altogether by the time we got home, *If I Should Fall from Grace with God* had been released and had gone in at No. 3. We went on tour in support of it. In the third week of February, we met, as usual, for Shane's convenience, in the Boot on Cromer Street before climbing onto the tour bus.

We were by now more than familiar with the circuit: the upholstered well of the dressing room at the University of East Anglia; the panelling and parquet of the De Montfort Hall in Leicester; the balconies and bar of the City Hall in Newcastle; the bulb-lined, theatrical mirrors at the Playhouse in Edinburgh; the treacherous aluminium staircase to the stage at Leeds University refectory; the cosily carpeted living room at the Apollo in Manchester; the freezing parlour at the Royal Court in Liverpool; the fibre-carpeting at Rock City, Nottingham; the metal gantries and modern wooden stairways at the Corn Exchange in Cambridge; the befuddling, corporate corridors at the Brighton Centre.

Frank had put together a tour programme, with individual photographs from the photo session for the cover of *If I Should Fall from Grace with God*. The booklet included the lyrics, a scrapbook page of photos from recent tours and a couple of pages written by our biographer, Ann Scanlon, in the style of racing form. Frank had devoted the first page to the rejected album cover of repeated reproductions of our faces as James Joyce's.

The arrival of MacColl in Edinburgh to sing 'Fairytale of New York' – a week into the tour and a couple of months adrift of the Christmas season – lifted the tour up and carried it down the country, to a week-long residency at the Town and Country in Kentish Town.

At the beginning of the day I stepped out of the glare of the spring sunshine into the darkness of the auditorium, out of the rumbling of the traffic on Highgate Road into the serial concussion of Scully sound-checking the drum kit. The stage was a black-painted plywood expanse framed at the front by the line of monitor wedges and microphones and at the back by ranks of amps and risers draped in black. Backstage the corridors smelled of disinfectant. The dressing rooms were empty but for the drinks coolers, cheese plates and bowls of fruit on layered napkins on the counters beneath the mirrors, and the now obligatory pineapple.

The gigs at the Town and Country were frenziedly kaleidoscopic. MacColl stepped out in a green blouse closed by a choker, her earrings swinging, and an abundance of red hair, which on St Patrick's Day was swept up in a large green bow. In 'Fairytale of New York', Shane and Kirsty's shuffling left a meandering track in the confetti snow which blew down from the lighting trusses. At the end of 'Turkish Song of the Damned', she hooked Spider by the arm, to hurl each other around. At the end of 'Fiesta', she was merciless with the Silly String.

At the end of each set, dressed as if against a chill in a black leather jacket, polo neck undervest and shirt, Lynval Golding from the Specials performed 'A Message to You, Rudy'. On a couple of nights, Strummer came out to perform 'London Calling' and 'I Fought the Law' – black shirt, black jeans, bolo tie and a clump of wilted shamrock dangling from his breast pocket.

At the end of each night, the auditorium was loud with the clatter of the clean-up crew shunting banks of beer tins and plastic glasses across the floor with huge brooms. The stage was strewn with fake snow. Silly String hung in festoons from the microphones, if they were still standing. Backstage, the dressing rooms smelled of booze and cigarette smoke. The coolers gaped empty. There was cheese and fruit everywhere and the pineapple smashed to pulp in the corner.

By the end of the week we had filmed the video for the next single, 'If I Should Fall from Grace with God', concurrently with filming the shows from St Patrick's Day to the end of the week for a documentary, including interviews. In between, we crammed in a recording session with Steve Earle for a song called 'Johnny Come Lately' on his third album, *Copperhead Road*.

⊹

For a year, Shane had been going out with a girl called Victoria. She had dark hair, green eyes and protrusive incisors. There was a distracted but watchful air about her. She had introduced herself to me in the Devonshire Arms as Victoria Cross – a joke I didn't get, but one which for months afterwards rendered me incapable of acknowledging that her surname was in fact Clarke. The joy she seemed to take over the joke reminded me of the discomfiture I experienced from girls at school. I took to regarding her with a certain wariness.

She started to accompany us on tour. One night, in France, we had just had dinner in a restaurant next to the venue. I happened to be sitting opposite Shane and Victoria at one of the long trestle tables. I was tired and laid my head on my forearms on top of the table. I could hear Shane sniggering but tried to put it out of my mind.

'Should I, really?' I heard Victoria say. I didn't know what they were doing but it didn't surprise me when water started to trickle in my hair and down the side of my face. I raised my head up to see Victoria setting a jug of water back down on the table.

'What the fuck are you doing?' I said.

'He told me to!' she said with a defiant pout. Her presumption astounded me. I found myself preferring to accord Shane the right to pour water over my head than what I took to be this hanger-on.

During Philip's hospitalisation the previous February, Frank, Shane and Terry had each had a cameo in a *Comic Strip Presents . . .* production called *Eat the Rich.* Adrian Edmondson, one of the members of *The Comic Strip,* agreed to direct our next video, for 'Fiesta', for release in July. In the second week in April we travelled to Barcelona to shoot it.

The locations were a dusty colonial plaza, a restaurant outside the city with blinding-white tablecloths and an awning entwined with vines, and lastly the hallucinatory roof of Gaudí's Casa Batlló in the centre of Barcelona.

The morning of the shoot on the roof of the Casa Batlló, before going on to the location, I went in a car with Shane to a radio interview. I sat in front. Shane sat in the back with an assistant from the local publicity company.

On stage we came across with nineteenth-century lawlessness. Off stage we were civil to a fault. Shane, too, when it suited his purpose, was a stickler for etiquette. This morning, though, he complained petulantly and at length about the earliness of the hour, interrogating the driver about how long it was going to take to get to the radio station, questioning the necessity of the interview.

The assistant reiterated the prior commitment with the radio station. Shane started to bellow, leaning forward to the driver. I turned towards him.

'I bet you were spoilt as a child,' I said.

No sooner had I said it than Shane's forearm clamped across my throat and his knuckles bored into my cheekbone.

'You cunt!' he yelled with his face against my ear and his foul breath in my nose. 'You cunt! You cunt!'

As I fought to free myself from his headlock, the memory came rushing back to me of my first conversation with Shane on the evening of my audition for the Nips. He had described, if I had understood him properly, a childhood which, as much as it had been unusual, had also sometimes been difficult.

For the rest of the drive, I rebuked myself for the times I had succumbed to the temptation of disparaging his lyrics as products of a puerile fascination with horror and degradation, goaded by self-loathing and harried by the ineluctability of pain and death. Though I was sure he would have been the last to admit it, behind them all, I sensed Shane's prayers for some sort of respite. I should have reminded myself of the anxiety I knew he lived with daily. It was something I should have known since my first visits to his flat on Cromer Street.

The Casa Batlló was fitful with mosaics, swirling staircases, tiled light-wells and ranks of rib-like arches. Up on the roof the ridgeline soared and plummeted like a spine of a dragon. The chimneys veered up out of the craze of mosaic, banded with stars and topped with candlesnuffer spires. With the exception of Philip who had ordered ahead a blue knickerbocker suit with a swirly design, we were kitted out in dark suits. We waited for Shane.

He appeared at the doorway onto the roof in a matador outfit of tights, tassels and gaiters – and a *chaquetilla* with epaulettes of bronze thread and covered in dark stars. He stopped, took one look at the jackets and ties we were wearing and started screaming to be dressed like everyone else. Frank stepped across to calm him, but he was beside himself. Edmondson – a quiet, assured man with thinning blond hair which the wind blew about – waved someone to go and help.

A while later, Shane returned in shades, a dark suit, white shirt and red cummerbund but in no less a state of agitation. Though it was yet early afternoon and we hadn't started, I wanted the day to be over and done with. Shane frightened me, not so much on account of my remark earlier in the day, but because he seemed to be losing his mind.

Edmondson assembled us in a line against an undulating wall at the rear of the roof. We mimed to the backing track blasting through a couple of wedges on the tiled floor. Spider pretended to empty his lungs into a trombone. Jem and Joey Cashman, who was now a permanent member of Frank's management team, blew into saxophones. Philip ducked and weaved. Andrew did some sort of soft-shoe shuffle round the solitary snare drum. I hoisted the accordion. Shane strode up and down gesticulating as the camera followed him on a dolly. I loathed the exaggeration to which the camera required us to commit, particularly in view of the precarious state of mind Shane seemed to be in.

I happened to be histrionically bending over my accordion when Shane grabbed my hair and thrust my head down until the ground was inches from my face. I tried to lift up my head, but his arm was bolt-stiff. I managed to twist myself out of his grasp and resurface. With his other arm he pretended to brandish an *estoque*, as if I were the bull and he the matador. For the sake of the camera I carried on the ridiculous disporting though I was careful to put some distance between Shane and myself.

After the shot I went up to Edmondson.

'Yes sir!' he said. He half-turned to me from another matter, his thin hair snatched by a gust.

'I'd like you not to use that shot in the actual video,' I said.

'Sorry?' he said.

'The shot we did,' I said. 'I'd like you not to use it in the actual video.'

'Really?' he said. 'Seemed good to me.'

Edmondson and I stood together for a moment in the wind.

The headlock in the car that morning and the episode up on the roof of the Casa Batlló had been the first time Shane had assaulted me. For the rest of the spring, I kept him at a distance.

⊹

In the third week in April, we went to Thames Television's Euston Road studios to perform on a programme called *Friday Night Live*, hosted by Ben Elton. He had been the invisible journalist for London Weekend Television's *South of Watford* in the March of 1984. Now he ran the show in front of the camera. We set up on a stage between large, pink fibreglass hands with our feet swathed in a layer of dry ice.

A couple of months before, in January, after a six-week appeal hearing, Lord Lane had upheld the conviction of the Birmingham Six, in prison since 1975 for the Birmingham pub bombings. We made it known that we would be performing 'The Streets of Sorrow/Birmingham Six' to close the show. The camera rehearsal went without comment. We were in the middle of the song on the live broadcast when the producers cut to commercial. Rather than having simply gone over time, it seemed Thames Television had been cowed by the political climate engendered by the

326

Thatcher government. As early as 1985 Thatcher had used the words 'the oxygen of publicity'. Already, moves were afoot to restrict the media's coverage of acts of terrorism, which obviously included our performance on *Friday Night Live*.

⸙

We played throughout Europe and Scandinavia, from the snow and smoked fish of Norway to the rain and *Hackfleisch* of Germany. The warming Mediterranean brought carafes of vino tinto and fried squid. The cacophony of Rome brought grilled aubergines and penne all'arrabbiata.

In Germany we had had news that, in May, we would be embarking on our third tour of North America, this time starting off on the West Coast. As promised, I had written to Strummer's American girlfriend – a letter each from Sydney and Rome.

When I got home from Italy there was an envelope with a Los Angeles postmark in the hall. The letter inside contained a beautiful description of the gun-metal surface of the roads and the clear skies after the rain, together with an alluring one of herself sitting on what she called a 'chaise lounge'. I loved her canny self-deprecation as she described herself in a short black dress and wearing lipstick having come in from an audition where she'd waited an hour or two in a corridor with girls identically dressed. It was as if to say that though there might be hundreds like, *of* her there was only one.

Twenty-Seven

I was anxious to meet my bi-coastal correspondent, she of the 'chaise lounge' in Los Angeles, she of the wisteria-draped top-floor apartment in the West Village. I struggled to remember what she looked like, but could only come up with a memory of blonde hair and Nordic beauty.

The John Anson Ford Theater was in the open air, set into the hillside. The auditorium was made of concrete, the stage framed by a pair of towers with trees receding up the hill behind, luridly orange, then red, then green in the stage lighting.

After the show, Danielle von Zerneck came to the dressing room. She was lovely, and more so now that she was by herself, without Strummer, backstage, and to meet me. Hardly covertly I refamiliarised myself with her near-as-damn-it symmetrical features, her bangs, blonde hair and strabismus. The tiny blue dot on her left eyelid was where she'd been stabbed with a pencil when she was at school.

If Danielle typified the Hollywood ingénue, my yen for a blonde American actress typified the English rock-and-roll musician. I hadn't considered myself to be so predictable, but when I thought about Heather, my blonde American performance artist friend, and the other dalliances I had had on the road, all at least ten years younger than I was and all blonde, it was clear I had resorted to type.

I wasn't alone. Shane, while not quite sloughing off the skin of the poet-drunk, was now taking on the traits of a rock-and-roll prima donna, as I had seen on the roof of the Casa Batlló. Frank, from the outset, when he had turned up at the Windsor Castle in Camden in his blue blazer, faded jeans and loafers, had typified the rock-and-roll manager. In Charlie McLennan, with his Mick Ronson coiffure and skintight jeans and his presumption of indestructibility, we had the quintessential rock-and-roll roadie. Most of the rest of the band seemed immune from such predetermination.

Resorting to type too, Danielle and I ended up at the Hyatt on Sunset – the rock-and-roll hotel in Hollywood – in Spider's room. P.V. had already gone to bed and we needed somewhere to go. Spider lounged next to Danielle on his bed. His arm lolled over her shoulders. He started to complain about the bothersomeness of sharing rooms on the road and had asked could he come back to Danielle's apartment with her, when I got up.

'Can I have a quick word with you?' I said to Danielle. 'Outside?'

'Sure,' she said. We went out into the corridor. I closed Spider's door behind me.

'Have you anything in there you need?' I said.

'No,' she said.

'You want to go somewhere else?' I said.

'You want to come to my place?' she said.

'Yes,' I said.

Her apartment was a ten-minute drive down the hill from Sunset Boulevard. The windows were covered with wrought-iron bars. The living room was dark. Neither of us switched on the lights. She walked across to her record player and put on a Thelonious Monk record. When she stepped into my arms to dance to 'Crepuscule with Nellie,' she led us both out of the resort of type.

She had to get up for a flight to New York the following morning. I had her apartment to myself. The band wasn't due to leave for Dallas for the next date of the tour until the following day. I didn't much want to go back to the hotel and attempt to make light of the taunts that were sure to come my way that I had bedded Joe Strummer's girlfriend behind his back, nor had I much stomach for any encounter with Spider. I sat in Danielle's kitchen, content with the thought that I would be seeing her again at the end of the tour when we finished up at Roseland Ballroom in New York City.

⊹

The South in June was stultifying with heat. I had brought my baggy, cream-coloured linen, country vicar's suit. It wasn't much use. After the show in Dallas we threw open all the windows in the dilapidated dressing room. No wind came through them. A distant thunderstorm crackled, but even as it exploded overhead half an hour later and passed on its way, the air remained just as still and just as oppressive. I watched Andrew panting with his head hanging between his shoulders. His dripping hair darkened the dusty floorboards between his feet. P.V. came in and looked down at Andrew.

'It's too hot for man nor beast,' he said.

In Austin we played in the middle of the afternoon, at a venue which was half-inside, half-outside. The auditorium was a rectangle of dust divided down the middle into blazing sunlight and sweltering shade. Halfway through our set, all the lights in the trusses above us went out. It made little difference in the daylight. I looked out to where P.V. should have been standing at his lighting desk under his corrugated roof. We were told afterwards that he had fainted from the heat.

'But that's not why the lights went out,' Frank said. P.V. had been sweating so much that his desk had shorted. To drain the desk they had had to remove the top and pour P.V.'s perspiration out.

It was just as hot in New Orleans. The stage at Tipitina's was cramped, the dressing rooms airless. On a day off we lounged round the pool. In the evening, I found myself having dinner with Frank and Terry. We ate outside. The evening was warm and scented with jasmine. As we sat down to dinner, Frank gestured to his new suit. It was a linen suit the same colour as mine, but tailored and with what looked like suede gun-patches on it.

'Linen,' he said. 'In this weather, you have to have linen.' He lounged in the wicker chair with the air of a plantation owner.

'James,' he said despairingly, gesturing at my suit. My suit was rumpled and a size too big for me. Terry had taken to calling it my Kowloon Ferry suit. It made me feel literary. I put Frank's disparagement of it down to his sheepishness over the amount of disposable income he earned from our touring, combined with not having immediately realised how like mine his new suit was.

Though it hadn't been long since we had renegotiated Frank's commission to fifteen per cent of gross, there were yet eight of us in the band to be paid from the net income from touring. We had a crew of five, sometimes six. Four of them – Charlie, Scully, P.V. and D.J. – were paid on a permanent basis whether we were working or not. Our accountant, a blunt, frowning Manchester man called Anthony Addis, went through our accounts with us after each tour. For some time now, Frank's salary had exceeded our individual incomes from touring. We had lately signed a contract with WEA, but, still, money always seemed to be tight.

We drove in a yellow Silver Eagle with the head sign 'No One

You Know', from Birmingham and Atlanta up through the Midwest – Cincinnati, St Louis, Chicago, Detroit – and into Canada. The venues ranged from the casting shed of a blast-furnace plant amid pipes and gantries and ore-bridges and furnaces, to a club by the river from the back door of which we could see the Gateway to the West, rising over the Missouri. The closer I got to New York and the end of the tour, the more excited I became about my reunion with Danielle.

When we got to Boston the day before travelling down to New York, I rang Danielle at the number she had given me and described the lingering loyalty I had to my New York girlfriend Heather.

'But I want to be with you,' I said. 'Do you want to be with me?'

'Yes,' she said.

I had loved Heather's company in New York whenever I had arrived in the city. I had enjoyed the ranging letters she had written to me on mismatched stationery and crammed into an envelope. I was in debt to Heather for her catalysis of the end of my relationship with Debsey. The evening we got to the city, I went to see her at her apartment.

'That's okay,' Heather said. 'If you're in love with her.'

'I don't know if I am,' I said.

'It's okay anyway,' she said.

For two nights the Pogues played the Roseland Ballroom. It was an enormous place reminiscent of the Hammersmith Palais with its stage situated on one of the long sides of the hall and its dowdy gold-painted balcony.

The days before the gigs, I spent in Danielle's company. She took me zigzagging through Manhattan, reading the flashing WALK and DON'T WALK signs ahead of the traffic lights changing colour. New York traffic seemed to part before her. I bobbed in her wake.

After the first night at Roseland she hailed a cab with the voice of a carney barker and when it tried to drive off with her, leaving me on the sidewalk, she held the door open, preventing it going any further. She filled the interior of the cab with invective.

On my last day before going home to London – other than Danielle's outing to a deli in the neighbourhood for bagels, cream cheese, red onions and lox – we spent the day in bed. Even as the daylight started to fade, I knew the day hadn't been wasted. I left her to meet up with the Pogues' transport to JFK airport. Danielle and I made no plans to see one another again.

Festivals in Europe and Scandinavia – Roskilde, Oslo, Milan, Lorelei, Annecy, Lorient, Madrid – took up the rest of the summer. At the end of July, for the last and most nerve-racking gig, Jem and I turned up with our instruments to play a handful of songs for Ella Finer – nearly five years old – and her nursery schoolmates in Coram's Fields.

Danielle and I continued to write to one another. In August she rang me, to invite me to an island in the Caribbean. We spent ten days on St Martin. A ceiling fan wafted the scents of hibiscus and the morning rain through our palm-fronded villa by the ocean. In September the Pogues were due to start rehearsals for the next record. When Danielle and I parted company at JFK airport, I waited until I had rounded the corner of the corridor to the plane, before I gave myself to uncontrollable weeping.

⊹

The summer of 1988 had already been touted as the 'Second Summer of Love.' England was febrile with acid house, raves, Ecstasy and LSD. Darryl rediscovered an appetite for dance music that was gluttonous. He would give a couple of us lifts to rehearsal in his Volkswagen and treat us to mixes he'd come across, fresh from clubs as far apart as Ibiza and Birmingham. He extolled the virtues of the Roland TR-808 above all other drum-machines, and dropped names like Frankie Knuckles and Paul Oakenfold.

Not only was acid house all the rage in London, but Jem was concerned that I should know that jazz was too. He ushered me in the direction of artists like Courtney Pine and Wynton Marsalis, along with the usual suspects, the Charlies Mingus and Parker. Jem's keenness for jazz was urbane. Darryl's enthusiasm for house music was irrepressible.

In homage to the psychedelic, 1960s flavour of the 'Second Summer of Love', we took to wearing patterned shirts. On our festival tour that summer, Jem seemed to have been on a mission to uncover as many shirts with crazed patterns as he could. He had found a shop in Milan airport. Whenever we passed through, Jem was sure to pick out something brightly coloured, mosaic, dense with addled geometry. Darryl favoured T-shirts more in keeping with the youthful demographic of the country's rave culture. Though I was persuaded, in the odd photo shoot and on stage, to put on something fittingly riotous, I clung to my white shirt and my suit.

We started a couple of weeks' rehearsal at the end of September. Jem had written a handful of songs. There was a jazz instrumental he and I had played a few times in dressing rooms on the road in Germany – he on saxophone, myself on accordion. It was vaguely blues-based, but angular and with unapologetic flattened notes. He'd written a Cajun-country-rockabilly song called 'Train of Love' with a hurtling succession of chord changes in it and which modulated precipitately, flinging me into a bewildering realm of black keys on the accordion. He brought forward a song inspired by our tour of Australia, with minimal chord changes and full of drones, which Terry was going to sing. Lastly, there was a love song, in 6/8 time, with a melody full of longing, in the style, and following pretty much the parameters, of 'A Rainy Night in Soho'.

Philip had written a song inspired by the legend of Lorelei, one of the rock-bound Rhine maidens who lured passing navigators to their doom. Philip had always had a Wagnerian bent which turned on the pivot of desire and loss, love and death. His song, 'Lorelei', was no exception. A guitar jangled against a Phil Spector beat.

The songwriter who kept the flag flying for Irish music was Terry. He came to rehearsal with a song whose lyrics swore vengeance on Oliver Cromwell. We submitted it to a ska backbeat. The other song he brought in was a galloping one about the alcoholic antics of a band he used to be in. The tune was so complicated to play and the jig rhythm so unswerving that we had no other option but to play it straight.

I yearned so much for what I hoped would be the superiority of Shane's songs that when he came to rehearsal it was a struggle to prevent myself lavishing praise on all of them.

335

At first hearing, 'London You're a Lady' and 'White City' were luminous with ancient melodies. The middle eight of 'London You're a Lady' was from the turn of the seventeenth century – a section from 'Planxty Fanny Power' by the harpist Turlough O'Carolan. The melody for 'White City' was the tune of a traditional song called the 'Curragh of Kildare'. The chord sequences of both songs were majestic.

The lyrics were another matter. The writing in 'London You're a Lady' didn't seem so sure of itself. The personification of London as a prostrate whore was as lurid as a penny dreadful. 'White City', which Shane had written about the demolition of the West London greyhound-racing track, seemed to be the counterpart to 'Bottle of Smoke' – from *If I Should Fall from Grace with God* – but for dogs.

A couple of other songs he had written were scant of melody. They were formulaic, encrusted in rock idiom and dependent on extended sequences of improvisation. The song called 'USA' was morbidly oriented around the heroin imagery of Dr John's 'I Walk on Gilded Splinters'. Shane sang it in a humbug American accent. The pedestrian and vaguely magisterial chorus of '*It's the same wherever you go*' saddened me. The chorus of the other song, lifted from Lead Belly, was '*In those old cotton fields back home*'. Things didn't look good.

In rehearsal I found myself indulging in a technique I had come to resort to when I felt uninspired, which was to rock the bass-end of my accordion back and forth, holding down the chords. The effect was moody and atmospheric, but it was an indication not only of how little real cause there was for an accordion to be played at all, but how dull the song was.

To my relief, Shane had written an unrepentant soul song called 'Yeah Yeah Yeah Yeah Yeah', heavy with onbeat. The song was even further distant from what I knew Frank was concerned should be the Pogues' brand. Ironically, its novelty made it an instant candidate for release as a single.

I loved to play the song. It reminded me of my days as a soul guitarist. I made my accordion a Hammond B3, painted glissandi up and down the keyboard with my thumbnail, stabbed out soul figures full of minor sevenths and blue notes.

We found time at RAK at the beginning of October to record 'Yeah Yeah Yeah Yeah Yeah' with Lillywhite. Shane wanted strings. Fiachra Trench brought an orchestra to the studio. Shane described an ascending scale which would climb through the chorus like the boys' choir on the Stones' 'You Can't Always Get What You Want'. Fiachra pointed out that the end of the scale as it rose up through the chords would end up clashing. The boys' choir on 'You Can't Always Get What You Want' jumped a third, up to the tonic at the end of the scale to avoid the same problem. I sided with the Rolling Stones and our orchestral arranger. I doubted Shane's capabilities. Shane tapped impatiently on the ledge of the mixing desk in a show of restraint before his patience wore out.

'Of course it's going to clash!' he cried. 'That's the *whole point!*'

Trench went back to his orchestra leader to make adjustments to the score. When it came to a run-through against the backing track, the strings rose in inexorable steps one after the other. Instead of the jarring crash I expected, though, the prow of Shane's line cleaved cleanly through the chords.

Danielle came to visit me in London for my thirty-fourth birthday. After renting a room in Hampstead for eighteen months, I had just moved into a flat near Great Ormond Street Hospital. We went around buying things for the flat as if we were newly-weds.

She organised a birthday party for me in a room above a pub in Farringdon. Debsey came to it. I saw her talking to Danielle.

'Well,' Debsey said to me afterwards, 'I wanted to be able to complain how bloody predictable she is. But I can't really.'

A couple of days later, Danielle had gone back to Los Angeles. I was bound for Japan.

⚜

There was a gloomy desperation about Andrew on the flight to Tokyo. As short as the tour was going to be, it had been difficult to leave his lifetime companion, Deborah. For some time they had been trying to have a baby. The latest ordeal had been an ectopic pregnancy which had needed emergency treatment. To leave her during her convalescence made him miserable.

Tokyo was a monochrome confusion of aerial walkways, expressways and overpasses choked with black or white cars. Men in white helmets and facemasks, grey overalls and cloven footwear pruned the leafless trees down to knuckles. The only colour seemed to be the purple of ornamental kale in the flower-beds beneath the trees.

By nightfall, however, driving to our first gig in Ariake, the city had exploded into a conflagration of neon. Hoardings rippled, cascaded, flickered and flared. Beneath them swirled complicated currents and crosscurrents of people. In the middle of them, men in yellow overalls frantically waved luminous sticks.

Shane sometimes liked to change the set round at the last minute and without warning. Arms on his knees, stabbing with a marker, wiping his nose with a forearm, impatiently cuffing the paper, he would scribble over the set list we'd been happy with for a couple of weeks at least. We would swap looks over the top of his head, preparing for conflict.

For the Japanese audience, Shane wanted to do a melody by a jazz saxophonist called Pharoah Sanders. The piece was called 'Japan'. None of us had heard it before. We buckled under Shane's growing petulance and unpredictability and agreed to learn it.

One of my study courses at college had been 'Introduction to Psychology'. We studied human cortical processes when confronted by the Boring Figure – the image of the provocatively turned cheek and ear of a young woman flipping to represent the nose and eye of an old crone – and the Rubin Vase – the classic figure/ground, ground/figure dichotomy. Like the Rubin Vase and the Boring Figure, a stable perception was never reachable as to whether Shane was a genius or a fucking idiot.

With the customary stops and starts, misunderstandings and misconceptions, 'Japan' turned out to be a simple pentatonic melody which we could do nothing else with, but play it round a few times.

The suddenness, ferocity and brevity of the Japanese audience's applause took me by surprise. So did the expectant silence which followed, as they waited for us to play again. It happened song after song. If the time or key signature changed, a collective shriek went up. Other than that, at the end of each song, the applause vanished as precipitately as it had erupted.

Pharoah Sanders's tune was met with the same forbidding silence. With childlike ceremony we built it up from its initial iteration on the mandolin, adding instruments as we went. At the end of the piece Shane stepped up to the microphone to balance wordless chanting on the top of the foundations we'd made, like a capstone, wobbly as it was. His vocalisations were delivered with a boyish solemnity and conjured up an Indian pow-wow.

⊹

A couple of weeks after our return to England, after a few dates in the Eissporthallen of West Germany, we were depressed – but at the same time flattered – to play the vast and belittling venues of the Scottish Exhibition and Conference Centre in Glasgow, the National Exhibition Centre in Birmingham and the Leisure Centre in Brighton. The tour bus crept through their subterranean concrete galleries. We bleated in echoing corridors, lost. When we found them, the stages were hanging in black and of a scale worthy of William Wyler. They were erected in a huge expanse of cement, with railings and cables, flight cases and forklifts. At sound check, heater-fans roared like jet-turbines. At show time, once we had been led through the labyrinth backstage, an audience murmured darkly beyond the sable draperies hanging from the trusses. In Glasgow, it felt like desertion not to play at our stamping ground, Barrowland.

It was a relief to turn up for sound check at the Royal Ulster Hall, familiar from our tour with Costello four years before – until men from security, accompanied by the Royal Ulster Constabulary, came to tell us that a bomb warning had been called in and that we had to vacate the building.

The RUC performed a sweep. Though they came to tell us that they'd found nothing, Frank asked us if we wanted to cancel the gig. We said no.

My family were justifiably worried about the danger I had put myself into.

'First and foremost,' my dad said, 'you should remember you're just an entertainer.'

'I play the songs that get written,' I said.

·✠·

When we had been in Paris, a journalist had offered me the use of a house she and a friend were fixing up on an island off the Beara peninsula on the south-west coast of Ireland. Danielle flew over from Los Angeles to meet my family. After Christmas, we flew to Cork airport, drove over the Ring of Kerry and took a local one-car ferry from Castletownbere to Bere Island. At the end of a slurried road a quarter of a mile from the jetty we let ourselves into a freezing and dilapidated hovel. In the kitchen stood a rickety table, a tiny pot-bellied stove and an upside-down boat. We spent four days making St Brigid crosses from the reeds that grew everywhere, washed our dishes in the hand-numbing stream which flowed past the house and huddled round the stove drinking vodka. By the end of our stay, we had decided to get married.

'What are you thinking?' Frank said. 'Your wife-to-be lives six thousand miles away. You're in a band that tours seventy-five per cent of the year.'

'Congratulations would have been nice,' I said.

'Congratulations,' he said. 'You're fucking mad.'

✠

We started work on the next record at RAK, with Steve Lillywhite, in February 1989. Shane arrived at the studio, took one step into the control room from the corridor and released the contents of his stomach into a wastepaper bin. He sat to the side of the room struggling to take us all in, a meek expression on his face.

We went through the backing tracks quickly enough. In 'USA', we made a voodoo soundscape, braided with freewheeling, Jefferson Airplane improvisations, haunted by the sounds of wah-wah pedals, helicopter rotors and an explosion which evoked *Apocalypse Now*. By exposing the dark side of the original 'Summer of Love', we were proud to have our finger on the cultural pulse. We recorded Jem's jazz instrumental. It exploded into being with an Elvin Jones drum solo and blasted with alto, tenor and trombone solos, note-clusters stabbed on the piano, chords on the accordion straight from Mickey Baker's *Complete Course in Jazz Guitar*. We added ska, highlife and Romani to our stock-in-trade. To join the welter of new influences and the heterogeneity of the new soundscape, Jem added the hurdy-gurdy which he had bought on mail order. On the strength of my abiding enthusiasm for Hungarian gypsy music, and because the banging of teaspoons on a mandolin lacked the range, I had bought a hammered dulcimer. We also brought spoils from our visit to Australia the previous February to the studio: clap sticks and a bull-roarer. Everything we had in our arsenal, we used and unsparingly.

The magic-marker ink on the genre divider in the record shops that read 'World Music' was hardly dry. At the beginning of our career, when we bashed out waltzes, reels, polkas, hornpipes on ridiculed instruments and went around in second-hand suits, we exuded such a timelessness that we could easily have been plucked from any decade since the 1900s. Now, wearing our influences on our sleeves, with our Antipodean souvenirs, in our kaleidoscopic shirts, we exuded such a timeliness that it mired us up to our necks in the Nineties.

There was one stowaway song on the record, a reminder of the terra firma from which we had banished ourselves and which some of us were happy to see recede into the mists. Though it started out with a signature Count Basie Big Band motif, 'Boat Train' was a rattling procession of verses – the words unmistakably, inimitably and unapologetically MacGowan's. The song told of a journey by ferry and train from Ireland to London via Holyhead, narrated by the figure of Napper Tandy, an associate of Wolfe Tone in the Irish Rebellion of 1798. 'Boat Train' seemed to be from another, suddenly distant incarnation of the band.

Lillywhite had difficulty getting vocal performances from Shane. In Jem's song 'Misty Morning, Albert Bridge', he slurred

syllables and botched consonants. He attempted to inject enthusiasm into singing someone else's lyrics by means of the now
inevitable American accent and an intonation gravelly with fake
emotion. 'White City' and 'London You're a Lady' fared better,
but Shane's diction only served to highlight the platitude of the
songs' conceits, despite the daring of some of the imagery. Lillywhite tried different set-ups, from a booth in the studio, to sitting
Shane in front of a music stand in the control room. One evening,
as we were about to break for dinner, one of the engineers pro-
grammed a basic drumbeat, handed Shane a microphone with
a large chamber of reverb on it and set a full spool of three-inch
tape on record. We left to go and have dinner. When we got back,
Shane was still at it, sitting in Lillywhite's chair, chanting through
the studio monitors, over and over, his face lit up with childish
delight.

You've got to contact yourself
You've got to contact yourself
You've got to contact yourself
You've got to contact yourself

To compensate for the disengagement of Shane's vocals on the
album, we drafted in the other singers in the group – Philip for
the most part, but also Andrew and Spider – to prop up Shane's
ailing voice which dangled like a wounded staff-officer from the
shoulders of his adjutants. Andrew stepped up for 'Cotton Fields'.
He sang, like Shane, in an American accent and had been persuaded that an 'uh-uh' in the manner of Elvis Presley was a good
idea. Spider gave good account of himself in 'USA'. Philip's tenor
soared harmoniously in a couple of songs.

When Danielle had left to go back to Los Angeles, I would
leave my new flat every morning to walk up past Coram's Fields

and around to Russell Square station to catch the tube up to St John's Wood. As I turned the corner of Lansdowne Terrace into Bernard Street, repeatedly, more and more urgently as the recording proceeded, I found myself looking up into the sky into the west, where Danielle had gone, aching to be finished with this record and to be where she was.

Twenty-Eight

Andrew had become victim to cluster-headaches. They came without warning in volleys of regular and debilitating attacks. Without warning too, the episodes stopped, only to start again weeks or months later. Frequently we would find Andrew curled into a ball on the sofa in a darkened dressing room in pain.

Andrew petitioned to be granted a room to himself. We all wanted a room to ourselves, but the economics – the burden of Frank's commission and the number of people in the band and in the crew – wouldn't permit it. In Andrew's case, though, we had no problem.

Philip moved in with Darryl. It wasn't long before he had formed an attachment – as he had to both me and, after me, to Andrew – to this new roommate, and had become just as devout a fan of Nottingham Forest as Darryl was, if not more so. When they could, the pair of them travelled to see Forest play. On the 15th April 1989, a month after we had finished the album we had heavy-footedly entitled *Peace and Love*, Darryl and Philip went up to Sheffield to watch Nottingham Forest play Liverpool in the semi-final of the FA Cup at Hillsborough Stadium. A few minutes into the game, with fans spilling onto the pitch and police officers racing to form a cordon, the referee stopped the match. The weight of thousands of fans coming out of a tunnel at the rear had caused the compaction of those already on the terraces, squeezing them up against the fencing. Though many managed to escape by climbing or being pulled onto the grass, that day ninety-four people died from asphyxia.

The photographs of those gasping for breath behind the bars of the fence along the perimeter of the pitch were disturbing. When I saw them next, Darryl and Philip were wretched with horror from their experience. We dedicated the record to the memory of those who died in the disaster.

⽓

My and Danielle's wedding was set for the beginning of October. It was going to take place in the Cotswold village where the von Zernecks' cottage nestled in a crook in the no through road. The village couldn't have been more picturesque. It consisted of mostly Cotswold stone houses – with names like Tumbledown Cottage and Rose Cottage. A thirteenth-century church stood on a rise next to a manor-house-turned-hotel, the leaded windows of which gazed across patterned lawns, beds of impatiens, tennis courts and, beyond the inky copper beech at the end of the drive, the Vale of Evesham. Only jackdaws and the chimes of the church clock broke the silence – or an occasional RAF Harrier from Brize Norton which would come tilting over the wolds and rend the hush.

Danielle's dad was the paradigm of a Hollywood producer – tanned to the colour of a hazelnut, a coppery hue to his thinning hair, an Errol Flynn moustache and predisposed to navy-blue blazers. Her mum had small, blue, vivacious eyes, girlishly short hair, the cut and colour of which were tastefully expensive. Her infatuation with rural England was manifest in her predilection for tweed flat-caps and sleeveless quilted jackets.

We had a wedding planner. The wedding was going to be lavish, with a marquee erected in the rectory garden. A bus would be laid on for those living in London. Since it was going to take place in October, there would be quiverfuls of umbrellas. Against the threat of ruffling the slightest feather in the village at the prospect of a rock-and-roll wedding bringing along with it drunken hordes of Irish, an invitation would go out to the last inhabitant. More than a significant contribution would be made to the Church Roof Fund.

⋅✠⋅

Shane in the meantime had discovered Thailand. My familiarity with Thailand was tethered to Rodgers and Hammerstein's *The King and I* and the picture of Yul Brynner and Deborah Kerr on the sleeve of the soundtrack album – he in a crimson gold-braided pantaloon suit, foot up on a footstool, finger pointing skyward, she in a gigantic lilac crinoline at his feet. Otherwise my understanding of Thailand was restricted to a series of stereotypical images: the stiff, hindered choreography of tiny women with faces immobilised by smiles balancing miniature golden temples on their heads; rotting shantytowns made of laths, built on stilts in fetid estuaries crowded with filthy boats; thousands of square miles of sweating jungle in which labyrinthine ruins were hidden; lurid arcades crammed with child-prostitutes whose self-esteem was never likely to rise above that of a blow-up doll.

He returned to us extolling the benefits of Pattaya Beach. I couldn't imagine him ever leaving his hotel room. He was smug with beatitude and had a childlike belief in the chubby benevolence which radiated from the huge, golden and ubiquitous Buddhas. He wanted us to believe that Thailand was Shangri-La, Cockaigne, Tír na nÓg. A glaze of mysticism twinkled in his eyes for a week or two, to be clouded once more by sullenness and resentment. He became irascible, unpredictable, rudderless and unmanageable.

At the end of May, we travelled to Portugal. Between shows in Lisbon and Oporto we were taken down to the banks of the River Douro for a photo shoot. We stood around a skiff that was beached on the shingle downstream from the latticework of the Arrabida Bridge and the jumble of buildings on the opposite bank. Shane was in a dark and precarious state. There was a piratical dishevelment about him, reinforced by the eye-patch he had taken to wearing. When it came to taking the photographs, he was intractable. He clambered up on board the skiff and screamed at the photographer, and screamed at us. We waited, ransom to his dementia.

He failed to show up at a photo session for the cover of our album in London. The Scala at King's Cross had been rented for the day. The stage had been dressed with scores of church candles. The photographer and his assistant had set up their gear. We had all put on our best suits. In the end, dispirited, we pointlessly shot a roll or two and then went home.

On a night off in Madrid, a couple of weeks after our visit to Portugal, some of us were having dinner in the centre of town when we had word that Shane was wandering around the Barrio Salamanca with a samurai sword. The image of him staggering through the crowded, crepuscular streets, having obviously lost his mind, was appalling. I was thankful to be out of the clamour. We had become so inured that none of us interrupted our dinner.

The following day we arrived at San Sebastián airport at the same time as UB40, both bands on our way to play at the Velódromo Antonio Elorza. Discovering that our buses were parked next to one another, we agreed that, in exchange for Spider going on UB40's bus, we would invite their singer Ali Campbell onto ours.

Campbell climbed on the bus and went straight to the back lounge to sit with Shane. He had a pugnacious face with narrow eyes, a wide mouth and prominent canines.

By the time I took a seat in the next row forward from the lounge, Campbell had already started up a confrontation with Shane. He sat opposite, leaning forward, forearms on his knees, hands clasped. Shane was sitting in what passed for a comfy chair with his legs stretched out, his head back, sunglasses on, and a bottle of gin between his knees.

Campbell goaded him about whether or not Shane meant what he said in his lyrics, if he was being true to his upbringing, if his money was where his mouth was when it came to Ireland. Campbell started to go on about how much money he made, about his hometown of Birmingham, about how he helped the community he came from. I pretended to take in the lush landscape and red roofs of the Spanish Basque Country as the bus drove the fifteen miles to San Sebastián, wishing that we hadn't traded Spider for this brute. I would sooner have listened to Spider's wittering than to Campbell's aggressive apologia for his career, demanding from Shane a mutual account. Now and again, I looked back at the two of them. Campbell flicked the backs of his fingers against Shane's knee at every point he made, as if he thought Shane might fall asleep. Campbell's Birmingham accent made his brutality even uglier.

To begin with, Shane treated Campbell with the indifference he deserved, replying with noncommittal grunts and the occasional nod, preferring no doubt to have sat by himself with his drink and dozed off. Campbell's prodding continued. At one time, Shane could have run rings round such a thug as Campbell, but he was down and the resources he once had seemed to have left him. I willed Shane to come back at Campbell and shut him up with a definitive *coup de grâce* but, to my dismay, he had nothing.

'Shut up,' I heard Shane moan. It had no effect.

I continued to listen, becoming more and more resentful of Campbell's presence on our bus, more and more disheartened by Shane's defencelessness.

A guttural and anguished sound issued from Shane – part-scream, part-whimper. It had the effect of intensifying my battered but abiding loyalty to Shane to such a pitch that I got up, knelt on my seat and leant on the seatback.

'Hey!' I said to Campbell. 'That's enough. Please leave him alone.'

Campbell stiffened and turned his pugilist's face to me.

'Shut the fuck up and sit down, fuck-face! What do you know about anything?' he shouted. Confronted by such immediate and intemperate antagonism and knowing that to pursue anything with him at all would be pointless and could possibly make things worse for Shane, I sat back down in my seat, my forearms and shins prickling from adrenalin.

The release party for *Peace and Love* took place at the Boston Arms in Tufnell Park, the venue of our first rehearsal with Terry Woods. Mystifyingly, though the relentlessness of our touring schedule ebbed, *Peace and Love* climbed to No. 5 in the charts anyway. Throughout the summer, for weeks at a time, I was able to join my fiancée in California.

Los Angeles was a constant source of amazement to me. It was no longer a malevolently twinkling grid guarded by a thirty-foot cut-out of Arnold Schwarzenegger. Much of it turned out to be a vast suburb of family apartments and houses: Spanish colonial, English country, bungalows, craftsman; painted white, blue, puce, lilac; with roofs of pantile, wood shingle, asphalt. The trees

– ficus, fir, palm and oak – never shed their leaves. Day after day, the sun shone without abatement. It was as if time never passed.

During my absence, the band shot the video for 'Yeah Yeah Yeah Yeah Yeah.' Charlie McLennan stood in on accordion. I had not been able to afford to return from Los Angeles for it. The cost of the flights was punishing. I had locked horns with Jem about the band contributing half of the cost. I hoped to clinch my argument with the fact that Danielle and I were engaged to be married and had rented an apartment in Los Angeles. I implored him to acknowledge that Los Angeles was now my home, not London, though Danielle and I kept the flat on Great Ormond Street. In the end, it was Frank who ushered through the arrangement to split my airfares.

The Pogues had no money. Frank's commission was still fifteen per cent of gross. At a meeting with Anthony Addis after one of our tours, Terry complained in a voice piping with emotion about how difficult it had become to make ends meet.

'Terry,' Addis said in his flat Manchester accent. 'As much as I hate to say this, you have to live within your means.'

'I don't have any means to live within!' Terry replied.

⋅✠⋅

After a series of festivals in Europe, in July we travelled to the United States to co-headline what was called a 'shed tour' – a tour of small amphitheatres, half-covered by a cantilevered roof. Our co-headliners were a band called the Violent Femmes. They were darlings of college radio and deemed to be our counterparts in the United States. The tour went without incident with the exception of the first gig in Chicago, when the stage filled with acrid smoke from the transformer Terry needed to power his amplifier, and, at the last show in Fairfax, Virginia, Shane

352

being assisted from the stage after managing to sing just three songs.

While we were in New York we shot the video for our next single: Shane's song 'White City'. Such inertia had started to encroach that there was no storyboard or artistic conceit. We allowed a film crew to point their cameras at us while we sound-checked before a gig at Pier 84 on the Hudson River. Since first playing the song, in the instrumental breaks, Shane had taken up a shuffling sort of caper, away from the microphone, across the stage, jerkily pointing his fingers skyward at each step. It was as sophisticated as the video shoot got.

When the tour was finished I flew back to Los Angeles with Danielle who had accompanied us. The rest of the band went home.

Word had come during the recording of *Peace and Love* that Bob Dylan wanted us to open for him for six shows at the beginning of September on the Californian leg of his so-called Never Ending Tour – starting at the Greek Theater in Berkeley and ending at the Greek Theater in Los Angeles. The recognition by such a laureate was thrilling, but the pairing seemed late in coming. Frank saw it as a vindication of Shane's stature as a songwriter. If Shane did, none of us were aware.

In the third week of August, we reconvened for a handful of shows in Ireland. Shane had just returned from Thailand. At Leisureland in Galway, in a flocculent white flat-cap, he stared blindly and for long periods out at the audience, not knowing what to do. He became lost in the middle of songs.

We had become adept at responding quickly if he should augment a verse or simply excise a peculiarity of the arrangement. When we heard him start singing the words to a chorus over what should have been an instrumental section, or sometimes the words of another song altogether, a tremor radiated out from

353

the centre mike through all of us. Terry stepped forward into what he hoped was Shane's peripheral vision. He exaggerated his height in an attempt to bring to Shane's attention that he was singing the wrong song. Darryl pulled his face into an angry grimace. His instinct was to step forward too, but standing right behind Shane, he knew it was futile. Instead he swung his bass from side to side as if to sweep away all the wrong words Shane was singing. Beyond Darryl, Jem's mouth would adopt a resolute pucker, accompanied by raised eyebrows and eyes full of misery. Spider quivered, ramrod straight, his whistle clenched in his fist, looking at Shane in disbelief. Philip would look from Terry to me and back to Terry to try to get a fix on where we were supposed to be in the song. On his drum riser, Shane's fuck-ups darkened Andrew's eyes with fury. His arms seemed to hurl the sticks against the drum skins and the cymbals. He stared balefully at the back of Shane's head, beyond which, on the Saturday night at Reading Festival in August – a week before flying over to San Francisco for the first date of our tour opening for Dylan – fifteen thousand people receded into the twilight past the scaffolding above the mixing desk, towards a dim horizon of tents and the line of trees.

I flew to Los Angeles ahead of the beginning of our tour. Danielle and I made our way to Berkeley. On the day of the first show we drove up through lawns lush with grass and dense with trees to the amphitheatre, the concrete stage dwarfed by three walls of half-columns.

When the rest of the band arrived from the hotel, Shane was not among them. He had been too drunk, I was told, to be allowed on the plane. Not only that, but Charlie McLennan had also been debarred from getting on the plane at Heathrow. Charlie's signature was required to release our equipment from customs. As a consequence, we had neither singer nor gear.

We set about distributing the three-quarter-hour set between those who could sing, as we had done in Malmö nearly four years before. Again, Spider volunteered to sing most of the songs. Andrew would take 'Cotton Fields' and 'Star of the County Down', which we had recorded during the making of *Peace and Love*. Terry sang the couple of songs he'd written, 'The Gartloney Rats' and 'Young Ned of the Hill', and Philip, 'If I Should Fall from Grace with God' and 'Lorelei'. We borrowed a couple of guitars from somewhere. Dylan's backing band lent us their drum kit. A friend of Terry's was sent to scour Marin County for instruments.

I played a guitar belonging to Dylan's crew for three songs until Terry's friend appeared in one of the doorways at the side of the stage with an accordion.

It wasn't until after Labor Day that Charlie showed up with our equipment. Shane, it seemed, could not be persuaded to travel out with him and had stayed at home.

Backstage at the next gig opening for Dylan, at the Starlight Bowl in San Diego, Frank teased Dylan's crew about the charm stones each of them wore hanging on thongs round their necks.

'Yeah,' one of them said. 'We got charm stones. We've also got a singer. You got a singer? I don't see you wearing any charm stones.'

As we left our dressing room to go on stage, their singer was leaning against the wall outside his dressing room with a foot tucked behind him. His hands were in the pockets of a grey hoodie, the hood pulled up over his head. As I passed him on my way up the stairs to the stage, I took in his aquiline profile, papery face and wiry stubble. He met no one's eyes as we filed past.

Most nights after our set, I went into the audience to watch Dylan play. I struggled to recognise the songs. It was only when the unmistakable choruses of such songs as 'Mr Tambourine Man' or 'Positively 4th Street' managed to break free from the otherwise arcane arrangements that I knew what I was listening to.

At the Pacific Amphitheater in Costa Mesa, he sang a Van Morrison song, 'One Irish Rover.' The lyrics were addressed to someone far away, lost at sea. I couldn't help but think he'd chosen it for Shane, who remained resolutely in London.

Again, the heat of an American summer was intolerable – daylong and without relief. Day after day the sun beat down.

P.V. suffered worst. He complained all the time, not just about the heat but about the Puccini arias we had taken to listening to in the Econoline. He grumbled about the 'screeching', sank down into his seat at the back of the van and covered his head with his unseasonable leather jacket.

There had always been an air of the indoors about P.V. He had never been a person who cleaned up nicely, but we had noticed how much worse he was starting to look. Gradually, over the course of the tour, a jaundiced pallor had replaced his mottled and usually stubbly complexion. I would come across him backstage with his face in his hands or sitting with his back up against the wall cradling his head in his arms. I put his malaise down to the heat and road-fatigue. The crew's schedule was more punishing than ours, with early mornings and long days. That he drank a lot was common knowledge, though I hadn't seen much evidence in all the months I had shared a room with him.

By the time we arrived in Costa Mesa for the penultimate show on the Dylan tour, the yellowness of P.V.'s face had spread into the whites of his eyes and he was immobile from lethargy.

The weekend of the last date at the Greek Theater in Los Angeles, P.V. suffered a gastric attack of such violence that it dashed the walls of the bathroom in the hotel with blood and excrement. He was admitted to Cedars-Sinai Medical Center.

Now I realised what the source was of the vapour which had filled the rooms I had shared with him on the road. It wasn't so much the drink on his breath, nor a leaky bottle in his luggage. It was the smell of acetone coming from him. I was embarrassed at my naïvety.

When the tour supporting Dylan was finished, we had no other option but to leave him behind and go on to Phoenix where our own tour was going to continue and where we grimly expected to be reunited with Shane.

Shane turned up in Dallas. When he showed up backstage before the gig, there was no confrontation, no demand that he explain his absence. We welcomed him back in the dressing room as if he had returned from a day out. We went about the business of our sound check with an enclosed, self-preserving earnestness. It was hardly intended to punish him, merely to show him how little his absence had affected us.

That night we found ourselves standing out in the car park of the hotel in our nightwear. A burning cigarette in Shane's room had set off the fire alarm.

Our tour took us through the South and up into the Midwest.

We were on our way to a gig at the University of Michigan in Ann Arbor when Shane insisted we stop at a bar. We indulged him as we always had. Since turning up from England there was a mardiness about him which brooked no contradiction. The bar was a small lilac-coloured room with louvred shades. It was the middle of the afternoon and we were the only people in there. Shane made a great clatter with the stool which had been set against the bar with its legs on the other side of the foot rail. When Shane was eventually settled, the Hispanic barman came across.

'What'll it be, sir?' he said.

'Lo'i'lan'icetea,' Shane said. The barman set a paper napkin in front of his customer.

'Sorry, sir?'

'Lo'i'lan'icetea!' Shane shouted. 'Lo'i'lan'icetea! Lo'i'lan'-ICED-TEA!' We helped the hapless barman to understand he wanted a Long Island Iced Tea.

'Dago cunt!' Shane said, as the guy went down the bar. Either he didn't understand or chose not to.

'Shut it!' Spider beseeched.

'Dago cunt,' Shane said. 'He's a fucking dago cunt.'

I watched the barman make the Long Island Iced Tea. It was basically the same as a Black Zombie but with the substitution of triple sec for pastis. After the third or fourth, we managed to prise him out of the bar and get him back onto the bus. After the gig, he was so drunk that four of us had to carry him from the dressing room. We grunted with his dead weight across a car park. As we heaved him up the steps and onto the bus, he looked up at us and cackled as if the whole thing was a joke. We threw him onto the plastic leather sofa in the back lounge.

⁘

A week after the end of the tour, on the presentation of Danielle's Certificate of Approval to Marry, I picked up my and Danielle's marriage licence from the Faculty Office at Westminster Abbey.

For the weekend of our wedding, a striped tangerine-coloured marquee had been erected in the gardens of the rectory. All bed-and-breakfast accommodation in the locality had been taken up by Americans, the Pogues' entourage from London and my family from the north of England – and Twiggy, whom the von Zernecks knew. Jem was my best man. He took me, hung over from the rehearsal dinner the night before, to a café in Evesham for breakfast. I loved Jem and was grateful for his solicitude, and for a glass of champagne along with the bacon, eggs and black pudding in the Crown Tea Rooms on Bridge Street.

As I stood with Jem at the chancel-rail, Julie my soon-to-be mother-in-law came down the aisle to touch my arm with unsuppressed excitement. She was wearing an elaborately embroidered dress in creamy white and a cartwheel hat. When she'd gone to her pew, my uncle John came up.

'Tha'll not be living in a shoebox in t'middle of t'road then,' he said and went away.

At the exchange of vows, Danielle fought briefly with the vicar in order to say her vows without the impediment of her veil. At the reception, children tugged at the tails of my morning suit as Danielle and I cut the cake. Among them were Jem and Marcia's daughters, Kitty, now four, and Ella, two days away from turning six, along with Strummer's two daughters, Jazz and Lola. They had come with their mum, Gaby. Strummer himself was on tour with The Latino Rockabilly War, an hour down the M5 in Bristol. When Danielle and I had fed each other cake, Philip took his place on the stage with the swing band to sing 'Summer Wind', which since our ten days on St Martin had become our song.

The speeches had been made. Darryl had won £42 in the sweep as to how long the groom's speech would be. My aunt had threaded her way through the tables and chairs to sit and give me the one piece of advice which had sustained her in her thirty-year marriage to my uncle. My dad had finally had a dance with Twiggy. I had persuaded Rick Trevan to get out of the Bentley parked outside the rectory which he was convulsing with prolonged pressure on the accelerator pedal.

A watchful hush followed the procession of Shane and Victoria as they made their way between the backs of the rented chairs, towards where the rest of the Pogues were sitting. Shane was oblivious to the stir he caused. Victoria seemed at pains to deny it. I was annoyed at the shift in the centre of gravity. I was chuffed, though, that he had shown up at all.

He came over to my table with a gift for Danielle and me.

'Sorry I'm late,' he said. He and Victoria had been to a few villages of the same name. There were four others – in Surrey, Hertfordshire, Oxfordshire and Kent. 'I didn't go to the one in Kent,' he said.

He dropped his wedding present on the table. It was wrapped in maroon tissue paper. It obviously contained a record.

'Open it now if you like,' he said.

It was a bootleg of the Buzzcocks. With it was a stack of stills from the video of 'Yeah Yeah Yeah Yeah Yeah' which had been laminated into place mats. For the most part they were pictures of himself in demented attitudes of imperiousness wearing a coolie hat.

I tried, but couldn't persuade myself that there was no significance in his choosing stills from a video shoot I had not taken part in. Everything Shane did was imbued with significance. I was glum at the prospect that someone was eventually going to have to figure out what he was trying to tell all of us, as he continued to lurch into decline.

Twenty-Nine

When I got back from honeymoon, in November 1989, we managed to get through a two-and-a-half-week tour of sports halls and ice-hockey stadiums in Germany. Most nights Shane delayed our going on stage. He sat morose and intractable on a bench in the echoing locker room backstage, or gave himself to apoplexy over some petty concern, often enough the position of a particular song in the set list. His obduracy exhausted our supply of tactics. By the end of the tour we had beseeched, bartered and bellowed. In a couple of cases we had left him staring at the rubberised floor of the changing room and gone on stage without him. Spider took hold of the centre microphone with such a fever that it could have been Shane's neck. He spat out the lyrics into it with such violence that it could have been Shane's face.

In December, the now obligatory Christmas tour was cancelled in favour of what we hoped would be the restorative project of recording demos for a further record. We met at a studio off Highgate Road.

Jem brought in a couple of songs, both of them spleenful. One was called 'Bastard Landlord' and was about Marcia's mum's situation in rented accommodation and the hiking up of her rent. The other one was called 'The Wake of the Medusa' – a haggardly lit cautionary tale on the theme of theft, full of howling wind, lightning and empty caskets. I wondered if it was about Frank.

The material of Shane's we worked on included an instrumental called 'Lust for Vomit' and a song tentatively entitled 'Mexican Funeral in Paris.' They were nothing more than sketches. There was a pastiche of Van Morrison, which Shane had dedicated to Victoria.

Three songs stuck out: a heroin-inspired meditation on Thailand called 'Summer in Siam' and a couple of tenderly elegiac songs, both harking back to Shane's youth in London. One of them was called 'Five Green Queens and Jean.' The other was called 'NW3,' the melody of which was beautiful and made us nostalgic for the days when everything was in front of us.

We took Christmas off before our second tour of Australia. The holiday only deepened Shane's detachment, which, by the time we met again in Perth, had turned into isolation.

In Perth, Shane performed for only a fraction of the show. We were lucky if he managed to get all the way through any of the songs. I saw Spider turning at his microphone, sneering with loathing as Shane lurched, confused, through the songs. Shane staggered away from the microphone and towards the side of the stage where he slumped onto a chair next to Charlie McLennan's chest of drawers. Without missing a beat Spider stepped across to the centre microphone to take up the singing. Playing suddenly became untrammelled. Spider's voice might have lacked the sonority of Shane's but at least he knew all the words. In spite of that, once Shane had gone, our performance felt empty, lightweight, lacking in substance.

As with our last tour of Australia, Vivian Lees was the promoter. We all liked him and regretted the condition in which we had brought Shane back to the Antipodes. When we came off stage, Lees's face was glazed over.

Frank strode into the dressing room. He pushed Shane away from where he was bungling the opening of a bottle of wine. Frank stood inches away from his face.

'You think you can do what you fucking want and fuck every-one else?' Frank shouted. 'You want to go to fucking Thailand? Go to fucking Thailand! Well, I've got one last card, right? I can make fucking sure you never get in that fucking country. I know two princes, right, associated with the fucking Thai royal fucking family, right, and I can make fucking sure you never get into fucking Thailand. All it takes is one phone call and you're fucked as far as going to Thailand. You and Thailand? That's fucking his-tory, right? You're fucking history, man.'

'History Man?' Spider said. 'Didn't Malcolm Bradbury write that?'

'Shut the fuck up,' Frank said. 'Not helpful.'

By the time we had done the first couple of gigs, Lees had star-ted to clap pointedly as we filed off stage. Backstage we sat in various attitudes of glumness, our forearms on our knees, staring at the floor. Spider strutted up and down the dressing room re-peating the word 'fuck' to himself.

In Canberra it was raining. Frank was eager to let us know that the Irish Ambassador to Australia would be coming to the gig.

'Would he be after bringing a couple o' sticks o' gelignite and an owld alarum clock?' Spider said.

'When are you going to fucking grow up?' Frank said.

Again, Shane only managed to get through a part of the set. Spider took over his microphone, cutting short Shane's increas-ingly wrathful helplessness. When we came off stage, to our re-lief, Shane was gone.

The dressing room was a corner of the auditorium-bar screened off by black felt curtains. Exhausted, Spider sat hunched with his elbows on his knees, pressing his face into a towel. The heads of a couple of lads appeared above the curtain rail. They waved a slopping brown flagon around. They had crew cuts, slimy with sweat. A camera flashed.

364

''ERE WE GO! 'ERE WE GO! 'ERE WE GO!' one of them sang to the now chronically iterated tune of 'Stars and Stripes Forever'. More and more heads appeared above the rail. We all sat staring at the concrete floor.

'Hey! Hey! Philip! Where's Shane?' they called down.

'Give us twenty minutes, will you?' Philip called up to them in a surprisingly cheery voice. He wiggled his hands by his ears and looked for something he pretended he'd dropped on the floor.

'Where's Shane? Has Shane gone? He's bloody pissed, ain't he? Hit the turps again! What a bludger!'

Joey shone a torch along the line of heads above the curtain.

'Give the band a couple of minutes, please,' he said. 'Just be nice and fuck off, will you?'

Spider pulled his face out of the towel and kneaded it in his fingers. He was clenching and unclenching his jaw.

'FUCK OFF!' Spider yelled, with so much force that his voice broke into bleating. 'JUST FUCK OFF AND LEAVE US ALONE!'

No sooner were the words out of Spider's mouth than he clasped his towel over his face and started to wave, frantically. I handed him a bottle of water from the table next to me. He took the towel from his face.

'Bin!'

I managed to slide a large vinyl bin lined with plastic between his knees. He hugged the rim and gave himself up to violent retching. When he'd finished, he wiped his face. I was horrified to see that the towel was stained with blood.

'You're throwing up blood,' I said.

'Am I?' he said. He looked at the towel, glanced inside the bin. He quivered with wrath.

'Cunt! Cunt! Fucking cunt! Waste of fucking space!' Spider said.

'I'd like to say that as soon as Viv's back with the van, we'll get the fuck out of here,' Joey said. 'But I can't, because Frank wants you to meet the Irish Ambassador.'

Not only did we have to wait for Lees to come back with the van, but also we had to wait for Andrew who was still in the kimono he put on after gigs. We were further delayed by Ambassador Burke's wife who wouldn't let go of Andrew's hand, so concerned was she about how much weight Andrew lost in the course of a gig.

Charlie Malcolm, our new roadie, a guy from Dublin with crossing front teeth, announced the van's arrival. Saying nothing to Frank or to the ambassador and his wife, we left for the hotel.

We climbed into the van. The air inside smelled of recent cigarette smoke. 'Where's the cunt?' Spider asked.

'I took him back,' Lees said. 'Charlie helped him onto the van and I helped him off.'

'You should have heard the fucking crack when he hit the pavement,' Charlie Malcolm said.

'He bumped his head slightly,' said Vivian.

I thought so little of Shane that I couldn't care less. I laughed with everyone else at the idea of Lees, who was otherwise so even-tempered, who had once held Shane in such high esteem, who loved our music, being driven to such a length as chucking him out onto the pavement outside the hotel.

We all went to the room Jem and Darryl shared. We were grateful for one another's company, grateful for Darryl's beloved house music, grateful to be away from Frank, and Shane, to be by ourselves. Spider seemed to have recovered. He hoisted himself onto one of the beds and started to roll a joint.

There were two loud raps on the door. Darryl turned the cassette player down and got up to answer it but Frank was somehow already standing in the room. His face was red. He moistened his lips with his tongue.

'Guys!' he said. Though his face was haggard and his eyes dull with drink, there was an edge about him. His mouth was adhesive. He sucked air through his teeth.

'I just want to express my distaste at the shoddy way you treated the ambassador at the gig tonight,' he said.

'What?' Andrew said.

'Coming backstage like that can be intimidating enough at any time,' Frank went on. 'The least you could have done would have been to show a bit of civility.'

'Civility?' Andrew snorted. 'The Irish Ambassador is the equivalent to Les Patterson. His wife wouldn't let go of me.'

'Is this a joke?' asked Jem.

'For once, this is not a fucking joke!' Frank said. He put a finger beneath his nose, as if to take a moment or two to calm himself. 'These people are important people to be polite to,' he said.

'If they're so important,' Spider said, 'where was Shane?'

'The fucking Brits can have him,' Frank said. 'He's no use to Ireland.'

'What are you talking about?' Spider said. 'Shane's on a roll!'

'I'm going to fucking hit you, Spider!' Frank said. 'Fucking smart-arse digs all the fucking time, all the fucking time!'

'Oh Frank,' Spider said. 'Just fuck off, will you?'

Before I knew it, Frank had lunged at Spider and with the heel of his hand in the middle of his chest had stuffed him into the pillows on the bed. Spider began gasping. I jumped on top of Frank, locked him around the neck and pulled him backwards off the bed. I dumped him on the floor and fell backwards over the chair at the vanity table.

'DON'T YOU FUCKING DARE!' I shouted.

'For fuck's sake, Frank,' Spider grunted. Jem and Andrew clambered over the spare bed to stand over Frank in case he got up. Terry stood shaking his fists.

'You fucking idiot! You fucking idiot!' Terry said.

'Get out, Frank,' Jem said. Frank hooked his elbow over the corner of the bed, crouched and heaved himself up.

'You don't know what a mistake you just made,' Frank said.

'No!' Jem shouted. '*You* don't know!'

Frank stood staring at us all.

'I'll fucking hit who I fucking want in this group!' he shouted. 'I'll do what I fucking want with this group! You don't fucking know anything!' He chopped the air. 'You-don't-fucking-know-anything!'

Terry went over to him holding his arms out, tilting his head and smiling and closing his eyes.

'You're wrong. You're wrong,' Terry said. 'You're wrong, Frank. You're wrong.'

'Fuck off away from me, Terry,' Frank said.

'I think it's time you left, Frank,' Andrew said. Frank snatched his sleeve from Terry's grip and strode out of the room.

Spider felt around for his packet of cigarettes, pulled one out, ruffled his hair, propped himself back up against the pillows. He adjusted the magazine in his lap and carried on rolling the joint.

'Frank ought to be the Irish Ambassador,' Jem said. 'Canberra's his kind of town.'

⁂

Over the next week, Frank put on a show of bonhomie and optimism that was so buoyant that I felt sorry for him.

'Just go up on that stage and do your best,' Frank said as we lined up along the wall before the gig in Wellington, New Zealand. 'Play to his strengths.'

'What strengths would those be?' Andrew said.

It had become Shane and Charlie McLennan's custom, each

night before the gig, to find a room and lock themselves in it for twenty minutes. A couple of lines of amphetamine would at least give Shane a wire to walk. That night, Charlie McLennan didn't come to lean out behind the curtains to wiggle his Maglite at the back of the hall. The house lights sank the auditorium into darkness without Charlie's cue. A roar went up. We held back, waiting for Shane.

'He's on his way,' Joey said. 'Go, go, go!'

We stepped up between the high black curtains and out under the lights. Terry held out a hand in greeting to the horde receding into the dark. Spider weaved up to the centre mike with his head bowed and then held aloft his tin whistles in a clenched fist. Frowning against the lights, he looked out into the crowd – a stew of sweating faces, rat-tailed hair, oily and bare arms, gaping mouths and someone whirling a pair of trousers above his head.

''OW ARE YA?' Spider said. 'YAWRIGHT?'

Plainly, amid the roaring of the crowd, someone below him shouted out:

'FUCK OFF! WE WANT SHANE!'

We stood around waiting. There was no sign of Shane. I dragged a chord or two out of my accordion, pretending to make sure it was working. Jem was standing at the far side of the stage with his hands folded over the top of his banjo, waiting. With his cheeks stained by the puce blotches of his stigmata, his face was even more lugubrious. Darryl paced about with his bass, going over to his amp to adjust something. Andrew, sleeves rolled up, bent down to tighten a lug nut on the rim of one of his drums and then looked up at the empty place where Shane should have been. Philip stepped back and forth in his tight suit, tweaking a string into tune. Terry with a slightly pursed mouth peered at the row of knobs along the top of his amp.

Alerted to a movement at the side of the stage, I watched Charlie McLennan and Charlie Malcolm drag Shane out of the gloom, an arm slung round each of their necks, between flight cases, over cables, to the side of the stage where Charlie McLennan's chest of drawers stood. Charlie Malcolm stood Shane on his feet to face the stage and steadied him for a moment. Charlie McLennan wiped the powder from Shane's nose. I saw Shane hold out his hand. Charlie McLennan looked at him, baffled. Shane wafted his arms and then buckled over, shouting. Charlie patted his pockets, looked round in panic and shone his Maglite over the top of his chest of drawers. In the end, while Charlie Malcolm held Shane up, Charlie McLennan bent down to rummage through Shane's trouser pockets. He fished out a pair of sunglasses. Shane snatched them out of his fingers.

When Shane had teetered to his microphone, he grabbed it to his mouth and screamed into it.

'YAAAAAAAAAAAGH!'

I had to clap my hands over my ears. Terry retracted his head like a tortoise. With a knitted brow, D.J. located a button on his mixing desk and, with a forefinger, prodded out most of the noise. It continued through the front-of-house speakers and only stopped when Shane's lungs gave out, when he twisted round to glare at Andrew, histrionic in his fury that Andrew hadn't yet counted in the first song.

'COME ON!' he shouted. He lifted up the stand to bang it back down onto the stage. Andrew sat for a moment, taking his time, making him wait.

'ONE TWO THREE FOUR!' Andrew eventually shouted.

In the middle of the set, in the middle of a song, what energy Shane had, gave out. He dropped to the ground and sat splay-legged with his back to the audience. We looked from one to the other. We didn't stop playing. Shane bent over, brought the microphone to his mouth and gave vent to a desperate, anguished and lung-emptying howl, which, once finished, started up again, and again, relentlessly, as if he feared interruption.

I became aware of Jem walking slowly across, still playing his banjo. He stopped to stand over Shane, the stigmata under his eyes livid in the stage lighting. Shane became aware only when Jem stopped playing to touch him on the shoulder. Shane looked up. Jem shook his head slowly.

With the microphone stand for support, Shane managed to heave himself up to tower above Jem. Ignoring Jem, he staggered round, staring balefully at each of us. He started to drive the base of the stand repeatedly onto the boards. With each bang I saw the speakers in the front wedges flutter. It was all I could do to ignore the pounding, focus on Andrew's drumming, Philip's guitar, and confine myself to the song it seemed wholly pointless to continue playing but impossible to bring to an end.

Eventually the song staggered to a standstill. Yet Shane carried on driving the base of the microphone stand against the stage.

'Get that fucking thing off him!' I heard Frank shout from the side.

Jem stood in front of Shane, his hands folded one over the other. Shane stared with malevolence at him for a while until a haggard contrition began to suffuse his face. He mauled the stage with the base of the stand one last time and finally relented. The crowd roared – with disapproval or ridicule I couldn't tell. A shoe bounced off the edge of the drum riser.

After the gig, in the tiny dressing room at the foot of the couple of steps from the stage, we sat for a long time, stunned, dejected and exhausted. At the near end of the grimy plum-coloured velvet sofa, Andrew sat in his kimono, leaning on his knees, pulling angrily on a cigarette. Next to him Frank, his face in his hands, stared into middle distance between his fingers. Jem and Darryl stood with their arses on the edge of the table opposite. Philip squatted on the top step from the stage next to a grimy wash-stand. I sat with a towel wrapped around my waist on one of the metal-framed chairs and waited to see what was going to happen next, if anything. At the far end of the sofa with his head in the corner of the wall, Shane slouched in an attitude of defiant incorrigibility, opaque behind his shades.

Still wearing his black suit and with a glass of champagne trembling in his fingers, Terry spoke up.

'Don't you understand?' he said. 'We try and try and try, Shane. That's all we can do.' He had already had a couple of drinks. He was on the verge of tears.

'Give it a rest, Terry,' Frank said. Terry went to sit down next to Philip, shaking his head. He stared at Shane with mournful eyes.

Shane sniffed scornfully and said:

'Sawon giyia si-rett!'

There was a brief silence.

'What!?' Spider laughed.

'CI-GA-RETTE!' Shane enunciated elaborately. 'SAWON GIMME A CI-GA-RETTE!'

None of us went to our pockets. None of us wanted to give him anything. To come forward with a cigarette would have been tantamount to treachery. We sat ranged against him in mute hatred.

Suddenly his back arched, his elbows dug into his sides and he lifted his face to the ceiling. The thud of his head against the wall made me jump.

'SAWON GIMME A SI-RETT!' he screamed. The artery at the side of his throat swelled with the effort. Frank uncovered his face.

'Jesus,' he said. 'Give the twat a cigarette, will you Andrew?'

'I'm not giving that cunt a cigarette!' Andrew shouted. He dashed ash from the end of his cigarette onto the carpet and glowered down the sofa at Shane.

'Why should I do anything any more for that cunt piece of shit waste of fucking time doesn't fucking do anything for fucking us does he piece of shit waste of space MACGOWAN!'

Shane wiped his forearm under his nose, coughed, clawed up his bottle which was standing on the floor between his feet and upended it in his mouth. He shook the last of the wine into his throat and then let the bottle dangle between his legs.

'Cunt,' he said, bored.

Andrew exploded across the bench behind Frank to get at Shane and when he did, he pummelled him with the heels of his hands, pushing Shane off the bench onto the floor. A galvanised bucket had been standing under the washstand. Shane's mouth hit the edge of it with a clank. Andrew continued to shunt Shane further under the sink with his palms.

Frank and Joey jumped up. There was a scuffle with grating heels, clatters and grunts, after which Andrew ended up lying on top of Joey's hips and Joey face down on the floor. Frank knelt over Andrew with his hands on his knees, panting and red-faced. Shane lay twisted under the sink.

'Calm down, Andrew!' Frank shouted into Andrew's face. 'Just calm the fuck down, right?'

Shane's mouth had filled with blood, bubbling through the stumps of his teeth. He sat up a bit and felt his face for his shades. They had fallen off somewhere. His eyes were swimming. He closed them, it seemed from pain. When he opened them again, he looked across at Andrew, in defiant puzzlement.

'What's matter with you?' he said.

Spider burst into a cackle of disbelief and stared at the floor, barring his face with outspread fingers.

'Christ!'

It took Shane a moment to locate Spider's voice.

'What?'

'Are you fucking DENSE?' Spider said. Shane pursed his lips and shrugged. Cradling the bucket, his head dithering, he attempted to get up but the bucket spun out from under his arm. A second attempt resulted in his bonking his head against the underside of the sink. He sat back down against the wall.

Frank and Joey hoisted him out and up by the armpits and began to walk him back to the bench. Shane, catching sight of a packet of cigarettes on the table, wriggled Joey and Frank off and sidestepped to pick the packet up. It had been floating in spilt drinks. The cigarette that was in it was sodden and split. Shane stood shivering for a moment looking at it. He slammed his hands down on the table, bent forward towards the wall and screwed up his eyes.

'ALL I FUCKING WANT IS A FUCKING CIGARETTE!' he shouted. His voice had gone and he was crying. 'CAN'T YOU UNDERSTAND ALL I FUCKING WANT IS A FUCKING CIGARETTE!'

'Here!' Andrew shouted, digging into his kimono pocket. 'Have a fucking cigarette!'

He brought out his packet and, one by one, pelted Shane with all the cigarettes there were in it. Shane tried to catch some of them but they tumbled through his fingers and rolled across the carpet, under the sink, under the bench. He gave up trying and stood as they hit him in his bleeding mouth, in his eyes and bounced off his chest.

Charlie Malcolm and Lees came in to take Shane back to the hotel. We watched in silence as they helped him out of the dressing room. Charlie handed him a cigarette and lit it for him. When they had gone we started to try and talk about something else but it was no use.

Charlie Malcolm and Charlie McLennan husbanded Shane through the rest of the tour. During the day the former watered down his drinks. In the evenings, before each of the remaining gigs, the latter ushered Shane into an empty room and locked the door behind them. A grim lassitude descended on us. We were desperate to get home, ruefully counting the days until we could be rid of Shane, however temporarily, full of fear for the future.

Thirty

In the third week of June, four months after coming back from Australia, I packed up my clothes, a couple of instruments, notebooks and my typewriter, and headed out on the Great Western Railway past Oxford and across the Severn, to record at Rockfield Studios. Rockfield was a refurbished farmhouse a couple of miles outside Monmouth. Not only had the likes of Van der Graaf Generator, Hawkwind and Black Sabbath made records there, but also it was where 'Bohemian Rhapsody' had been recorded.

Charlie McLennan picked me up from Newport railway station. We sped up the A449 to Monmouth. He sat nibbling the fingers of one hand. His other lolled on the steering wheel. Neither of us spoke much. Charlie wasn't a person for talking. Charlie went about his life seemingly sealed off from what was going on around him, his blue eyes absent, inwardly focused, preoccupied with some business or other, his layered blond hair carefully coiffed.

The rationale for recording at a residential studio in the Welsh countryside echoed the one behind a season at a sanatorium as a cure for tuberculosis. In order to reconstitute Shane as either a functioning artist or a human being or both, I wondered if it was Frank's strategy to provide plentiful amounts of fresh air and good nutrition. On the other hand, Frank's intention might well have been to imprison him out in the Welsh Marches in order to get a record out of him before it all went to shit.

As far as sanatoria went there was plenty of food. Every evening a covey of cooks clattered and clanged in the kitchen and served up roasts, mounds of stew and bologneses on a long wooden table, with vegetarian versions of each. As far as sanatoria went there was plenty of fresh air. On many an afternoon throughout June and July and into August we took ourselves on walks through the hayfields, along Offa's Dyke, or along the river into Monmouth, to village fêtes and jumble sales, or on outings to Symonds Yat. The weather was unremittingly clement. What other similarities there were between Rockfield Studios and, say, the Berghof at Davos-Platz ended with the lack of altitude and, after the first couple of weeks, with the absence of the one person Frank might have thought would benefit the most from the seclusion or the incarceration.

There had been a problem about who was going to produce. The lacklustre success of *Peace and Love* had emptied our dance-card. Steve Lillywhite had declined. At the last minute Strummer stepped up. He skidded to a halt in the courtyard in his green Morris Minor.

I hadn't seen him since our week at the Town and Country in March 1988. In the meantime, he had made a couple of re-cords: a soundtrack for an independent film and his own album, *Earthquake Weather*. He had been on tour with his group The Latino Rockabilly War which featured guitarist Zander Schloss, who had played Karl in *Straight to Hell*. Strummer had had a small part in Jim Jarmusch's film *Mystery Train*, and, in the last couple of months, an even smaller one in a film by Aki Kauris-mäki called *I Hired a Contract Killer*. I had spoken to him once, in February 1989. I had answered the phone to him as he was clear-ing out of the studio on Sunset Boulevard after recording *Earth-quake Weather*. He had wanted to talk to Danielle. He climbed out of his Morris Minor wearing a bent cowboy hat tilted back on his head. We greeted one another civilly.

As we recorded, Strummer made copious and minuscule notes in a hard-backed notebook, with drawings of the positions of the microphones and the angles of the wooden acoustic vanes in the drum room. A line from one of Shane's songs, 'Hell's Ditch', appealed to him so much that he scrawled it in huge letters on a banner and posted it on the beam over the veranda:

NAKED HOWLING FREEDOM!

Before showing up at Rockfield, Shane had been, as we expected, to Thailand. What guide vocals he managed to accomplish in the first couple of weeks were slurred and indistinct. We recorded as much as we could with him, before he slipped the snare and disappeared to London.

The songs he left behind dwelled on imprisonment. The song 'Hell's Ditch' was set in a Spanish prison, with chains, bunks, buggery and execution. A version of Culture's 'I'm Alone in the Wilderness', which featured Spider singing the chorus, was a rap by Shane about pindown, a method of punishment similar to lockdown in prisons but used on children. Its practice in a Staffordshire children's home had recently been the subject of a public inquiry.

Unsurprisingly too, a lot of the songs he left behind no longer dealt with Shane's idea of Shangri-La, Big Rock Candy Mountain or Tír na nÓg as a place to aspire to – as 'Streams of Whiskey' had. Now he seemed preoccupied with Paradises Lost and Gardens of Eden he had been cast out from. Shane's fall, as a Catholic, echoed the original Fall. Now, though, more than ever, the lyrics he was writing were haunted by regret or yearning for abnegation. 'Five Green Queens and Jean' described a time when, to Shane, poker dice and a bin bag were all that mattered. A tender song, it reminded me of Eeyore's happiness with the gifts of a popped green balloon and an empty honey jar which Pooh and Piglet brought to Eeyore's Gloomy Place on his birthday.

'Summer in Siam' stood at the core of Shane's desire to be done with everything. It was a meditation on the nullification of self. 'House of the Gods' – with an introduction ironically lifted straight from 'You Still Believe in Me' from the Beach Boys' *Pet Sounds* – contained lyrics which were unmistakably directed towards us: he had finally found a place we could never reach, a place where no mongrels preach.

'Sunnyside of the Street' seemed to explain that the drunkenness which prevented Shane from boarding the plane for San Francisco, for the West Coast leg of our tour opening for Bob Dylan, had in fact been sheer recalcitrance. He had wanted to stay right there, on the sunny side of the street. Later in the song, as I came to understand what it meant, a line gave me the chills.

He sang that he would not be reconstructed. It was then that I knew we were going to lose him, if we hadn't already.

Shane had also written a song called 'Sayonara'. The message was obvious.

For the first couple of weeks I had been billeted with Darryl above the room with the television in it. It was noisy with the World Cup. It was apt that the BBC should have chosen the aria 'Nessun Dorma' for their coverage of the Italian World Cup. It meant 'none shall sleep'. When Shane had gone back to London and it had become apparent that he had little interest in returning to Wales, I took the room Charlie had set aside for him – a quiet suite above a storage room. It had a south-facing window overlooking a hayfield. Each morning I watched a troop of foxes skulk between the hay bales.

The recording went on without Shane. Terry had a couple of songs and an instrumental. Jem's song 'The Wake of the Medusa' took its inspiration from Géricault's painting *Le Radeau de la Méduse*. The song seemed to illustrate the correlations between our predicament and that of the victims on the raft, substituting Frank for Viscount de Chaumereys, the captain of the *Méduse*, and ourselves for the hapless crew members cast adrift.

We carried on with the recording – Terry's and Jem's songs, a song Strummer had written for Kaurismäki's film, overdubs and even a jam or two – as we waited for Shane to return. The World Cup ended. We travelled to Reggio Emilia in Italy to play a couple of communist festivals without Shane. When we got back Strummer and our engineer Paul Cobbold – a Hereford guy with vaguely seafaring features: a prominent nose and windswept blond hair – worked on our overdubs and repairs in turn. Jem went around the buildings with a DAT recorder, hitting old bits of farm machinery he came across. Spider fell in with a local band called the Monmouth Pumas. In the late afternoon a beaten-up old van would skid into the courtyard throwing up dust. Spider would fall out of it cackling with drink. Andrew seemed to spend his time off hiking. For the most part I lingered in the control room, listening and suggesting overdubs. I put myself forward to play a thumb piano on 'Summer in Siam', an electric sitar on 'House of the Gods', Spanish guitar on 'Lorca's Novena', Stratocaster on 'Rainbow Man', handclaps on 'The Wake of the Medusa', piano wherever I could. I wished I'd come up with Andrew's idea to mike up the engine of Strummer's Morris Minor for the beginning of the instrumental section in 'Rain Street'.

The day Shane was due to come back to record vocals there was a palpable air of expectancy around the studios. When Charlie McLennan's car crunched across the gravel in the courtyard I was sitting on the sofa in the control room, listening back. I heard the sound of the car doors. If it had not been Shane, I would have gone out to greet them. I was scared of seeing him, weary of the complexity of what should have been ordinary social congress with him. I stayed put, my forearms on my knees, my head down.

I became aware of Shane's latticed shoes in my field of vision. When I saw the bottom of a dove-grey pair of trousers with a more or less sharp crease in them I remembered the grey suit he had always worn when he meant business – during the rehearsals for 'A Rainy Night in Soho' and 'The Broad Majestic Shannon' and for the video of 'Dirty Old Town'. My heart rose. I looked up at him standing next to me in the control room. I took in the suit, the rings on his brown fingers, his black shirt – until I got to his head.

It dithered senescently on his neck in an attitude that was simultaneously sheepish and judgemental, nominally guilty about his absence but demanding to know what we had been doing while he had been away. He was smoking a cigarette. Through

381

the wreaths of smoke which escaped through his nostrils, his eyes were incapable of focusing and his lids were heavy. Strummer swivelled in his producer's chair and greeted him robustly. Shane let out a cackle that was supposed to have been ironic. I wanted to leave the control room but didn't want my departure to come across as too much of a gesture of disappointment, anger or of my feeling of doom.

Strummer and Paul Cobbold set about painstakingly recording Shane's vocals. I relieved myself of the compulsion always to be down in the studio and spent the afternoons up in my room, playing my guitar or writing, and then taking a walk along the river.

Cobbold and Strummer's job wasn't easy. It was standard practice to compile multiple vocal tracks. Once they had got a handful of takes they let Shane go in order to piece together a master track of such bits as they could use. Charlie whisked Shane away to London. I happened to go down to the control room one afternoon to find Cobbold in the process of copying a *t* consonant from elsewhere on the vocal track, to insert it where it was needed. He did it over and over again, until it sounded as natural as he could make it. Once he'd finished, he moved on to another one.

At the end of August, we finished the record and went our separate ways for the rest of the summer. I packed my things into a hired car and drove back to London. A couple of days later I was back in Los Angeles. Soon after, I was horrified to hear that on a seaside holiday with her family, Frank's fourteen-year-old daughter Shannon had dived into shallow water and broken her neck.

We released two singles from *Hell's Ditch* – 'Summer in Siam' and 'Sunnyside of the Street'. The former gave rise to a regrettable video, which was cluttered with as many stereotypical images of Thailand as my prejudices were. Along with the dancers with small temples on their heads, an enormous Buddha and vaguely underage girls in hot pants, was the addition of kick-boxing. Shane, wearing a beard reminiscent of Rolf Harris, made a hackneyed attempt at bringing his recorded vocal performance to life. The rest of us looked miserable. 'Summer in Siam' reached the upper sixties in the charts. 'Sunnyside of the Street' made no showing at all.

At the end of September we started a five-week tour of England – playing many of the same halls we had when we had opened for Elvis Costello in 1984. Although P.V. had resumed working for us and was to be seen regularly at Rockfield, his condition was precarious. When we came off the stage at Glasgow Barrowland, before the customary encores, he had already left his lighting desk and had come to the dressing room. His face was leeched of colour and his mouth fixed into a senile smile. By the time we had to go back on stage, he had collapsed in the dressing-room doorway. We were forced to step over him on our way to the stairs. As we did, he looked up at us, seeming both to recognise us and not to know who we were at all. It was the last time I saw him alive.

In November and December, with Kirsty MacColl, we toured a succession of ice-stadiums and civic centres, and otherwise suffered a sleet-lashed and freezing Germany.

Andrew let us know that Deborah, his childhood sweetheart and lifetime companion, was four months pregnant. Bearing in mind Deborah's ectopic pregnancy two years before, it hadn't been a particularly calm passage to parenthood. Andrew's pride and abashment when he made his announcement made me adore him, though I feared for him and Deborah – as I had for Jem and Marcia when they were expecting a baby in 1982 – embarking on parenthood in circumstances that were more or less hostile.

⊹

On an unseasonably sunny afternoon between Hanover and Offenbach, Jem and I were sitting by ourselves in the back of the bus, on either side of the lounge, each at our own table, when Jem leant across the aisle towards me, holding what turned out to be the management contract, with his thumb on a particular clause.

'Read that,' he said. 'Does it mean what I think it means?'

The clause seemed to indicate that we would be entitled to terminate our contract with Frank, if, after six months of the expiry of our recording agreement, we had not signed a new one. On the delivery of *Hell's Ditch* in September, we had fulfilled our contract with Warner's. Jem reckoned that, if Frank had not come up with another record deal, we could let him go by the end of March. We swore each other to secrecy and strove to see out the remainder of the six months.

The bitterness of our decision to let Frank go turned all our stomachs when, in the second week of December, after our tour

384

of Germany, we performed a benefit show for Frank's daughter at the Electric Ballroom in Camden with Kirsty MacColl and Joe Strummer. After spending several months at Stoke Mandeville Hospital Spinal Injuries Unit, Shannon had come home, with the prognosis that she would never walk again.

The year turned. Duly, in March, at a meeting at Frank's office on Kentish Town Road, we let Frank go. Hill 16 Ltd's office had always been cluttered. Frank and Joey's desks were strewn with papers. Our silver records leant against the wall. The windows were filthy. A plastic extractor propeller set into one of them whizzed whenever the door opened. Plastic pots of noodles stood on the ledges. Down the corridor was a filthy bathroom where they used the hot-water geyser to make tea. The meeting was excruciating. Frank's usually swift and steely blue eyes suddenly turned inward. I was relieved to part company with him, and relieved that Jem had volunteered to give Frank the bad news.

After that, but for a couple of shows in France which Frank had set up for the second week in March, we had nothing to do – for months. We had asked Joey Cashman to take over from Frank, as caretaker-manager, to be paid a share of the tour profits rather than the percentage of gross, the means by which Frank had steadily let erode whatever good feeling we had had towards him.

The only work we had coming up was a handful of festivals, spread haphazardly throughout the summer, starting off at the Fleadh in Finsbury Park in June and culminating at the end of August in the WOMAD festival in Yokohama. Despite Shane's condition, we looked forward to the weekend jaunts in Europe, out in the open air, among our peers. We were excited, too, to return to Japan.

Up until then, I had the entire months of April and May with which to do what I wanted. With Danielle away on location, I packed a couple of changes of clothes and my typewriter in a holdall and took the train up to the Yorkshire Dales to write for a week, before taking the train again, down to a writers' retreat in Devon. As Debsey and I had, when we had spent time up at my parents' cottage, I checked in to see what developments there might be with the Pogues at the public telephone box up the road. I didn't expect any. The summer in the Yorkshire Dales was beautiful. The fields were layered in luscious sheets of sedge, cranesbill and buttercups. Meadowsweet crowded the dry-stone walls. Greenfinches danced over the hedges.

On a trip up to the phone box, Jem answered the phone and told me the news that Deborah Korner was dead. She had given birth to a son, Daniel, and five days later, at home, while taking a shower, had suffered an aortic aneurysm.

The funeral took place at Golders Green Crematorium. I took the train to London, changed into the one suit I kept at the flat and went up to the crematorium. All of us had made the trip to the memorial service, but Shane.

Predictably, halfway through, a heavy door on the far side of the chapel grated open and Shane came in assisted by Charlie McLennan. Shane was wearing a pinstripe suit, dark glasses and had slicked his hair back. He let Charlie guide him to an empty pew.

A wake took place at the house of a friend of Deborah and Andrew's in Hackney. At the end of the night I held their barely two-week-old son in my arms, asleep, his head in my cupped hand. I walked with the little thing around their living room, wondering how Andrew was going to be able to cope.

Back in Los Angeles, not two weeks later, the phone rang.

'You need to come home,' my sister-in-law said. My mother had suffered a subarachnoid haemorrhage and had descended into a coma. That night, with Danielle, I flew back to England.

The following morning, my two brothers and my father, grim in a car coat, greeted us at the foot of the escalator at Manchester airport. My mum had died during my flight over. They took me to the funeral home where, at the sight of my mum in the coffin, her mouth slightly open, her teeth biting her bottom lip, it was as if my legs had been cut from under me.

✠

At the end of the month, that the first gig of our career with Joey Cashman should have been Leeds University seemed a bitter joke. For time immemorial now, it seemed to have been the first gig of every damn tour of the United Kingdom we had ever done. We had grown to hate the place: the cramped and dingy corridors, the crashing acoustics and the stage built of scaffolding. After the sound check, Terry lost his footing at the top of the aluminium steps from the stage and, cradling his mandolin, rataplanned down to the bottom, causing him to limp through the next couple of gigs. It was not a good start.

Every alternate weekend for the rest of the summer we travelled out to play a festival – in Switzerland, Spain, Denmark, Italy. There were welcome distractions from the darkening abyss into which Shane was inexorably being sucked – alpine tarns and the low-eaved farmhouses above Lake Konstanz, the shaded arcades in Turin, a gleaming slice of Lake Geneva between the mountains, the medieval brickwork of Pamplona – but each of the festivals seemed a reiteration of *Le Radeau de la Méduse*, with the stage as the raft. Echoing the canvas, a couple of us continued to wave. I continued to show off – hoisting the accordion into the air, bending, hunching, stamping – in a wanton effort to distract the audience and myself from Shane's perdition.

387

Such a model of abandonment had Shane become that on stage he barely moved. Now and again he would lift a hand up to the microphone, the fingers curled so stiffly that we wondered if he might have had a stroke. When he sang, his mouth hardly opened. The decrepitude of his voice required his microphone to be set to such a level that I feared at any moment the screaming of feedback would rend the air and damage my ears. If Shane had nothing to do, during an instrumental break or between songs, he either bent down to pick up one of the plastic pint glasses of vodka and tonic which Charlie stationed at the foot of his mike stand, or stood with his arms hanging limply by his sides, staring across the stage. When Terry or Philip or Spider sang, Charlie came to get him, to escort him into the wings. It was a relief to be rid of him from the stage, but despite our best efforts, into his place rushed a banality that was crippling.

If an omen were needed for the imminence of the end, I had only to look out of the window of the tour bus as it inched down Parnell Street away from the Féile Festival at Semple Stadium in Thurles, County Tipperary – not fifty miles from Shane's hometown. A post-apocalyptic twilight had descended on the town centre. The bus threaded through knots of the staggering drunk, around a pile of burning rubbish, past a shattered phone box and a bus stop the roof of which was bent and twisted out of shape. It was the beginning of August, three weeks before what would turn out to be our determinative tour to Japan.

Thirty-One

Tragically, we filed out of our meeting in Jem's hotel room in Yokohama, in time for a couple of minutes' reflection in our own rooms before going down to the van to take us across to Seaside Park, and to our evening performance at the WOMAD festival. With grave ceremony, in my darkening room, I rolled up my stage trousers and shirt in one of the bath towels. I stood for a second or two, wondering if and how I should mark the event, but ended up, as was my custom, patting my pockets for picks, pass, fags and lighter, tucking the rolled towel under my arm and leaving the room.

Throughout the gig I was torn between, on the one hand, solemnising the occasion of firing our singer by keeping my movements to a mournful minimum and, on the other, in deference to the audience, pretending that nothing had changed and showboating as normal. Either way, I was incapable of not stamping my foot, jerking my body to recapture a wayward accordion strap, or wobbling my head in time to the music. Whenever I did, though, I thought everyone else in the group might think I was faking it or was just crassly insensitive. In the end, I thought, fuck it. Despite having little desire to loft the accordion skyward or descend to my knees at the final flourish of any of the songs, I did it anyway. I wasn't indulging in the occasion. I wasn't pandering to the audience. I wasn't rallying the troops. I wasn't unaware of the significance of what we'd done. I flung the accordion up and twitched my head. I pounded the boards with my heels and tried things on – ridiculous and inapposite Tex-Mex lines, couplets reminiscent of music hall, slathering glissandi with my fingernails – because I made the assumption that these last remaining gigs in Tokyo, with Osaka and Nagoya yet to get through, were the last I was going to do with the band.

On stage, we could barely look at one another. Darryl, in his youthfully stripy T-shirt, half of it tucked into his jeans, stepped back and forward with his bass, avoiding looking at Shane. His hair was long now and fell over his face in tatty ringlets from the swimming pool. The expression on his face was one of brooding anger. Despite our concerns that he simply had not been cool enough to replace Cait as our bass player, a nobility seemed to have attached itself to Darryl. I loved his authority and kindness, his indefatigable enthusiasm and his quintessentially English eccentricity.

Now that he had grown his hair long, Andrew, sweating behind his drum kit, looked like someone from the Iron Age. He had tied his hair into a rudimentary ponytail. He stared too at nothing, distracted and dissociated, but played with just as much heft as he always had, the sticks held awkwardly in his otherwise craftsmanly hands. I could have wept at the tribulations he had suffered and still did and would likely for years to come, but he looked indomitable, elemental, hewn from granite. I loved his dependability, the ruminative rhythm of his utterances and the pastoral tranquillity which came with him wherever he went.

Spider, in a shirt open to his waist, cast sidelong looks at Shane, full of betrayal and anger, but regret too. I remembered Spider and Shane's riotous exchanges in the kitchen at Burton Street, their explosive cackling in dressing rooms, on buses, on stage. I lamented their broken brotherhood. Though I hated the way Spider had exempted himself again and again from the bother of the consequences of what he did, I cherished him. I looked at his blotchy and swollen face. Part of me feared that before long – in the next couple of years – I'd get a phone call from Jem to tell me of Spider's death. Another part of me knew, though, that Spider was too inventive a guy for such an outcome.

Terry at first seemed to have been untouched by the events of the afternoon. He stood where he always had, in his cheap black suit. He played as he always had, lifting his head now and again to a patrician angle. When he wasn't looking at his tiny fingers on the frets of his cittern, he studied, with the intensity of a shill, what my fingers were doing on my keyboard. Throughout our set he avoided looking at Shane. If he happened to, I saw him look away.

Despite having barbarously lashed my ears for years and maddened me with the sanctimony of his experience, I loved Terry too. It might have infuriated me that he never played the same thing twice, was incapable of keeping to the book and made a meal out of the simplest lines, but I loved to play with him, so attentive was he to what I played. I basked in his sometimes lofty and avuncular goodwill towards me.

Philip, in a misshapen blue suit and plantation tie, hair tousled by the wind coming in off the Pacific Ocean, stared most of the time at the floor. He played his guitar with little exaggeration and avoided throwing shapes. I owed so much to Philip. If it hadn't been for him I would have stayed cemented to my position at the far side of the stage like a post, resentful of the attention I wasn't getting. Despite his hangdog yearning for me and his virtual imprisonment of me during those first couple of years, I admired his perseverance and his loyalty.

Jem hung back behind the line of microphones next to the flight case on which his hurdy-gurdy stood. Though often detached at the far side of the stage, he and I, now and again, in the course of a gig, would exchange a look prolonged both by the distraction of playing our instruments and by our fondness for each another. Tonight though, Jem had isolated himself behind Darryl. When I looked over at him he was staring into the middle ground, his eyes wide and sad, his lips protruding. He played gazing out, seeming not to take in the audience, which bounced in front of us, impulsively ebbing and flowing, orange from the lights: the bobbing black heads of hair, the seemingly uniform faces. It was an expression I had seen on Jem's face many times when the unpredictability of circumstances and people conspired to frustrate his idealism and inventiveness. Tonight, his face was unbearably sad, resigned, full of fear, angry and resolute.

Guessing that circumstances would prevent me afterwards, I longed for the opportunity to convey to him how grateful I was to him – my best man, my counterpart – to let him know how much I loved him. He did not look back at me. I looked away.

Philip came up to sing 'Thousands Are Sailing'. He stood sad and stern at the microphone. A frown knitted his brow. His scutiform face was handsome, his lashes lush. Behind him, the blue vaguely zebra-print banners began to snap in the wind.

I had always adored his song. Now, the events of the afternoon imbued it with such significance that tears filled my eyes. I knew the song was not specifically about the band's circumstances, nor about those of any particular member, not Shane's, nor mine. The fact, though, that in a couple of days, like the addressee in the song, I would be making a similar transformative trip to America caused the lines to turn round to address me and my circumstances.

The words of the song always had, but tonight they devastated me with their ghosts haunting the waves, the old songs taunting or cheering or making you cry. I knew, when it came time to go to my empty room at the end of the night, I would close the door behind me and look out over the lights of Yokohama Bay and the ocean beyond. I supposed I would cry too.

As Philip sang 'Thousands Are Sailing' I caught sight of Shane, sitting next to Charlie McLennan on a flight case in the darkness in the wings. His arms lay slack on his lap. His crippled hands clutched a plastic glass. His face in dark glasses was inscrutable.

I didn't know much about Jewish teaching but I did know of the creation myth. As Adonai contracted to make room for the physical world, the vessels containing the divine light broke, letting the light out. It crossed my mind that my life with Shane so far had been a matter of watching his breakage. The gratitude I felt for him at that moment outweighed my feeling that, on his path of self-destruction, he had just betrayed us.

Author's Note

I have known most of the characters in this book for as long as it has taken to write. Jem pointed out that I have lived with the Pogues longer than I lived with my own family. The people in the book are my family. My dreams have featured Shane more often than my dad for some time now.

This book is a work of creative non-fiction. I have tried to revivify the events and characters in it using the tools and the sensibilities of a fiction writer. According to the demands of the narrative I have recreated episodes, conversations and environments. In order to reproduce the spirit of an event, I have conflated a number of similar, recurring situations and exchanges.

Above all, it is a memoir. It is how I have remembered the twelve years of my life it covers.

Acknowledgements

I would not have been able to write this memoir without the patience and abstention from judgement of my wife, Danielle von Zerneck. I would like also to thank my daughters, Martha and Irene, for their unfailing enthusiasm for what I have been doing up in our home office for months, years on end.

Much of the material found form under the inimitable guidance of my mentor Nancy Bacal and the members of her writers' group 'The Writer's Way'. I would like to thank Marisa Silver for helping me further shape it.

I am more than grateful for the generosity of the following: Bob Ahern, Terri Cheney, Ron Comley, Dave Cripps, DzM, Adam Evans, Marcia Farquhar, Gill Ford, Andrea Gibb, J. Maizlish Mole, Biddy Mulligan, Deirdre O'Mahony, Steve Pyke, Tom Sheehan, Neil Titman and Debsey Wykes.

I would like to thank my agent, Caroline Wood, and my editor, Lee Brackstone, along with Dave Watkins and Ruth Atkins at Faber and Faber.

I am wholly indebted to all my raw materials: Stan Brennan, Jem Finer, Darryl Hunt, Shane MacGowan, Frank Murray, Cait O'Riordan, Andrew Ranken, Paul Scully, Spider Stacy and Terry Woods. I wish Philip Chevron, David Jordan, Kirsty MacColl, Charlie McLennan, Joe Strummer and Paul Verner were still around to thank.

Index

JAMES FEARNLEY was born in 1954 in Worsley, Manchester. A multi-instrumentalist, specializing in guitar and accordion, he was a founder member of the Pogues and has played with the London-Irish folk-punk band throughout its thirty-year career. In 1993, he moved to California to form the critically acclaimed Low and Sweet Orchestra. He rejoined the Pogues upon their reunion in 2001 and continues to perform with them throughout the world.

Fearnley has also participated in writers' programs at the Arvon Foundation in Great Britain, and in the United States he has been a Fellow at both the Virginia Center for the Creative Arts and the Hambidge Artists' Residency Program. He is currently working on a second book, his first work of fiction.